Anthropological Theory
in North America

6

Anthropological Theory in North America

Edited by
E. L. Cerroni-Long

Foreword by Vesna V. Godina

BERGIN & GARVEY
Westport, Connecticut • London

149853

Library of Congress Cataloging-in Publication Data

Anthropological theory in North America / edited by E. L. Cerroni-Long
; foreword by Vesna V. Godina.
    p.   cm.
  Includes bibliographical references and index.
  ISBN 0–89789–684–X (alk. paper).—ISBN 0–89789–685–8 (pbk. :
alk. paper)
    1. Anthropology—Philosophy.   2. Anthropology—North America.
3. Ethnology—Philosophy.   4. Ethnology—North America.   I. Cerroni-
Long, E. L., date.
  GN33.A444   1999
  301′.01—dc21   99–15406

British Library Cataloguing in Publication Data is available.

Library of Congress Catalog Card Number: 99–15406
ISBN: 0–89789–684–X
       0–89789–685–8 (pbk.)

First published in 1999

Bergin & Garvey, 88 Post Road West, Westport, CT 06881
An imprint of Greenwood Publishing Group, Inc.
www.greenwood.com

Printed in the United States of America

The paper used in this book complies with the
Permanent Paper Standard issued by the National
Information Standards Organization (Z39.48–1984).

10 9 8 7 6 5 4 3 2 1

CONTENTS

Foreword
Vesna V. Godina   vii

Introduction

Anthropology at Century's End
E. L. Cerroni-Long   1

Critical Issues

**Paradigms Refound: The Structure
of Anthropological Revolutions**
Paul Bohannan, Mari Womack, and Karen Saenz   19

**The "World System" of Anthropology
and "Professional Others"**
Pamela J. Asquith   33

Maladaptation: A Challenge to Relativism
Robert B. Edgerton   55

Science, Objectivity, Morality
Marvin Harris   77

Culture Is Not Everything
Roy D'Andrade   85

Theoretical Perspectives

Causal Individualism and the Unification of Anthropology
  Tim O'Meara   105

A Realist/Postmodern Concept of Culture
  Joseph A. Maxwell   143

Immanent Holism: On Transfer of Knowledge
from Global to Local
  Peter Harries-Jones   175

Toward an Anthropological Theory
of Natural Resource Management
in Indigenous Communities
  Daniel M. Cartledge   197

Recapturing Anthropology in Marginal Communities
  Parin A. Dossa   213

Human Materialism: A Paradigm for Analyzing
Sociocultural Systems and Understanding
Human Behavior
  Paul J. Magnarella   235

Conclusion

Forecasting Theory: Problems and Exemplars
in the Twenty-First Century
  Stanley R. Barrett   255

Index   283
Contributors   295

FOREWORD

"Anthropology is either truly international or not at all!" This philosophy, which is behind the creation and ongoing activities of the International Union of Anthropological and Ethnological Sciences (IUAES), is particularly relevant to anthropologists concerned with matters of theory. Theory can only be refined through an ongoing process of comparative discussion and understanding. It is to facilitate this process that the IUAES Commission on Theoretical Anthropology (COTA) was founded in 1993, establishing a varied program of activities. Such activities include the development of a series of publications which document current theoretical developments in our discipline from a worldwide perspective. The first volume, titled *Horizons of Understanding*, was published in 1996, and it surveyed the European landscape in the field of anthropological theory. As current COTA chairperson, it is a great pleasure to now introduce this new volume, dedicated to an overview of recent theoretical developments in Canada and the United States.

Although American anthropologists sometimes identify a concern with theory as particularly European, some of the most influential theoretical debates in modern anthropology have originated in North America. The ideas introduced by Morgan or Boas, Harris or Geertz, have had a tremendous impact on the worldwide development of the discipline. However, the historical trajectory of American theoretical innovations is nonlinear; sometimes these innovations did not have any major impact outside the Anglo-Saxon world, sometimes their influence came from a process of much-delayed rediscovery (the cur-

rent European interest in Sapir's ideas is a case in point), and sometimes—as in the case of postmodernism—it took the American elaboration of European ideas for them to really have an impact throughout
the discipline.

The history of the anthropological debate between North America
and other parts of the world—and especially Europe—has often been
marked by competition and jealousy, and sometimes even mockery and
rejection. Nevertheless, the overall results of the debate have been
positive. Not only new theoretical models, concepts, and hypotheses,
but also excellent criticism, and brave positing of new questions and
points of view, have emerged from the process. This volume carries
forth the debate, bringing to international attention the views of com-
paratively new authors, as well as those of scholars who have already
marked the discipline with their provocative theoretical influence.

Various circumstances—not least of which are the financial stric-
tures COTA has to contend with on a regular basis—have often put in
question the publication of the present volume. It certainly would not
have been produced so soon after the first one if not for the hard work
of its editor, Liza Cerroni-Long, who took up the challenge of
documenting the state-of-the-art of North American anthropological
theory with enthusiasm and dedication. Her efforts are acknowledged
with gratitude by all the COTA members, and especially by the representatives of COTA's Steering Committee. Support from the IUAES is
also gratefully acknowledged.

Our project to document worldwide theoretical developments in
anthropology will go forward. We plan to publish at least three more
"regional" volumes: one each for Latin America, Asia, and Africa.
Work on one of them, surveying anthropological theory in Latin
America, has already been started, and we hope to bring it to publication in the near future. The international dialog on anthropology
must continue; we can all learn a great deal from it, and it is only
through it that our discipline can move on to play a central role in the
intellectual life of the twenty-first century.

Vesna V. Godina
COTA Chairperson
Ljubljana, Slovenia, 1999

Introduction

ANTHROPOLOGY AT CENTURY'S END

E. L. Cerroni-Long

In January 1959, the Voice of America introduced a special series of radio broadcasts called "Forum: The Arts and Sciences in Mid-Century America." Sol Tax was asked to develop a set on anthropology, and he did so by inviting a number of young specialists to discuss what they thought were the most relevant issues in their specific subfields. The lectures were subsequently published under the title *Horizons of Anthropology*, and the book's "Preface" ends with the following words: "As one should expect in a growing science, anthropology has ever new horizons. Students who read this book are invited to work now on its successor" (Tax 1964:6).

Indeed, anthropology's horizons have changed quite dramatically since mid-century, and this volume harks back to that now classic compilation of state-of-the-art assessments both to pay homage to its vision and to take up its invitation: to look at contemporary developments with the aim of documenting disciplinary growth.

This might seem a rather unorthodox objective in these postmodern times, as the ongoing debates on anthropology's scope, range, and scientific validity appear to indicate a major disciplinary crisis. However, I would suggest that the sense of impending disciplinary doom one may perceive in the tone of many recent professional discussions[1] has more to do with the "millenarian malaise" driving postmodern nihilism than with a real crisis.

In fact, from my personal perspective—derived from being an Italian, academically trained in Europe, Asia, and North America, and professionally based in the United States since 1978—it seems highly ironic that it is *American* anthropologists, and especially American *cultural* anthropologists, who seem most anxious about the future of their discipline. No matter how sincere these feelings, they utterly belie the fact that North America is still the part of the world in which anthropology in general and cultural anthropology in particular have the strongest and broadest academic bases, the most numerous publishing outlets, and the largest number of professional affiliates (see Evans 1998).

On the other hand, it is also true that, as the century ends, American anthropology no longer occupies the assured position of intellectual hegemony it had at the time *Horizons of Anthropology* was published. Furthermore, the very growth of the discipline has inevitably set into motion centrifugal forces portending possible fragmentation. Finally and most importantly, intellectual perceptions and intercultural power relations have changed enough in half a century to challenge some of cultural anthropology's basic methodological assumptions (see Cerroni-Long 1995). Still, these can all be seen as signs and sources of creative ferment rather than of impending demise. The apocalyptic component of postmodern nihilism is obscuring this interpretation.

What cannot be denied, though, is that theory-building is again central to anthropology's disciplinary growth. It is also clear that the focus of theoretical development is sociocultural anthropology, rather than any of the other anthropological subfields. And the concept of "culture," that most American of the anthropological core concepts, seems still to be the grand prize of current theoretical contests.

Franz Boas is called the father of modern anthropology because of his seminal role in both suggesting a new meaning for the word culture—from evolutionist synonym of civilization to historicist summa of a people's way of life—and in putting it at the center of the anthropological research endeavor. This has led to the development of a powerful intellectual paradigm, based on the concept of cultural relativism, which has spread way beyond its American source. As Clifford has pointed out (1988:95), if the close of the nineteenth century seemed to focus Western intellectual life almost obsessively on matters of historical change and progress, the end of this century is characterized by a worldwide preoccupation with matters of cultural identity and diversity.

This is a world in which anthropology's relevance can only grow. But successful growth requires serious efforts at theoretically refining major disciplinary assumptions. This volume documents some of these efforts, both in the discussion of the most critical disciplinary issues, and in the description of particularly promising new theoretical approaches. To fully understand the scope of these contributions, however, it is necessary to briefly describe the context from which they emerge.

Historical Background

Writing at the beginning of the 1980s, Sherry Ortner argued that: "Although anthropology was never actually unified in the sense of adopting a single shared paradigm, there was at least a period when there were a few large categories of theoretical affiliation, . . . [while now we] are no longer sure of how the sides are to be drawn up, and of where we would place ourselves if we could identify the sides" (1984:126-127). On the contrary, I would argue that Boasian anthropology generated a very solid paradigm, that of cultural relativism, and while the sense of internal fragmentation plaguing the profession since the 1960s may be partly due to the slow emergence of paradigmatic inconsistencies (to be discussed more fully later), it mainly derives from the gap between theory and method which has been slowly widening ever since the heyday of functionalism.

My argument focuses on the fact that, in reference to research practice, the Boasian paradigm rested on loose functionalist premises ("cultural traits are perpetuated because of the function they fulfill") which were tempered and buttressed by historicism ("cultural specificity emerges from a complex historical process"). The aim of early Boasian anthropologists was to reconstruct this historical process through the description and analysis of the collection of traits characterizing a particular culture (Fox 1991:103). However, the psychologism that swept anthropology in the 1920s, partly through Freud's general influence and partly through the impact of Malinowski's theoretical approach, inevitably led to the development of types of functionalism that, while adopting widely different perspectives (in fact, some of them even rejected the functionalist label), had several common characteristics: they were theoretically abstract, they were ahistorical, and they were intensely preoccupied with how to correlate individual behavior to structural issues (Langness 1987:100).

This is the kind of implicit functionalism revealed in the pages of *Horizons of Anthropology*, and this is the type of functionalism which found its best expression in the classic ethnographic monograph. In other words, there is a direct link between a loose, implicit functionalism and both the research methodology which came to characterize sociocultural anthropology—involving fieldwork, participant observation, and informant interviewing—and the type of ethnographic writing emerging from it.

However, the various functionalisms driving decades of anthropological practice also contained a methodological conundrum: whether to pay more attention to the material context of adaptive practices or to the symbolic representations of the same. It is this dualism that came to the fore in the 1960s, splitting the anthropological camp into various factions linked to one side or the other of the materialist/idealist battleforce. As a result, by the late 1960s and early 1970s, a number of anthropological texts started expressing feelings of impending doom (e.g. Berreman 1968; Scholte 1972), or calling for disciplinary renewal (e.g. Leach 1971; Hymes 1972). By the mid-1980s, with postmodern nihilism in full swing, some anthropologists were rejoicing in the supposed collapse of scientific rationality, and advocated a new type of anthropology which "must break the whole spell of representation and project a world of pure arbitrariness without representation" (Tyler 1986:133).

While it is understandable that such developments have been interpreted by some as a terminal process of disciplinary involution (e.g. Nash 1997), it should also be kept in mind that the impact of postmodernism on anthropology may have been greatly exaggerated. In fact, I would propose that, by and large, American anthropology is still locked into the materialist/idealist impasse which by the mid-1970s became identified with the conflict between the cultural materialism of Marvin Harris and the symbolic interpretivism of Clifford Geertz. The impasse has not been really affected by postmodernism, and it continues because, paradoxically, each side has scored important victories.

Even a superficial review of the best-selling textbooks used throughout North America to introduce college students to anthropology, for example, reveals that they all partake of one or another version of cultural materialism, emphasizing the role of subsistence patterns (or behavioral infrastructure) in providing insights into sociocultural differences and similarities (see Kottak et al. 1996:Part 1). Also, as Harris points out (1994:62), cultural materialism continues to be very influential in archaeology and other anthropological subfields. On the other hand, the various types of interpretive approaches inspired by Geertz's metaphorically dense disquisitions (e.g. 1973) have stimulated broad interdisciplinary interest, so that anthropological concepts have now percolated to a large public and are being used—with various degrees of accuracy—in a number of fields, ranging from film criticism to theology.

In spite of these successes, however, neither approach has won the day as yet, chiefly because neither has managed to translate its theoretical premises into methodological innovations that can replace the traditional ways anthropologists conduct research. That is possibly why, in the last two decades, the approach that may have engaged the largest number of researchers is what Barrett has memorably called "no-name anthropology" (1996:178-184). This means that research is done, and ethnographic texts are written, without any overt reference to specific theoretical premises. In practical terms, though, the research techniques used are still those emerging from the loose functionalism implicit in the cultural relativist paradigm. And this, in turn, perpetuates the materialist/idealist impasse.

Such a protracted continuation of practice devoid of theoretical underpinnings has been problematized even further by the postmodern critique of ethnographic "essentialisms" and "appropriations." By proclaiming the fragmentary and "imagined" reality of culture, nation, community, or indeed any type of social setting which may be the focus of research, postmodernism denies the legitimacy of ethnographic generalizations (which get labelled as "essentialisms"), and thus conclusively undermines cross-cultural comparison. By calling attention to the power play that underscores any human transactions, but especially those across historically unequal groups—such as men and women, rich and poor, whites and people of color, heterosexuals and homosexuals—postmodernism denounces the ethnographic endeavor (as an attempt at "appropriation" of the "other"), insofar as it is directed at describing, comparing, and understanding human diversity.[2]

All of this could have truly dire consequences for anthropology, but the robust state of the discipline seems to indicate that while postmodernism has become the intellectual orthodoxy of the *fin de siècle* it has not affected anthropological practice in a substantive way. In fact, it may even have contributed constructively, on the one hand, by honing some aspects of our traditional methodology (see Cerroni-Long 1995:11), and, on the other, by calling attention to the role of discourse, context, perspective—and thus, by extension, theory.

As a matter of fact, it appears as if the flowering of theory-building that is beginning to emerge in contemporary North-American anthropology has been stimulated at least partly by postmodernism, whether as a reaction to its anti-theoretical skepticism, or as a response to some of the issues to which it has called attention. The major trigger, however, is certainly the growing perception of the need to bridge the gap between theory and method. There is also the fact that the Boasian paradigm itself is increasingly showing some internal inconsistencies, revolving around a set of critical issues that demand disciplinary discussion, and which are likely to affect all future theory-building. These critical issues emerge from anthropology's ambiguous comparativism, and its "adaptivism," moralism, and descriptivism.

Critical Issues

Cross-cultural comparisons are at the core of functionalist anthropology; and while Franz Boas called attention to the need to use cross-cultural comparisons only within a well-defined historical context, the discipline has been practically built around comparativism (Sarana 1975). Certainly, the assumption that anthropological research is conducted within a comparative framework is built into the Boasian paradigm; indeed, the very concept of cultural relativism derives from it ("cultural traits can only be understood relative to the cultural context in which they are observed"). Nevertheless, the comparative harvest of one hundred years of anthropology is rather thin. Even thinner is the record of research that directly engages the issue of comparativism and cultural relativism at the level of practice (Nader 1994). Where are the cross-cultural analyses of same-issue studies, or the research projects conducted by cross-cultural teams, or even the basic cross-cultural agreement on the anthropological terms and concepts to be used in research? In other words, where is the evidence that anthropology is not itself a culture-specific—or, at least Western-specific—intellectual product, irrelevant to other civilizations, and unlikely to live up to its universalist claims?

This issue is of course closely linked to whether the products of cultural anthropology are science or literature. The debate over this point has been largely instigated by postmodern nihilism, and, as will be argued later, it is utterly inconclusive. But comparativism also involves a different dimension which deserves attention. A crucial underpinning of the Boasian paradigm is the assumption of mankind's psychic unity ("there are no fundamental differences in the ways of thinking of people of different cultures"); in fact, Boas went on record with a full treatment of this topic (Boas 1938[1911]). Nevertheless, anthropology has undoubtedly emerged as an autonomous discipline out of the historical experience of Western colonialism, at least partly based on assumptions of "natural" superiority of the colonizers over the colonized. Indeed, colonialism provided anthropology both with its early intellectual justification and with the natural "laboratory" in which to conduct research (Cerroni-Long 1989). Consequently, it is perhaps not too surprising that the ethnographic endeavor may be regarded with a certain amount of suspicion, and perhaps even hostility, by social scientists operating in non-Western societies (see Nakane 1984).

What is puzzling, though, is that so little attention has been given within the Western tradition to seeking out, and engaging with, the cross-cultural dimension of anthropological research. A certain amount of parochialism in intellectual life is perhaps always to be expected, but anthropology must deal with the issue of culture-specific analytical perspective in order to steady its own theoretical moorings. And the need to take up this challenge is made all the more urgent by the fact that the postmodern critique of ethnography—with its denunciation of "essentialisms" and "appropriations" described above—is rapidly trivializing the serious issues at stake, and may end up hampering current attempts at even defining a "worldwide anthropology" (see Krotz 1997; Prah 1997).

The consequences of cultural relativism must also be clarified at a different level. The Boasian paradigm implies a moral message of cross-cultural tolerance which, while generally admirable—and practically necessary for the historical period in which it was elaborated—has led to disciplinary inconsistencies ultimately deleterious to research.

The first inconsistency has to do with the persistent confusion between cultural and moral relativism, a confusion that has greatly harmed the public perception of our discipline. While introductory texts of cultural anthropology invariably mention that "cultural relativity does not mean that all patterns must be judged as equally 'good'" (Nanda 1994:17), the implied functionalism of the Boasian paradigm, with its insistence on the adaptive value of cultural practices, has traditionally short-circuited comparative assessments of human adaptation. Consequently, anthropologists have contributed to the perpetuation of some of the very myths—of "primitive social harmony" for example—the discipline was supposed to explode through the accumulation of factual information.

The second inconsistency emerges from the expectation that, through the comparative study of different cultures, anthropologists can gain enough insights into the human condition to be able to benefit the subjects of their study as well as their own societies. Anthropology has traditionally posited itself as a reformer's science (e.g. Tylor 1871:410), and the great popularity of anthropological works such as those of Margaret Mead came from the fact that they used ethnographic evidence to present advice on how to improve the lives of contemporary Americans (MacClancy 1996:18). The problem is that, because cultural anthropologists typically engage in the kind of research that both alienates them from their own society and dramatically distances them from the type of knowledge and power that are the prerequisites of social reform (Bennett 1996), their contribution must limit itself to "speaking truth to evil," in an effort to establish "the primacy of the ethical" (Scheper-Hughes 1995). In other words, the champions of relativism are, paradoxically, also supposed to be "professional moralists."[3]

The preoccupation with the moral dimension of anthropology, which has become embedded in the postmodernist critique of the discipline (e.g. Clifford and Marcus 1989; Marcus and Fischer 1986), is the counterpart of the process by which ethnographic texts have been defined as literary rather than scientific. One must remember that, in postmodern nihilism, scientific knowledge emerges from rationality's "totalizing metanarrative," and is thus part of a discourse of domination. But the deconstruction of ethnographic texts did not derive directly from a critique of science. Rather, it was the natural by-product of extending the interpretive approach—according to which the focus of anthropological research must be the "webs of significance" men spin (Geertz 1973:5)—to the writings produced by it. The consequences of this procedure, however, have been rather unexpected.

"By exposing the artifice in ethnographic writing, Clifford Geertz opened to suspicion the very question as to whether the understanding of humankind was advanced by fieldwork" (Nash 1997:21). This suspicion triggered disciplinary discussions over the scientific validity of anthropology which, because of the incommensurable premises of the discussants, were as heated as they were inconclusive; if the universalist value of science is denied, the argument that a particular discipline is not scientific becomes celebratory rather than critical.[4] What is more significant is that this suspicion also called new attention to the concept of culture—the fulcrum of the Boasian paradigm—and to the limitations of ethnography.

A thorough reconsideration of the culture concept was also made necessary by the meteoric rise of a new field of study—cultural studies—which directly challenged cultural anthropology by seemingly appropriating its core concept. But the culture of cultural studies is adjusted for postmodern consumption, and is thus a determinedly atheoretical concept.   In fact, the intellectual trajectory of post-modernism itself is revealed in the transformation of this field, which emerged in the 1970s as the British version of Gramscian analyses of "folkways" as counter-hegemonic strategy and went on to become, especially in its American version, the celebratory documentation of identity politics.

Still, cultural studies call attention both to the performative, expressive aspect of culture—an aspect anthropologists have often bypassed—and to the limitations of ethnography as an end in itself. The relentless descriptiveness of cultural studies in its post-Gramscian phase is increasingly recognized as sterile (DiMaggio 1997:263). This, in turn, is stimulating anthropological interest in going beyond the "what" of culture in favor of its "why" and "how," which implies an attempt at problematizing the emergence, maintenance, and transforma-tion of cultural patterns.   Inevitably, this trend is likely to steer research on the one hand toward the cognitive underpinnings of culture-specific behavior, and on the other, toward the political assess-ment of cultural expression.   These trends are very promising, but it must be remembered that the discipline has structural tendencies that may severely limit their constructive potential.

Disciplinary Tendencies

In his Huxley Memorial Lecture for 1971, titled "Anthropology's Mythology," George Murdock denounced the limitations of the anthropological approach and suggested looking at psychology to find "an understanding of the underlying mechanisms of behavior, and their variations under different conditions of life" (Eggan 1977:2).   This rather extreme position can be interpreted as just another expression of the "gloom and doom" perspective characterizing Anglo-Saxon anthropology since the 1960s. However, I would suggest that it also reveals two other typical disciplinary tendencies: the enthusiasm for turning to other disciplines for purposes of internal revitalization, and the readiness to scuttle whole sets of views (even one's own previously held views) in favor of the latest fashionable approach.

Admittedly, many anthropologists have fully acknowledged these tendencies, and particularly the latter one, which Wallace called the "slash and burn nature of anthropology," Wolf described as "a project of intellectual deforestation," and the Norwegian Fredrik Barth related to the great "pressure toward a stereotyped originality" one finds in

American academia (Borofsky 1994:10-12). However, the swings in orientation characterizing cultural anthropology seem to have no counterpart in any other anthropological subfields, or indeed, in any other of the social sciences. It is because of the rapid alternations of these swings that one gets little sense of disciplinary continuity and accumulation of knowledge.

In view of these disciplinary characteristics, the growing interest in the insights into culture which can be derived from biology, evolutionary psychology, comparative ethology, or cognitive science may bring about a spiralling into scientism which may be as deleterious as postmodern nihilism (Cerroni-Long 1996). Furthermore, the current gap between theory and method requires a theoretical refinement of the core concepts of the discipline, rather than the wholesale adoption of extra-disciplinary approaches. The very enthusiasm of cultural anthropologists for self-criticism and interdisciplinarity may have a limiting effect on any efforts at internal revitalization.

Similarly, the anthropological interest in analyzing the political implications of action—or praxis—is severely limited by the marginal role assigned to intellectuals in general, and social scientists in particular, within the Anglo-Saxon world. The strong barriers American anthropologists encounter when attempting to apply their findings, especially when the findings have potentially subversive political implications (see Rappaport 1994), do not favor the development of the anthropological study of praxis beyond the boundaries of radical chic. Unsurprisingly, then, postmodern identity politics has provided the most fertile ground for this approach, which has become the idiom of feminist, ethnic, or gay self-promotion while it has consistently failed to engage issues of class (Ortner 1991), or neocolonial economic dominance (Sanjek 1995).

Gearing cultural anthropology toward the analysis of praxis has other important impediments, which gain further strength by being correlated. To begin with, the study of praxis calls attention to abstract levels of politico-economic organization, as well as to historical process (Ortner 1984:148-160). This shifts the focus away from the individual agent and toward systemic, structural social issues, which is an approach at variance with the traditional American penchant for an individual-centered social science. Furthermore, the obvious link between the study of praxis and Marxism ends up clashing with the unresolved materialist/idealist impasse. Consequently, practitioners of this approach have attempted to adopt "an interpenetration, almost a merger, between Marxist and Weberian frameworks" (Ortner

1984:147). This is a most unrealistic endeavor. The result is that a decade of anthropological experiments with "practice theory" reveals a gradual transition of the focus of study from historically situated collective action (e.g. Wolf 1982), to the life histories of specific actors, increasingly intermixed with the researcher's narcissistic self-analysis (e.g. Behar 1993).

In fairness, this shift cannot be related only to American individualism, or to postmodern aestheticism, even if these factors do play a part in it. The crucial impediment to structural analysis in cultural anthropology derives from the fact that our research methodology is rooted in the observation, documentation, and description of concrete human behavior in natural settings; our research techniques decidedly involve *micro* levels of investigation. And, to date, only the various kinds of functionalism encasing the Boasian paradigm have managed to offer models linking agency and structure, micro and macro levels of behavior.

To go beyond these models, and out of the materialist/idealist impasse, it may be necessary to look again at our methodology and gather inspiration from it. This means desisting from the attempt at modifying it to fit a particular theoretical approach, as various factions of the materialist/ idealist camps have repeatedly attempted to do over the last forty years, with uniformly poor results. Rather, it may be possible to inductively arrive at a refinement of the culture concept by assessing and clarifying the empirical realities we focus on in the actual process of research. This is an approach taken up in different ways by various contributors to this volume, and may well be setting the premises for a quiet theoretical revolution.

Volume's Composition

As mentioned at the beginning of this chapter, millenarian malaise and postmodern nihilism have combined to deepen the perception of impending disciplinary crisis shared by many cultural anthropologists at least since the late 1960s. A closer look at current anthropological practice, however, reveals a thriving discipline, which is nevertheless undergoing a process of theoretical renewal. This process is driven by the widening gap between theory and method on the one hand, and a basic theoretical impasse between materialist and idealist approaches on the other. Furthermore, the Boasian paradigm, which still provides the often unrecognized underpinnings of the discipline, has developed internal inconsistencies demanding attention.

All of this makes for a situation obviously full of creative ferment but which is also in flux. To creditably document such a situation is inherently challenging. In an attempt to meet this challenge, the composition of this volume emerged from a series of strategies. The standard, broadly disseminated, open call for contributions—first introduced at the thirteenth ICAES (International Congress of Anthropological and Ethnological Sciences) in Mexico City—was combined with a survey of the theoretical production of the past five years, both in terms of major publications and national-level professional presentations. From this survey was derived a roster of active theoreticians, to whom personal invitations were forwarded. Finally, a theory-focused session was organized for the fourteenth ICAES, held in North America, and the open call for participation to the meeting was combined with further special invitations to contribute to this volume.

The representativeness of this collection can only be assessed by its readers. However, as it began to take shape, I became pleasantly surprised by the many cross-references encountered in the texts selected for inclusion. While the contributors had not read each other's pieces, they often referred to each other's ideas, both positively and critically. This seems to indicate that these ideas, and these authors, are at the center of the theoretical flowering beginning to emerge in North American anthropology. Also, without any editorial guideline whatsoever, several authors contributed pieces that specifically focused on one or the other of what I earlier identified as the critical issues demanding disciplinary attention. Even more reassuringly, some of these contributors were Canadian, and others American, documenting the lack of sharp lines of national demarcation in the concerns shared by North American anthropologists.

Four chapters in particular address critical issues. Asquith takes up the discussions of anthropology's ambiguous comparativism and, using the comparison between Anglo-Saxon and Japanese primatology as a case study, builds a strong argument denouncing the lack of international dialog which seems to characterize anthropological practice. Edgerton and Harris respectively address the two major inconsistencies generated by relativism: the adoption of an uncritical "adaptivist" perspective, and the trend toward giving priority to moral concerns over scientific objectives. Finally, the topic of cultural anthropology's descriptivism is debated by D'Andrade, who argues for the need to turn away from studying what is determined by culture and toward studying what culture is determined by. In the author's words, the crucial question anthropologists should address is: "Culture is related to what, how?"

The chapters presenting full-fledged theoretical models—which are arranged thematically—also reveal similarities among the authors, whether they are Canadian or American. In fact, they all seem to share some basic perspectives, differently emphasized in each of the texts. These include: a realist epistemology (Maxwell, O'Meara), a behavioral view of structuration (Dossa, Magnarella), an inductive approach (Cartledge, Harries-Jones), a personalized interpretation of causation (Magnarella, O'Meara), a systemic understanding of the interpenetration of the micro and macro levels of reality (Cartledge, Harries-Jones, Maxwell), and a keen appreciation of the strategic consequences of social locus (Cartledge, Dossa, Magnarella).

Perhaps, the only national difference can be found in the fact that Canadian contributors seem rather more sanguine than their American counterparts about the positive influence of postmodernism on theoretical development. This is particularly evident in Barrett's "Forecast," which concludes the volume. After contributing a useful framework for predicting theory in general, and after a *tour-de-force* survey of the areas of anthropology most likely to demand theoretical treatment in the next century, Barrett suggests that "if sanity prevails" some of the innovations stimulated by postmodernism—such as interpretive, feminist, and dialogic anthropology—will endure. He also points out, however, that the discipline has an internal dynamic which leads to theoretical orientations "bouncing off each other," so that dialectical oscillations are unavoidable.

The temporal recursiveness of such oscillations is discussed in the chapter opening the "Critical Issues" section of the volume, in which scholars from three different generations reflect upon the "slash and burn nature of anthropology." By correlating the symbolic "killing of [intellectual] ancestors" to the structural characteristics of Western kinship, the authors provide insights into the possible cultural-specificity of anthropological practice, both in terms of research choices, and in reference to career-building and professional conduct. These insights dovetail particularly well with the argument presented by Asquith, and set the stage for an "anthropology-of-science" debate which is likely to affect very powerfully the theoretical dynamics described by Barrett.

Whether anthropology may emerge from this debate, or from the other ones delineated above, with a broadened focus, clarified premises, and enhanced applicability, remains to be seen. There is no doubt, however, that as the Boasian century closes, the entire world is acknowledging "the relevance of culture" (Freilich 1989), and demanding a better understandings of its various dimensions and dynamics. For better or for worse, the concept of culture has become popularized and politicized (Wright 1998), and anthropologists must respond to this development.

One of the three authors of the opening chapter, Paul Bohannan, was also a contributor to *Horizons of Anthropology* (Tax 1964), the volume this collection commemorates. In reflecting upon his long career span, he points out that: "We all know that history has to be rewritten every generation. Even if the historical 'facts' do not change, the context in which they are to be read and interpreted does change" (Bohannan 1998:415). That context, of course, is influenced by anthropology itself. A hundred years of research have tremendously affected the way we look at human behavior. If we have not yet provided many answers to the puzzles our research documents, we have at least stimulated some good questions, and this is what ensures a discipline's future.

Notes

1. I am referring in particular to several of the plenary sessions held at the American Anthropological Association Annual Meetings over the last five years and to the thematic discussions published by the *Anthropology Newsletter* in the same period.

2. Barrett gives an extremely useful example of the consequences of measuring ethnography through postmodern orthodoxy by describing the variety of reactions stimulated by a recent study of the Okanagan people of British Columbia (1996:185).

3. In 1995 *Current Anthropology* published the text of a major debate among a number of anthropologists on the topic of "Objectivity and Militancy." Roy D'Andrade (1995) and Nancy Scheper-Hughes (1995) provided the texts for the opposing viewpoints.

4. The *Anthropology Newsletter*, the most broadly circulated anthropological publication in North America, dedicated an entire year of issues (1995-1996) to such a debate, which also included the publication of highlights of an "e-mail dialog" it sponsored during the summer of 1995. These highlights were published in the March,

April, May, and September 1996 issues of the newsletter.

References

Barrett, Stanley R.
  1996   *Anthropology: A Student's Guide to Theory and Method.*
          Toronto: University of Toronto Press.
Behar, Ruth
  1993   *Translated Woman.* Boston, MA: Beacon Press.
Bennett, John W.
  1996   "Applied and Action Anthropology." *Current Anthropology*
          36(Supplement):S23-S53.
Berreman, Gerald D.
  1968   "Is Anthropology Alive?" *Current Anthropology* 9:391-396.
Boas, Franz
  1938   *The Mind of Primitive Man.* 1911. Reprint, London: Mac-
          millan.
Bohannan, Paul
  1998   "Passing into History." In Mari Womack, *Being Human.*
          Upper Saddle River, NJ: Prentice-Hall.
Borofsky, Robert,
  1994   "Introduction." In Robert Borofsky, ed., *Assessing Cultural
          Anthropology.* New York: McGraw-Hill.
Cerroni-Long, E. L.
  1989   "Child of Colonialism: The Primitivist Premises of Western
          Anthropology." *North Dakota Quarterly* 57(3):76-98.
  1995   "Insider or Native Anthropology?" In E. L. Cerroni-Long,
          ed., *Insider Anthropology.* Arlington, VA: American
          Anthropological Association.
  1996   "Human Science." *Anthropology Newsletter* (January):52,
          50.
Clifford, James
  1988   *The Predicament of Culture.* Cambridge, MA: Harvard
          University Press.
Clifford, James, and George Marcus, eds.
  1989   *Writing Culture: The Poetics and Politics of Ethnology.*
          Berkeley: University of California Press.
D'Andrade, Roy
  1995   "Moral Models in Anthropology." *Current Anthropology*
          36:399-408, 433-436.

DiMaggio, Paul
   1997   "Culture and Cognition." *Annual Review of Sociology* 23:
           263-287.
Eggan, Fred
   1977   "The History of Social/Cultural Anthropology" In A. F. C.
           Wallace et al., eds., *Perspectives on Anthropology 1976*.
           Washington, DC: American Anthropological Association.
Evans, Patsy
   1998   "Who We Are and What We Want." *Anthropology Newslet-
           ter* 39(2):1, 6-7.
Fox, Richard G.
   1991   "For a Nearly New Culture History" In Richard G. Fox,
           ed., *Recapturing Anthropology: Working in the Present*.
           Santa Fe, NM: School of American Research Press.
Freilich, Morris, ed.
   1989   *The Relevance of Culture*. New York: Bergin & Garvey.
Geertz, Clifford
   1973   *The Interpretation of Cultures*. New York: Basic Books.
Harris, Marvin
   1994   "Cultural Materialism Is Alive and Well and Won't Go
           Away Until Something Better Comes Along." In Robert
           Borofski, ed., *Assessing Cultural Anthropology*. New
           York: McGraw-Hill.
Hymes, Dell, ed.
   1972   *Reinventing Anthropology*. New York: Vintage.
Kottak, Conrad P., J. J. White, R. H. Furlow, and P. C. Rice, eds.
   1996   *The Teaching of Anthropology*. Mountain View, CA: May-
           field.
Krotz, Esteban
   1997   "Anthropologies of the South." *Critique of Anthropology* 17
           (3): 237-251.
Langness, L. L.
   1987   *The Study of Culture*. 2nd edition. Novato, CA: Chandler
           & Sharp.
Leach, Edmund R.
   1971   *Rethinking Anthropology*. London: Athlone Press.
MacClancy, Jeremy
   1996   "Popularizing Anthropology." In J. MacClancy and Chris
           McDonaugh, eds., *Popularizing Anthropology*. New York:
           Routledge.

Marcus, George E., and Michael M. J. Fischer
  1986   *Anthropology as Cultural Critique*. Chicago, IL: University
         of Chicago Press.
Nader, Laura
  1994   "Comparative Consciousness." In Robert Borofsky, ed.,
         Assessing Cultural Anthropology. New York: McGraw-
         Hill.
Nakane, Chie, ed.
  1984   *Social Sciences and Asia*. Tokyo: Institute of Oriental Cul-
         ture/UNESCO.
Nanda, Serena
  1994   *Cultural Anthropology*. Belmont, CA: Wadsworth.

Nash, June
  1997   "When Isms Become Wasms." *Critique of Anthropology* 17
         (1):11-32.
Ortner, Sherry B.
  1984   "Theory in Anthropology since the Sixties." *Comparative
         Studies in Society and History* 26(1):126-166.
  1991   "Reading America." In Richard G. Fox, ed., *Recapturing
         Anthropology: Working in the Present*. Santa Fe, NM:
         School of American Research Press.
Prah, Kwesi Kwaa
  1997   "North/South Parallels and Intersections." *Critique of
         Anthropology* 17(4):439-445.
Rappaport, Roy A.
  1994   "Disorders of Our Own: A Conclusion." In Shepard
         Forman, ed., *Diagnosing America: Anthropology and Pub-
         lic Engagement*. Ann Arbor: University of Michigan Press.
Sanjek, Roger
  1995   "Politics, Theory, and the Nature of Cultural Things." In
         Martin F. Murphy and Maxine L. Margolis, eds., *Science,
         Materialism, and the Study of Culture*. Gainesville: Univer-
         sity Press of Florida.
Sarana, Gopala
  1975   *The Methodology of Anthropological Comparisons*. Tuc-
         son: University of Arizona Press.
Scheper-Hughes, Nancy
  1995   "The Primacy of the Ethical: Propositions for a Militant
         Anthropology." *Current Anthropology* 36:409-420, 436-
         438.

Scholte, Bob
    1972   "Discontents in Anthropology." *Social Research* 38:777-
            807.
Tax, Sol, ed.
    1964   *Horizons of Anthropology*. Chicago, IL: Aldine.
Tyler, Stephen
    1986   "On Being Out of Words." *Cultural Anthropology* 1:131-
            137.
Tylor, Edward B.
    1871   *Primitive Culture*. London: John Murray.
Wolf, Eric
    1982   *Europe and the People without History*. Berkeley: Univer-
            sity of California Press.
Wright, Susan
    1998   "The Politicization of 'Culture.'" *Anthropology Today* 14
            (1):7-15.

Critical Issues

PARADIGMS REFOUND:
THE STRUCTURE OF ANTHROPOLOGICAL
REVOLUTIONS

Paul Bohannan, Mari Womack, and Karen Saenz

The Hopi, indigenous people of the U.S. Southwest, say: "This has happened before; it will come round again." The same might be said of anthropological theory. Paul Bohannan notes that a long career in anthropology allows one to witness a virtual parade of paradigms that cross and recross the anthropological stage. "As I write, . . . literary criticism is having considerable impact on cultural anthropology—again. My problem with that is not that I consider it wrong, but that I know it to be old hat" (1998:415). Bohannan remembers when literary critics like F. R. Leavis and William Empson had a profound impact on social anthropology. When you remember that, it is hard to think that the same ideas, under new authorship, with more recent publication dates, championing a new set of philosophers, are an original advance.

The difference between the Hopi concept of the return of the ancestors and the parade of ancestral paradigms across the anthropological stage is significant. The Hopi believe that when loved ones die, their last breath floats upward to become a cloud, a significant contribution in a land where rain is scarce, and every drop of moisture is cherished. The ancestors are remembered when the clouds return, bringing much-needed rain for growing crops. The Hopi say: "It will come round again." Anthropologists say: "Our ancestors were blind and wrong; we now know better." That is, anthropologists kill their ancestors, then sneak the essential ideas back in, with new names.

Rediscovery of overtly discarded models, however, is common. Leslie White (1949), for example, drew on the first accepted, then rejected, models of Lewis H. Morgan and E. B. Tylor to develop his apparently radical model of cultural evolution based on the use of technology for conversion of energy. It is significant that White acknowledged his ancestral debts. White's model was rejected in turn by many of his contemporaries, although his cultural evolutionary model provides the implicit and often unacknowledged foundation for more recent economic models, including the cultural materialism of Marvin Harris or the idea (pretty generally accepted at the moment) that knowing subsistence patterns is essential to understanding other aspects of social organization.

There is a decidedly Western bias against rehabilitating previously rejected paradigms in the same field. For example, Bronislaw Malinowski's angst while in the field, recorded in his diary, is one familiar to every anthropologist who conducts fieldwork. Malinowski writes: "Feeling of absurdity less intense. Strong impression that my information about fishing is very inadequate" (1967:145). And a few days later: "Sitting in the dinghy I enjoyed being alone. Then a dominant feeling of ethnographic disappointment came back" (1967:149). Like Malinowski, we have all asked ourselves whether the ethnographic enterprise we have undertaken is really worth the effort we have put into it. Only now we call it postmodernism or the "new ethnography." Why is it so difficult for us to acknowledge that the sense of "ethnographic disappointment" we now experience was also experienced by our anthropological ancestors almost a hundred years ago? This "ethnographic disappointment" is neither new nor postmodern. It is a condition of conducting fieldwork, often alone, frustrated, and insecure.

It is not, however, the rehabilitation of previously rejected theories that strikes the eye here; it is the fact that the names of ancestral scholars are not rehabilitated along with their theories. Recognizing the contribution of others to our work does not detract from the significance of our own contribution. In fact, it makes us appear more scholarly. The process of ancestor killing is not based in logic; rather, it is embedded in the social and conceptual context of constructing new analytical models.

In his pivotal book *The Structure of Scientific Revolutions*, Thomas Kuhn deals with one conceptual basis for the killing of ancestors:

> at times of revolution, when the normal-scientific tradition changes, the scientist's perception of his environment must be re-educated—in some familiar situations he must learn to see a new

gestalt. After he has done so the world of his research will seem, here and there, incommensurable with the one he had inhabited before. That is another reason why schools guided by different paradigms are always slightly at cross-purposes (1970:112).

Kuhn's view of the adoption and rejection of scientific paradigms sounds remarkably like religious conversion, and Kuhn does not dispute this. In fact, he describes the initial period of questioning an established paradigm as a time when scientists "may begin to lose faith" but "do not renounce the paradigm that has led them into crisis" (1970:77). Kuhn notes that beginning to doubt an accepted paradigm brings angst:

> Because it demands large-scale paradigm destruction and major shifts in the problems and techniques of normal science, the emergence of new theories is generally preceded by a period of pronounced professional insecurity. As one might expect, that insecurity is generated by the persistent failure of the puzzles of normal science to come out as they should. Failure of existing rules is the prelude to a search for new ones (1970:67-68).

Kuhn frames his model of scientific revolutions primarily in intellectualist terms. However, there is also a strong political and economic basis for maintenance and rejection of paradigms. Academic communities that share a paradigm also control a great deal of political power in terms of ensuring that their shared paradigm is passed on to new generations of students. This political power is reinforced economically through control over admissions to universities, granting of Ph.D.s, hiring, granting of tenure, and awarding of research grants, as well as control over publications and literature reviews. Competing paradigms challenge a type of control that can become almost monopolistic. Discrediting competing paradigms allows a scholarly lineage to maintain control over important political and economic empires. Kuhn writes: "The very existence of science depends upon vesting the power to choose between paradigms in the members of a special kind of community" (1970:167). He adds: "A paradigm is what the members of a scientific community share, *and*, conversely, the members of a scientific community consist of men who share a paradigm" (1970:176). The "professional insecurity" described by Kuhn is reflected in the reluctance of young scholars trying to make a name for themselves to become identified with previously discredited models for fear of making themselves appear naive or unsophisticated.

At the same time, scholars can make a name for themselves by attacking dominant elders. An example in anthropology is Derek Freeman (1983), whose most significant contribution to the discipline consists of repudiating Margaret Mead's work in Samoa. The discrepancy between Freeman's and Mead's analysis of Samoan socialization and adolescent behavior is based in their differing paradigmatic stances (Shankman 1996), in that Freeman favored biological explanations for behavior whereas Mead asserted the primacy of cultural factors. However, Freeman and Mead also studied different villages and occupied different social statuses that may have given them differing aspects of data on the behavior of adolescent females (Womack 1998:128-129). Freeman was addressed by the title *manaia*, signifying his leadership within a group of untitled, unmarried men. As a young woman, Mead was a frequent companion of unmarried females. Freeman, however, framed his debate with Mead as a means of discrediting "an anthropological myth," thus reinforcing the cultural construct that biologically based paradigms are incompatible with culturally based paradigms.

Another example is Kenneth Good, whose career is based largely on attacking Napoleon Chagnon's work among the Yanomamo and on the publicity generated when Good married a Yanomamo woman. Good's book on the subject is described by the publisher as "The fascinating adventure of an American among the Yanomama—a Stone Age people of the Amazon rain forest—and one of the most remarkable love stories of our time" (1991).[1] Good's report of his "adventure" among the Yanomamo emphasizes the killing of his anthropological ancestor rather than the advancement of a new or competing paradigm.

Though it is difficult to topple reigning anthropological monarchs, doing so can provide a young anthropologist with a secure career foothold. Building a career (or "making a name") in academic anthropology in the United States is essentially a two-step process: First, the would-be careerist must ritually kill his or her intellectual ancestors; and, second, he or she must forge alliances with powerful contemporaries. Ideally, both steps must be enacted publicly in front of an audience of professional colleagues or peers. Walter Goldschmidt speaks of the first step, in Oedipal terms, as the "killing of the father" (1980, personal communication).

Is it always necessary, however, to "kill the father" in every system of kinship reckoning? Why do anthropological revolutions so often combine ancestor killing (refuting our own intellectual traditions) with borrowing from other traditions (or intellectual lineages)? Some clues may be found in the time-honored anthropological study of kinship, even though some anthropologists feel it is time to kill off this venerable branch of the family altogether.

As anthropologists have long been aware, the dynamics of kinship cannot be divorced, so to speak, from the cultural context in which they occur. Bohannan writes of his tutelage under E. E. Evans-Pritchard at Oxford in the African idiom, "He is my father and my mother" (1997: 123). In the Tiv kinship model, within which context Bohannan conducted his fieldwork, sons do not kill their fathers and mothers and, in fact, Bohannan speaks of his relationship with Evans-Pritchard in terms of filial piety (1997:123).

Malinowski (1927) rejected the idea that father-killing is a primal Oedipal urge rooted in a boy's desire to displace his father and possess his mother sexually. Instead, he said, competitive feelings toward the father are the product of patrilineal forms of inheritance, in which a man acquires his own place in society by displacing his father. Ironically, it was Malinowski who set the standard for father-killing in anthropology by turning against Sir James Frazer, the man who inspired him to become an anthropologist in the first place. Malinowski ridiculed Frazer's work, *The Golden Bough*, the very book that inspired him to enter the field of anthropology, calling its association of the succession of kings with the worship of trees "the vegetable hypothesis."

In yet another ironic twist to this primal episode in the development of anthropology, Frazer dealt in *The Golden Bough* (1890) with what he considered the widespread practice of killing kings when their powers began to fail, a ritual practice that often included sexual cohabitation with the king's wives by the successor or a mock king. Malinowski "killed" Frazer professionally by ridiculing his work, embraced Frazer's young bride Anthropology, and inherited his academic "crown" from Frazer, who gave the inaugural address when Malinowski was installed as the holder of the first chair in anthropology at the London School of Economics.

Malinowski was himself murderously assaulted by other social anthropologists, who preferred Radcliffe-Brown's "more sophisticated terminology and theoretical approach" (Lewis 1985:55) to Malinowski's "earthy, materialist view of man's motives" (Lewis 1985:53). I. M. Lewis writes: "Whereas Malinowski had invoked the aid of reductionist principles borrowed from biology, and concentrated on man's *cultural* adaptation, Radcliffe-Brown re-asserted the *social* basis of all customs and institutions" (1985:55-56). Adam Kuper writes: "For many of Malinowski's contemporaries his theoretical naiveté was apparent from the first, and his crude utilitarianism could arouse derision" (1983:34). Kuper adds: "[Meyer] Fortes has pointed out that Malinowski was always promising a book on Trobriand kinship, and he suggests that the book was never written precisely because Malinowski could not conceive of a 'kinship system.' But so far as Malinowski was concerned, *The Sexual Life of Savages* was a book on Trobriand kinship" (1983:28).

Anthropological kinship studies are themselves currently in danger of extinction by ancestor-killing within the discipline even though, across time and across theoretical boundaries, kinship has long held a privileged place in anthropology. It has been a focus of many of our discipline's most revered ancestors, including Evans-Pritchard (1951). Contemporary scholars still rely on Lewis Henry Morgan's (1870) model of consanguinity (descent) and affinity (marriage). For example, Womack (1993) uses this model to explain the intricacies of the troubled relationship between England's Prince Charles and Princess Diana, a dynamic that can only be understood in terms of the patrilineal descent system for inheritance of the throne combined with marriage rules that prescribe endogamy for religion and social class.

The concepts of consanguinity and affinity are also useful in explaining the phenomenon of ancestor-killing in anthropology. Kuhn takes an intellectualist perspective on the tendency of scientists to vigorously reject earlier paradigms, noting that "science" is inextricably allied with "progress." It is also instructive to note that science is itself a cultural construct, developed in the Western intellectualist tradition. Scientists, too, are embedded in their genealogies. As in all kinship systems, scientists are inclined to ally themselves with relatives who can provide them with the greatest source of benefit and ignore kinship ties that might bring upon them ignominy or reduction of social status.

In particular, the American scientific community is characterized by bilateral inheritance and neolocal residence. In other words, scientists feel it is their right to borrow from whatever discipline advances their status (the rich relative syndrome associated with bilateral inheritance), while maintaining the right to cut ties of descent—which also imply obligations—in favor of establishing an entirely new area of expertise, and restricting access to resources to a small and tightly controlled reproductive unit. This shifts the emphasis from consanguineal ties to affinal ties. It also confers the advantages of bilateral inheritance and neolocal residence, which include mobility, flexibility, and the ability to expand or contract kinship bonds as advantage requires.

There are disadvantages to this system of reckoning kinship, however. One must surrender the privileges associated with unilineal or ambilineal inheritance and the extended family. Just as we are not obligated to come to the defense of anyone but our spouses and offspring, we cannot call on the resources of anyone but our spouses and offspring. We are not obligated to other lineage members, but in turn, they are not obligated to us. We claim the right to invest our resources in our offspring; our ancestors claim the right to disinherit us. We surrender the cooperative advantages of reinforcing alliances within the lineage in favor of the competitive advantages of the nuclear family.

By way of contrast, the Chinese system of ancestor reverence, with descent traced through patrilineal clans, emphasizes responsibility to the descent group. This is based on the view that an individual isolated from others cannot fulfill his or her human potential, and this philosophy is expressed formally in the "five relationships": father-son, older brother-younger brother, husband-wife, ruler-subject, and friend-friend. Of these, only the fifth relationship—friend-friend—is based on equality. In all the other cases, the position on the left side is one of responsibility, the position on the right side is one of respect and obedience. Womack writes:

> Relationships within the family continue after death in a system of ritual observance that unites land ownership, the patrilineal inheritance system, and clan membership. The oldest son is responsible for "feeding" his parents even after they are dead by maintaining an ancestral altar in the family home and by ritual observances at the ancestral graveyard, which is expected to occupy the most auspicious position on the land (1998:213).

On the other hand, failure to respect and care for the ancestors brings misfortune and dishonor to the entire family.

The spirits of the dead who have no one to feed them or who are neglected by their descendants must go "hungry" in the spirit world. These "hungry ghosts" retaliate by preying upon the unwary and bringing misfortune to the entire community. It is the responsibility of the community to hold a hungry ghost festival, in which people who are living provide food and paper money for the spirits of the dead who do not have family to take care of them. Womack writes: "Ancestor reverence reinforces the responsibility of the individual to the family and extends that responsibility to the community as a whole in the practice of feeding hungry ghosts" (1998:213). Rituals associated with ancestor reverence reinforce the solidarity of the lineage and bind lineage members to the land, whereas hungry ghost festivals emphasize responsibilities of individuals to the community as a whole.

The Chinese system of ancestor reverence is well-suited to an agricultural society, where land ownership is essential to survival and the labor of every family member is necessary to work the land. The scientific community, in contrast, is a product of secular segmentation, and its growth has been spurred by European colonialism and by the increasing dominance of industrialization. Industrialization is a system in which land is a resource suitable primarily for exploitation and the ideal of individual entrepreneurship is actively promoted. This is consonant with the ideology that "ancestors" are in fact "ghosts." They confer no benefits and they stick around only because they have some grievance against the living. Of course, individual entrepreneurship is a luxury for the elite and is dependent upon an abundant supply of workers who can be exploited.

In anthropology, this elitism results in a system in which an upwardly mobile individual is expected to literally abandon the family of biological origin and strike out on his or her own, exploring new territory and collecting new data. The fledgling anthropologist does not form alliances by marrying into a closely related kin group. Instead, the rite of passage that conducts the anthropologists from adolescence to maturity rests on adoption into the group being studied, in effect forming a fictive kin relationship. This amalgamation with a new lineage is not sufficient for attaining high professional status, however. The ambitious anthropologist must also adopt a paradigm advocated by powerful elders in one of the currently accepted anthropological lineages. Gaining the protection of a powerful head of an accepted lineage is sufficient for survival—getting a Ph.D., tenure, and publications—but it is not sufficient for gaining high status within the discipline. Paying homage to one's anthropological ancestors is not enough; one must also supplant the powerful lineage head, either by killing him or her or through "neolocal residence," that is, by establishing a new lineage based on a newly generated or newly defined paradigm. Bohannan notes: "We all know that history has to be rewritten every generation. Even if the historical 'facts' do not change, the context in which they are to be read and interpreted does change" (1998:415).

In lieu of killing an ancestor in one's direct line of descent, it is also possible to make one's reputation by killing the head of another anthropological lineage. This confers the advantage of retaining the protection of one's own lineage head and, in fact, solidifying that bond by killing the head of a rival lineage. This is an ironic twist on E. B. Tylor's dictum of "marry out or die out." In this case, the individual reinforces ties within the lineage and severs ties with other lineages. Whether killed by their own descendants or by the descendants of a rival lineage, the result is the same: the loss or discrediting of essential elders in the discipline, along with the knowledge and traditions they represent.

It is doubtful whether this wholesale slaughter of ancestors is essential to the scientific enterprise or that it is beneficial to the discipline of anthropology as a whole. To draw on an evolutionary paradigm, it does not even benefit the individuals who temporarily reign supreme, though they may gain the perquisites of tenure and publications. They cannot transmit their ideas (genetic material) beyond a single generation and the name they have so carefully won is doomed to die with them.

To further delineate this kinship metaphor, it is instructive to compare American and Australian descent systems. On the surface, these two descent systems have one element in common: each has a descent rule that reckons ancestry through both male and female lines. However, the American rule of bilateral descent and the Australian rule of double unilineal descent have different effects on the production of local knowledge and "career-building" within their respective cultures. Following current convention in the anthropological study of kinship systems, here we distinguish between the descent rule, which specifies the organization of successive parent-child links, and the use of that rule as the basis for recruitment to a descent group.

The Australian system of double (or sometimes bilineal) descent, for example, recognizes that individuals simultaneously reckon ancestry patrilineally for some purposes and matrilineally for other purposes. In other words, both unilineal descent rules coexist and even intersect, but they are relevant to different circumstances. This is the case with Wardaman-speaking Aborigines, for example, who trace certain land relationships through the father and certain social relationships through the mother (Saenz 1994).

The American rule of bilateral descent, in comparison, holds that individuals reckon descent through both sides rather than both lines. This distinction may seem merely semantic when looking at the descent rule; however, when the resulting descent group is considered, the emergence of a distinction between ancestor-killing and ancestor-reverence comes into sharp relief. Specifically, the American rule of bilateral descent does not produce a descent group which is traced forward from a founding ancestor in the past, as is the case of Wardaman Aborigines who trace their corporate lineages and clans from ancestral Dreaming beings. Rather, the American bilateral descent rule produces a descent group which is traced backward from an individual ego in the present. The Australian system produces a corporate descent group, whereas the American system produces a kindred, a set of kinship relationships specific to an individual and not shared by any group.

This distinction between kinship corporations (like lineages and clans) and kinship categories (like kindreds) cannot be overemphasized. Bilineally produced corporations, on the one hand, maintain cohesion by keeping the name of the common ancestor alive in the present. In addition to a sense of shared community, there is also a sense of shared history, or at least of continuity between the present and the past, such that descent is strongly valued in the culture. This sense of community is reinforced by the custom of naming children after ancestors. In contrast, kindred membership differs for every sibling set, since it is an ego-centered construct. Consequently, bilaterally produced kindreds reduce the community to an individual and reduce history to the present, weakening the value of ancestry (and correspondingly strengthening the value of affinity).

Similarly, the impact of this distinction between Aboriginal corporations and American kindreds on their respective cultural constructions of knowledge cannot be overemphasized. Both Wardaman culture and the American culture of academic anthropology value knowledge as a commodity; *how* the two cultures value knowledge, though, relates directly to their differing structure of descent. For Wardaman-speaking Aborigines, certain types of knowledge about "country" or land is inherited patrilineally and transmitted through the communal religious system along lines of male mentorship. Knowledge, then, both defines and is confined within the descent group. Consequently, junior members—whose "careers" are dependent upon a knowledge-wealthy descent corporation—revere senior members of their lineage, including living human mentors, former or deceased human mentors, and Dreaming-being ancestors.

American academic anthropologists, in contrast, have a vastly different cultural understanding of knowledge production and career-building. First of all, the descent system of the American culture-at-large de-emphasizes the past in favor of the present (an emphasis that is reflected in anthropology's construction of the "ethnographic present"). Secondly, the descent system of the American culture-at-large de-emphasizes the descent group in favor of the individual (an emphasis that is reflected in anthropology's construction of the fieldworker-as-maverick). Finally, in the culture of academic anthropology, knowledge cannot be entirely inherited through mentorship. In the process of fieldwork, so the canon goes, one must collect one's "own" data and "make" (not inherit) one's name. In order to do this, knowledge must be produced anew (not merely reproduced), making ancestors and mentors problematic for the would-be careerist. At the very least, their existence must be denied, lest one be accused of not individuating from one's intellectual family-of-origin, thereby suffering intellectual condemnation through being labeled "derivative," a term that connotes lack of creativity and initiative. In other words, ancestors must be surpassed, when they are not killed, to achieve individuation and renown.

Ironically, we may trace both the tradition of killing our ancestors and the practice of fieldwork as a process of individuation back to our "dreamtime" ancestor, Bronislaw Malinowski. We have already noted that Malinowski established a pattern of ancestor slaughter with his attack on Sir James Frazer. In addition, he has become the very model of the intrepid anthropologist stalking the native in the field. As I. M. Lewis writes: "Although he was not the very first, [Malinowski] has come to be regarded as the pioneer, bushwhacking anthropologist, the originator of the doctrine that until you have lived cheek by jowl with an exotic tribe and spoken their language fluently you cannot claim full professional status" (1985:54).

Though bilateral inheritance and neolocal residence (combining the rich relative syndrome with the killing of ancestors) is the prevailing kinship idiom in American culture, it may not be the most beneficial idiom for the culture of anthropology. Malinowski once wrote that: "Much ink has flowed on the problem of blood" (1930:19). It may be equally true that, in anthropology, much "blood" has flowed on the problem of "ink," or publications, which may also be equated with status in the field of anthropology.

The Chinese recognize their ancestors as continuing members of one's lineage by feeding them and by acknowledging their continuing contribution to the family. It is a reciprocal relationship. Living descendants feed the ancestors to keep them from becoming "hungry ghosts" and causing trouble for the living. In return, the ancestors are expected to care for and protect their descendants. Australian Aborigines similarly recognize indebtedness to their ancestors through both matrilineal and patrilineal lines and acknowledge the continuing presence of ancestors in their lives through naming customs.

American anthropologists, on the other hand, allow their intellectual ancestors to become "hungry ghosts" and get angry when discounted theoretical models return to haunt the living. The very vehemence with which anthropologists reject what they consider outmoded theories testifies to their continuing "power" over "living" or contemporary theories. We may find that anthropologists, who have conducted such sophisticated studies and analyses of kinship, may have much to learn from the writings of their ancestors—and, indeed, from their own writings—about the importance of "blood" ties in promoting not only the survival of the living but the eventual victories of their descendants.

Notes

Writing this chapter has been a test of the value of combining respect for one's ancestors with the advantages of neolocal residence. Paul Bohannan, Mari Womack, and Karen Saenz represent three stages of the anthropological career: respected elder, mature adult, and emerging young adult. Each has made a contribution independently of the others.

1. "Yanomamo" and "Yanomama" are alternate spellings for the same connotative term.

References

Bohannan, Paul
    1997   "It's Been a Good Field Trip." *Ethnos* 62(1-2):116-136.
    1998   "Passing into History." In Mari Womack, *Being Human: An Introduction to Cultural Anthropology*. Upper Saddle River, NJ: Prentice-Hall.
Evans-Pritchard, E. E.
    1951   *Kinship and Marriage Among the Nuer*. Oxford: Clarendon Press.
Frazer, James George
    1890   *The Golden Bough*. London: Macmillan.

Freeman, Derek
  1983   *Margaret Mead and Samoa.* Cambridge, MA: Harvard
          University Press.
Good, Kenneth (with David Chanoff)
  1991   *Into the Heart: One Man's Pursuit of Love and Knowledge
          among the Yanomama.* New York: Simon & Schuster.
Kuhn, Thomas S.
  1970   *The Structure of Scientific Revolutions.* 2nd edition. Chi-
          cago, IL: University of Chicago Press.
Kuper, Adam
  1983   *Anthropology and Anthropologists: The Modern British
          School.* London: Routledge.
Lewis, I. M.
  1985   *Social Anthropology in Perspective.* 2nd edition. Cam-
          bridge: Cambridge University Press.
Malinowski, Bronislaw
  1927   *The Father in Primitive Psychology.* New York: Norton.
  1930   "Kinship." *Man* 30:19-29.
  1967   *A Diary in the Strict Sense of the Term*, N. Guterman,
          trans. Stanford, CA: Stanford University Press.
Morgan, Lewis H.
  1870   *Systems of Consanguinity and Affinity in the Human Family.*
          Washington, DC: Smithsonian Institution (Contributions to
          Knowledge 17).
Saenz, Karen Eilene
  1994   Space, Time, and Gender: An Archaeology of Human Rela-
          tions in Post-Contact Aboriginal Northern Australia, Ph.D.
          dissertation, UCLA, Los Angeles.
Shankman, Paul
  1996   "The History of Samoan Sexual Conduct and the Mead-
          Freeman Controversy." *American Anthropologist* 98:555-
          567.
White, Leslie
  1949   *The Science of Culture.* New York: Grove Press.
Womack, Mari.
  1993   "Introduction to Love, Marriage, and Power." In Mari Wo-
          mack and Judith Marti, eds., *The Other Fifty Percent.*
          Prospect Heights, IL: Waveland Press.
  1998   *Being Human: An Introduction to Cultural Anthropology.*
          Upper Saddle River, NJ: Prentice-Hall.

THE "WORLD SYSTEM" OF ANTHROPOLOGY AND "PROFESSIONAL OTHERS"

Pamela J. Asquith

Introduction

There is by now a large and steadily growing body of literature on the history and problems of the privileging of Western, especially European and American, discourses in anthropology. These range, among others, from discussions of different epistemologies, to colonialist discourses, to irresponsibility on the part of those in the "anthropological center" toward "natives" and native anthropologists. In the anthropological study of Japan many of the same issues are being voiced. Yet, as with anthropology as a whole, actual examples of sustained privileging of one discourse over another, and especially what has been lost to our stores of knowledge, are few.

A debate[1] on some of these issues was published recently between a Japanese and a Dutch anthropologist of Japan. For various reasons (the original paper being in Japanese, and the subsequent English version and responses appearing in a newsletter written for a particular membership) it may not be widely known. I was particularly struck by this debate since it reflected many problematical aspects of a subfield of anthropology—primatology—in Japan. What follows is an example of a sustained privileging of one discourse over another and reflection upon some of the things that are at stake in the current larger debates. This example (of primatology) is, I think, all the more interesting because although it began as two quite distinct traditions in the West and Japan, it gives by now the *appearance* of being a truly integrated discipline. However, as an anthropologist and participant-observer in the Japanese science community over a period of eighteen years, I have seen important distinctions between the two traditions being buried in the necessity to write Western-style reports, and I think that what remains distinct and largely unknown about it in international fora is very relevant to current concerns in anthropology.

In the debate on Japanese anthropology, American trained anthropologist Takami Kuwayama (1997a, b, c) contended that in the "world system" of anthropology, "core" countries such as the United States, Great Britain and France have dominance over "peripheral" countries, of which he considers Japan to be one. The dominance, he contended, takes the form of lack of recognition of, or interest in, contributions by scholars in peripheral countries. It also determines the kinds of discourse (what is desired knowledge and how it is to be expressed) that is acceptable. Where Japan itself is the object of anthropological study, Kuwayama opined that the views of the native anthropologist are ignored or at least omitted from research reports written for the "dominant discourse" back home. Native anthropologists are thus relegated to the status of "professional others" in Kuwayama's terms.

Jan van Bremen (1997b) responded, on the other hand, that there are instances of anthropologists who have been marginalized at one time or another in every country that has a tradition of anthropology. Van Bremen has researched the intellectual history of Japanese anthropology as well as the impact of anthropological traditions that are outside of European and North American centers (e.g. van Bremen 1988, 1997a). He questioned Kuwayama's contention that Japanese anthropologists are any more marginalized than anyone else and cited instances of acknowledged Japanese contributions to world anthropology. More importantly, according to van Bremen, we should move in the direction of an interactive discipline and avoid the pitfalls of separate ethnic anthropologies. I will return to this last point at the end of this discussion.

In his response to van Bremen in the same issue, Kuwayama (1997c) maintained that those Japanese acknowledged as having contributed importantly to world anthropological research functioned within the parameters of the dominant tradition, either through their foreign training, or by publishing in English, or by formulating ideas with reference to Western scholarship. He also reiterated his thesis that native anthropologists in the non-West (the professional others) have been posited, but excluded from the anthropological discourse in the West.

I was struck as much by the obvious sincerity of van Bremen's perception that all professional anthropologists are equally subject to the shifting vagaries of marginalization and hegemonies of dominant discourses, as by the many parallels with Kuwayama's contentions to be found in primatology. I would like to reflect on some of the thoughtful points made by both authors in reference to primatology as a subdiscipline within anthropology. I do not know whether Kuwayama's observations about Japanese and (social)[2] anthropological studies are systemic problems or only impressions[3] (however well justified), though I have opinions about them. I *can* martial solid evidence in primatology, however, that echoes several of Kuwayama's contentions about systemic marginalization and hegemonies so closely, he could as well have been discussing that field. I refer to the large body of field or ethological studies of primate behavior, rather than primate research for pharmaceutical or other medical applications.

My purpose in examining primatology in this context is threefold: (1) In his discussion, van Bremen called for a more accurate and comprehensive picture of anthropology than is commonly given in accounts of the discipline. He is absolutely right that corrective is needed. Most of what I write below is never discussed formally across nationalities at international meetings, much less published. Both the perceptions and the facts of the matter need to be stated so that those (perceived to be) in the dominant tradition are made aware of the perceptions and experiences of those (who perceive themselves) on the periphery and to permit open and cooperative steps toward resolution. Related to van Bremen's comment, too, is the addition of another area of anthropology to the discussion (see below on primatology's links with anthropology). (2) This instantiation raises additional questions and reflections to those of Kuwayama's and van Bremen's thoughtful prolegomena. In illustrating examples of, and bases for, systematic peripheralization of Japanese studies of primates that can be followed over a forty year history, we can see more readily what the social anthropologists are facing in tackling this issue. (3) Consideration of both disciplines leads to points which could profitably be examined across disciplines which, like anthropology, have Japanese (or other nationalities) as both object of study and as professional colleagues (e.g. literature, film, sociology, history, linguistics, religious studies, etc.). In other words, what is the nature of our knowledge in these fields that have such a rich potential for international dialog and input? Or perhaps some of them already manage to tap the best of both epistemological and cultural worlds, in which case we could see why and how they do so.

Primatology as an Exemplar

Primatology is, in many ways, a separate scientific discipline, but it is part of anthropology in seeking biological and evolutionary parameters to past and present behavioral and physical characteristics of humans. Most Western primatologists worldwide receive their training in, and are employed by, Departments of Anthropology or Psychology. They publish in some of the same journals as social anthropologists, such as *American Anthropologist* and *Current Anthropology*. In Japan, place of employment is more eclectic. Primatologists who study naturalistic behavior may work in primate, medical, African studies or other institutes, Departments of Anthropology or Ethology, centers attached to zoos, etc. That said, the scientific nature of the discipline in some ways highlights the effects of marginalization, and raises further questions about bias in such areas as editing by international peers for style and content that changes or even deletes what the nonnative speaker wished to express; ignorance of philosophical and intellectual background to "peripheral" scientists' traditions; lack of translation facilities at international conferences to allow real debate after the presentation of papers, and so on.

In contradistinction to social anthropology (cf. Ishida 1965),[4] primatology is one of the few modern fields of research that was initiated independently in Japan at approximately the same time as in Western countries—with minimal exchange between the traditions during the formative stages. Japanese, European, and American studies of primate behavior began within a decade of one another in the 1930s and 1940s, and yet have had fundamental differences from the outset. Japanese reports of naturalistic primate behavior were, for instance, more personal, anthropomorphic, and richly detailed as to individual animal's life histories. The questions that arose from their studies yielded far-reaching insights that the Western approaches did not.[5] However, potential directions for research generated by Japanese findings were largely ignored by Western researchers, even though the work was published in English in a readily accessible journal, *Primates*, produced by the Japanese. Only after two decades and more[6] were those insights, that "other" knowledge, subjected to mainstream European and American methodology for testing, and found to be valid (Asquith 1996). Likewise, the Kuwayama-van Bremen debate highlights the need for both the "silent discourse," and what members of each tradition perceive the other to be doing, to be brought into the open.

Areas to Examine

Although each of the following areas are inextricably linked in the development and dissemination of ideas in a discipline, the points may be better illustrated separately. This may also allow easier cross-disciplinary comparison of factors effecting marginalization. In the interests of keeping this to a reasonable length, the examples from primatology are brief and intended simply to indicate areas anthropology and other fields could consider.

Journals

I will consider two aspects of journal publication with reference to primatology.

1. The journal's (perceived) status:

The first international journal of primate behavior was *Primates*.[7] This was begun by the Japanese in 1957. Only the first two issues were published in Japanese. From 1959 until now, all articles have appeared in English. There are other international Western-based journals in which primate behavior articles regularly appear, such as the *American Journal of Physical Anthropology*, *Folia Primatologica*, and the *International Journal of Primatology*. These publications, as well as more inclusive journals such as *Nature*, *Animal Behaviour*, *Behaviour*, *Journal of Human Evolution*, etc., are ranked higher than *Primates* by many Western primatologists.

We have arrived at the point in this commentary where, as Ishida (1965:303) remarked with regard to European views of American anthropology: "[we] touch upon the fundamental but delicate point of the cleavage between them, which, in my opinion, is not simply a matter of different terminology, (and which) might be felt by both sides to be somewhat unpleasant, if not unconsciously tabooed." Some North American primatologists even today advise their graduate students not to publish in *Primates*; some current teachers who were students in the 1970s were advised against even citing research published in *Primates* in their doctoral thesis. Although specialist primatology journals began to be published in the West in 1962, not until 1976 did a Japanese-authored paper appear in one of them (Nishida 1976), and the dates for first publication of a Japanese-authored paper on primates in each of the other Western journals range from 1973 to 1988.[8] Prior to 1980 these number less than a dozen papers.

Of course, not all Western primatologists subscribe to the views expressed above, but the phenomenon has not gone unnoticed by their

Japanese colleagues. On taking over the position recently, the present (Japanese) editor-in-chief of *Primates* sent a letter to all members of the editorial board (which includes several Western primatologists) to ask for their input on how to improve the stature of the journal. He even wondered aloud if changing the cover would help.

2. Reviews/editing

Japanese primatologists also have a Japanese language professional journal[9] in which to publish their findings. I would guess that fewer than a half dozen non-Japanese in the world read it. Primatologists have often remarked to me that when they wish to write what they really want to say about primate behavior, they can publish in Japanese. I have heard many, many complaints by Japanese researchers that English speaking reviewers and editors cut much of the detail from their submitted articles and always ask that the paper be modified to address a specific topic (much like Kuwayama's "dominant discourse") if it does not appear to do so. Purely descriptive articles are rarely, if ever, accepted. On the other hand, Western primatologists and reviewers have told me that they often cannot discern what is the main point of the Japanese-authored articles. Some reviewers work quite hard to "improve" the papers to make them acceptable to the dominant discourse. At one level, it is a simple problem of English fluency or lack thereof. However, it is more fundamentally the case that the Japanese author often cannot express the different paradigm adequately in English. Kuwayama's (1997b:55) suggestion that Japanese could learn to "displace" their writing to produce subtle, yet perceptible, differences from the dominant discourse, seems not to have worked in this field. Japanese graduate students in primatology are told that they may as well not bother to publish in Japanese as it will not get them anywhere professionally. So what happens to all that data recorded in Japanese? It gets lost to international science.

Citation

Van Bremen provided examples of Japanese anthropological scholarship that has been cited and received due recognition in international circles, as against Kuwayama's claim of disregard for Japanese scholarship. Kuwayama responded that those Japanese who have been recognized worked within the dominant discourse, through publishing in English, receiving their training in the West, and so on. I have found in primatology that it is not so much citation that is a marker of acceptance. After all, the Japanese must publish in English and they publish data in major journals once it has been put into a suitable form for those journals. Rather, the estimation of the Japanese contribution can be measured by who is invited to select international fora, think tanks, and specialized meetings, who is involved in symposia at large meetings, who receives the international prizes (only one to a Japanese primatologist so far),[10] and so on. Unsurprisingly, these are Japanese who speak English well and who appear, in English language exchanges, to be "untainted" by a Japanese scholarly tradition. This leads to the concept of "token internationals."

Token Internationals

I suggest that most Japanese anthropologists who are well known and appreciated in the West are, as among primatologists, good at English or another Western language, spend time abroad or work with foreign researchers, and give the impression to Westerners that there is little difference in their approaches. They are usually pleased to have been accepted into the international club, of course. But among primatologists they either do not attempt to state what their colleagues at home are saying (raising some resentment on the part of those left behind), or they feel so estranged from their own national tradition that they leave the tradition altogether. There is an additional loss here: we do not get the diversity of Japanese opinion from these "internationals" in primatology.[11]

This is not intended to denigrate the scholarship or motives of those Japanese who move more easily than their colleagues in the international arena. Indeed, their non-Japanese-speaking colleagues are very fortunate that they have made this effort. I am suggesting that the scholarly environment as it exists now is not truly international when we cannot encompass diverse cultural views or means of expression.

Language

A lot has been written about the problem of language in international scientific discourse, and much of it is directed to how and why Japanese research has difficulties in reaching an English-speaking audience. I will give three examples of the effect of language in primatology.

1. Writing style

The criticism of overly descriptive writing has not been confined to certain Japanese fields of scholarship. European ethnography has been described as such by American anthropologists (see Hultkrantz 1968 for views of each other's traditions). So far as primatology is concerned, the fact that findings were presented in anthropomorphic terms and that they "followed an individual" or "followed a problem" over many years resulted in a mass of detailed description without apparently drawing out general principles about structure or behavior. This did not serve them positively. Yet Japanese primatologists have reasons for including a lot of description when they do so. Very often the data gathered on a group of a particular species has been a group effort covering many years, even decades, and generations of field workers, and who is to say what might not be useful in future. There are, in fact, a number of seemingly picayune observations that have proven central to later theorizing in the discipline. A notable example was the necessity for accurate genealogical records for troop members (kept by Japanese researchers) in order to test sociobiological theory later developed by Western researchers.

There is another aspect to this. Nakayama (1995:90-92) notes that most East Asian historians of science never intend to write in English. They communicate in their native language, forming a local citation group. Such groups often have local paradigms. Although they cite Western works, their own are practically never read in the Western world. A few who do write in English become aware of the culture-bound character of authorship, which, he says, imposes a number of limitations. Their concepts often can hardly be rendered into English. Nakayama mentions Kinji Imanishi and his anti-Darwinian evolutionary ideas as an example of a local citation group, while van Bremen (1997b:60) cites the important influence of Imanishi and Tadao Umesao (a "disciple" of Imanishi) on ideas in ecological anthropology. Both Nakayama and van Bremen are accurate in their seemingly oppo-site conclusions. Imanishi's ideas have been influential in some areas of research (notably, in ecology) and not in others. Yet Imanishi wrote very little in English and, like the East Asian historians, chose not to do so. Imanishi once said to me that he would prefer all of his work (running to some twenty volumes) to be translated at one time or not to be translated at all, so likely was it that it would not be understood if not available in its entirety.

2. Translation

I think that Kuwayama (1997b) is probably correct that if Japanese work was thought to be absolutely vital to the world discourse, more efforts would be made to have it translated into other languages. It is a fact that more Western works are translated into Japanese than the other way around. Japanese primatologists spend a lot of time translat-ing important foreign works into Japanese, or reading the original English, and current graduate students in primatology are told not to bother writing for publication in Japanese at all. At Kyoto University, one of the requirements for the D.Sc. degree in primatology is publication of three articles in international (English language) journals. Yet the fact that English is the dominant language in international scholarship does not, in itself, imply negative opinions about Japanese scholarship. In another century we would all have had to write and read in Latin. The more important question is why are more Japanese language works not translated into English? To some extent, it may be because the Japanese authors have been "willing" to do the work for English speakers in order to participate in the dominant discourse of scholarship. As Kuwayama, citing Gerholm (1995) said, the mainland can carry on without worrying about what goes on the islands, but not the other way around.

Ian Reader (1997:20) suggests that responsibility lies with (Western) anthropologists who work on Japan to provide the non-Japanese-speaking scholarly community with information on Japanese scholarship, through reviews, translations, or use of Japanese sources in their own studies. He notes that in the field of religious studies, a major journal (the *Japanese Journal of Religious Studies*) regularly translates important research by Japanese scholars, thus raising the profile of Japanese religious studies in the academic community. While this is an eminently reasonable suggestion for those fields in which a knowledge of Japanese is necessary in order to conduct research, it is less likely for other fields, such as primatology, or areas of social anthropology that, in this instance, do not have Japan as a focus. One might argue, with van Bremen (1988:256-257), that anthropologists working in any part of the world in any scholarly field should be aware of Japanese (or any other) scholarship on it; but this brings us back to precisely the current discussion of linguistic hegemonies and how to make room for other discourses that approach questions differently.

3. Debate

Giving "voice" to alternative viewpoints in publications is one thing; but even more importantly, at the fountainhead of scholarship, in the conversations and debates at academic meetings, out of which new projects arise and current ones are refined, Japanese do not have much voice. Even most non-native Japanologists cannot debate with equal facility in Japanese as in their native tongue. So either Japanese must do so in English (or German, or French, etc.) with the obvious attendant disadvantages to themselves in terms of fluency and in terms of being able to use a different cultural discourse, or they must decline to participate in the discussion.[12]

Intellectual Traditions and Epistemologies

Van Bremen expressed concern that we not develop isolated "ethnic anthropologies" (1997b). Indeed, his concern has long been shared by others, including some who attended a Wenner-Gren sponsored meeting held in 1978 on *Indigenous Anthropology in Non-Western Countries* (edited by Fahim, 1982). In this collection, Barnes (1982), Cernea (1982) and Mott (1982) argued that the concept of indigenous anthropology is fraught with the epistemological dangers of legitimizing a particularistic nationalistic approach to social facts. In the context of Japanese scholarship, *nihonjinron* (literally, discussions of the Japanese) has received much attention in this regard.[13] The three authors thought that such segmentation of the discipline along ethnic or national lines would be at cross-purposes with the goal of generating universally applicable and valid statements and could result in the proliferation of innumerable anthropologies on the same topic (Fahim 1982:xiv).

To my mind, a much more likely scenario is that put forward at the same meeting by, among others, Altorki (1982), in which bias is viewed as a problem of the discipline as a whole. Fahim (1982:xiv) summarized:

> According to this orientation, anthropology has been unduly influenced by the Western cultural perspectives of its practitioners in the selection of topics, approach to problems, and interpretation of data. . . . New concepts and explanatory models, generated from other cultural perspectives, might provide a better fit between social reality—as perceived by a scholarly member of that society—and anthropological paradigms.

Likewise, Nakane (1982) has argued, with reference to studies of Japanese culture, that concerns and concepts emanating from a Western background have influenced problem selection and the scope of research and methodology, which do not coincide with those prevailing in scholarly Japanese circles. Because of foreign anthropologists' lack of understanding of greater Japanese (scholarly) culture and tradition, their work fails to interest Japanese scholars. This is another sense in which there is a lack of knowledge, leading to lack of acknowledgment of research conducted by "professional others." If the context of the research is not known or understood, that data cannot reasonably be applied to another context. Explanations of assumptions and goals underlying Japanese studies of primates have largely fallen on deaf ears.[14] Indigenous anthropology implies to me that new cultural perspectives will be brought into play, not as obstacles to be overcome, but as new sources of understanding for the discipline.

This is not without its own difficulties, however. Kuwayama (1997b) suggested that one way to strike a balance of power is to publish a new journal in which native scholars could comment on articles by non-native scholars, who in turn reply to the comments they have received. *Current Anthropology* provides such a forum, though it perhaps is not utilized to the extent Kuwayama would like to see. One large problem with this is whether members of one tradition *understand* the other. Western primatologists have not understood what underlay Japanese approaches to primate studies and they are also largely unaware of that fact. Evidence for this was revealed in early responses to descriptions of their approach by the founder of Japanese primatology (Imanishi 1960) and more recently in a year-long series of letters to the journal *Nature* in response to a misrepresentation of the influence of Kinji Imanishi's anti-Darwinian views in Japan (Asquith 1986b; Halstead 1985; Sakura et al. 1986). Analogies with Western paradigms are unproven in Ikeda and Shibatani's (1995) description of Imanishi's biological thoght.

Marginality

Although I also have been using it, the term and concept of "marginality" may be problematical in relation to these problems, for reasons in addition to those raised by van Bremen. That is, Kuwayama (1997b:52) contends that the traditions that form the "core" of anthropology are the United States, Great Britain and France and that they dictate the anthropological discourse with which scholars from "peripheral" countries must comply if they wish to be recognized. Yet this surely depends upon individual perspective. In 1968 one could not have gotten the impression that American anthropology was the core from European Hultkrantz's (1968) remarks. His critique of American anthropology (as being too broad, etc.) seems to have been occasioned by Wenner-Gren's gift donation for the establishment of the Nordic Institute of Anthropology "to be fashioned after American anthropology" (1968:289, note 4; 290). This understandably elicited a reaction from the European ethnographers. At the same time, American indifference to other traditions of anthropological contributions were noted (perceived) by Scandinavian Erixon (in Hultkrantz 1968:298).

Hofer (1968) described European ethnographers to be like Japanese, descriptive and cumulative. However, he said, from the European perspective, while American approaches may be fresh, they dash through layers that European ethnographers find vital to their understanding of a society.

Primatologists who are members of anthropology departments in North America are without exception vastly outnumbered by social anthropologists. Rare is the department that has more than one primatologist. There are marginalizing consequences of this, but a single researcher can also be put in a better position to obtain different resources from those needed by the majority of his or her colleagues in the department. So far as the position of Japanese primatology within the "world system of primatology" is concerned, the situation is rather fluid. Attitudes run the spectrum from those Westerners who perceive no difference in the Japanese tradition (and who have worked with the "token internationals") to those who, as mentioned, avoid publication in the Japanese journal *Primates*, or who say there are two traditions in Japanese primatology—an "international" tradition and another which they do not think they would understand.

Besides the vagaries of individual or national perceptions, the term "marginalization" itself is problematic. Gieryn and Hirsh argued that the concept of marginality is "so ambiguous as to be almost worthless as a conceptual tool for systematic inquiry into the sources of scientific innovation." Although the authors were examining different criteria from those of citation, dominant language, etc., (theirs included such things as young age, recent migration from a different discipline, different training, being apart from centers of institutional power and orthodoxy, etc.), they found that "marginal scientists are no more likely than others to contribute innovations" (1983:87).

What van Bremen contends about the multiple origins of relativity in time and space of marginal status in anthropology I believe to be correct. Primatology had two (and European primatologists would perhaps argue four or more) independent origins. Yet most would consider the discipline a "world system" in Kuwayama's sense. This commentary is intended to illustrate that whether or not it is called marginalization or peripheralization, real silencing of ideas and approaches, and privileging of others, has and is occurring, often unbeknown to those in the "dominant" discourse, in some of the ways I have outlined above.

Conclusion

Of course, it matters that those who perceive themselves to be marginalized are angry. However, it is at least as important that different voices not be silenced because of perceptions of the value of those ideas based upon different conventions of expression, world views, or assumptions. It is perhaps easier to correct for such bias in science where the necessity of being able to independently replicate results is one measure of the utility of an idea. Yet, even in science, a recognition of bias can be slow in coming. In the case of primatology, not only were early findings by Japanese not believed, but most Western researchers had neither the will nor the ability to try to replicate or compare findings across species. This was because they were unwilling to use the conceptual tools (e.g. assumptions about complex mental abilities of the animals, importance of individual differences, etc.) required for it, and they had not developed their own hypotheses to the necessary extent to take the next steps.

Kuwayama's suggestion that there is an inherent discord between peripheral native and dominant center anthropologists was something that van Bremen (1997b:62) said he found "disturbing." That discord does not originate mainly in the marginal and thankless role scholars assign to the natives. Nor is it confined to what several anthropologists suggest is a lack of responsibility to help the native anthropologist (especially in Third World countries) with the political and economic fallout from anthropological study of them (see Moore 1996). I have been concerned to point out that it is just as much a lack of understanding, or lack of willingness to try to facilitate enunciation of other approaches, a narrow-mindedness caught in the duck pond of Western theory,[15] that is the root of the discord. That this should occur in anthropology of all places is a shame. Yet it is precisely the self-described comparative characteristics and goals of the discipline that equip all of its practitioners to give equal attention to different voices[16] and to provide an exemplar for other disciplinary areas undergoing parallel debates.

I would like to end with a question arising from concluding comments made by van Bremen. He wrote that "scholarship is a transnational affair, answering to universal codes of craftsmanship and professionalism" (1997b:63) and that "the reappearance in places of the idea that anthropological knowledge and scholarship is grounded in an ethnic membership, or even the property of a presumed race, as proclaimed by some anthropologists today . . . is the kind of behavior and thought that spells danger and death for scholarship, local and global" (van Bremen 1997b:64). My question is: "Is scholarship with universal codes of craftsmanship and professionalism desirable? More to the point, what aspects should be universal?" Perhaps that is more determinable in science where at the least you must be able to replicate results. But what about in humanities and social sciences? I agree with van Bremen that the formation of isolated "ethnic anthropologies" is undesirable. What I am getting at is a truly international discourse in which the voices, insights, perceptions, and questions from different traditions are equally privileged in being equally subject to critical scrutiny by anthropologists throughout the world.

Notes

1. Kuwayama's (1997a) article first appeared in Japanese. He then posted a message about its contents on the EASIANTH (EASt AsIAn ANTHropology) electronic discussion group. An extended English summary of the Japanese article and van Bremen's response to it were subsequently printed in the *JAWS (Japan Anthropology Workshop) Newsletter*. This exchange, along with a rather vehement (on the part of the Japanese) disputation between a Canadian anthropologist (Niessen 1994, 1997) and two Japanese anthropologists (Shimizu 1997; Ohtsuka 1997) about some of the same issues of apparently one-sided perception of Western hegemonies, prompted these reflections. I am grateful to these scholars for having the courage of their convictions and sharing them with the international community.

2. The term "social" is not meant to indicate any particular national view of anthropology, but merely to distinguish it from physical or biological anthropology, of which primatology is a subdiscipline.

3. As in anthropology, there are different perceptions about marginalization among scientists. For instance, Gibbs (1995:97) reported results of interviews with scientists, journal editors and publishers to the effect that: "Most people in Africa and Asia will say there is a tremendous bias against them, while most Americans and Europeans will say it is not true." On the other hand, he reported that the editor of the journal *Science* counters that: "In high-quality journals where I have been an editor or reviewer, we lean over backwards to help science being presented from developing countries wherever it is

possible," and that he has no real sympathy for allegations of bias (Gibbs 1995:97).

4. Eiichiro Ishida's open letter to European and American anthropologists was published in a 1965 issue of *Current Anthropology*. In it, he asked if any mutual approach had been found between the two traditions. He wrote: "in Japan—caught between the two traditions—and probably in other countries where anthropology or some anthropological science is yet to be introduced into higher education as an independent discipline, we do feel the necessity to have a clear idea of *what anthropology ought to be*" (Ishida 1965:303, emphasis added).

5. Details of the Western approaches and theoretical bases for differences between the traditions can be found in Frisch 1959 and 1963; Imanishi 1960 (and especially in the exchange of comments following his paper); Asquith 1986a, 1991, and 1994.

6. It is not unusual that an idea lies buried for twenty years due to being ahead of its time, its inaccessibility, or being misunderstood, but the reasons for the burial here are of the order Kuwayama has raised.

7. The journal *Primatologia*, first published in 1956, was a forum for papers on morphological studies of primates. Earlier Western-based journals in which papers on primate behavior very occasionally appeared, were more general animal behavior and psychology journals.

8. In chronological order, they include: Nishida 1973; Kano 1983; Masataka 1983, 1986, 1988; Matsuzawa et al. 1983; Matsuzawa 1985; Nakamichi et al. 1983. Two earlier articles published in Western journals by Imanishi (1960) and Miyadi (1964) were more general overviews of the state of research on Japanese macaques, rather than research papers.

9. *Reichôrui kenkyû* (Primate Research).

10. Junichiro Itani, then of Kyoto University, received the Thomas Henry Huxley Memorial Award in 1984 for his contributions to anthropology.

11. We could even speak of countries as token internationals, such as Gerholm's (1995:163-164) characterization of his native Sweden as

"a holiday resort for international anthropology."

12. Only one primatological meeting has provided translators (Fedigan and Asquith 1991). This occasion was the first time that Japanese and North American primatologists, who had conducted research on the same population of Japanese macaques (that had split into two sub-groups, one of which was sent from Kyoto to Texas), had *discussed* their findings since the troop's fission twenty years before. Any suggestion to organizers of subsequent international meetings that translation be provided even for a couple of panels where there is likely to be a lot of debate invariably meets with the response that it would be far too expensive. Yet it costs less than the expense of hotels, international travel, conference facilities rental, etc.! Why are we meeting together, anyway?

13. In practice, however, *nihonjinron* "may be defined as works of cultural nationalism concerned with the ostensible 'uniqueness' of Japan" (Dale 1986:i). In the decade following Dale's publication, virtually all Western anthropological publications on Japan made (negative) allusion to *nihonjinron*. For a different perspective on *nihonjinron*, see Yoshino 1992.

14. For instance, a report of an actual dialogue between Japanese primatologists and a Western-trained, Japanese speaking interviewer is, I think, very revealing of the differences in assumptions underlying what most biologists would have assumed were shared assumptions about evolutionary theory (Asquith 1991:87-88).

15. Moore's (1996:4) felicitous phrase.

16. Cerroni-Long (1995:10) remarked with regard to comparing native and non-native anthropological analyses of the same settings, that: "This type of comparison should have by now become a disciplinary routine rather than being exploited from time to time to attack particular authors or to wave the red herring of anthropologists' lack of 'objectivity.'"

References

Altorki, Soraya
  1982 "The Anthropologist in the Field: A Case of 'Indigenous Anthropology' from Saudi Arabia." In Hussein Fahim, ed., *Indigenous Anthropology in Non-Western Countries*. Durham, NC: Carolina Academic Press.

Asquith, Pamela
  1986a "Anthropomorphism and the Japanese and Western Traditions in Primatology." In J. G. Else and C. Lee, eds., *Primate Ontogeny, Cognition and Social Behaviour*. Cambridge: Cambridge University Press.

  1986b "Imanishi's Impact in Japan." *Nature* (323):675-676.

  1991 "Primate Research Groups in Japan: Orientations and East-West Differences." In Linda-Marie Fedigan and Pamela Asquith, eds., *The Monkeys of Arashiyama: Thirty-Five Years of Research in Japan and the West*. New York: SUNY Press.

  1994 "The Intellectual History of Field Studies in Primatology, East and West." In Leslie K. Chan and Ann Herring, eds., *Strength in Diversity: A Reader in Physical Anthropology*. Toronto: Canadian Scholars' Press.

  1996 "Japanese Science and Western Hegemonies: Primatology and the Limits Set to Questions." In Laura Nader, ed., *Naked Science: Anthropological Inquiry into Boundaries, Power and Knowledge*. New York: Routledge.

Barnes, J. A.
  1982 "Social Science in India: Colonial Import, Indigenous Product, or Universal Truth?" In Hussein Fahim, ed., *Indigenous Anthropology in Non-Western Countries*. Durham, NC: Carolina Academic Press.

Cernea, Michael
  1982 "Indigenous Anthropologists and Development-Oriented Research." In Hussein Fahim, ed., *Indigenous Anthropology in Non-Western Countries*. Durham, NC: Carolina Academic Press.

Cerroni-Long, E. L.
  1995 "Introduction: Insider or Native anthropology?" In E. L. Cerroni-Long, ed., *Insider Anthropology*. Arlington, VA: American Anthropological Association.

Dale, Peter N.
  1986   *The Myth of Japanese Uniqueness*. London: Croom Helm.
Fahim, Hussein, ed.
  1982   *Indigenous Anthropology in Non-Western Countries*. Durham, NC: Carolina Academic Press.
Fedigan, Linda-Marie, and Pamela Asquith, eds.
  1991   *The Monkeys of Arashiyama: Thirty-Five Years of Research in Japan and the West*. New York: SUNY Press.
Frisch, Jean
  1959   "Research on Primate Behavior in Japan." *American Anthropologist* 61(4):584-596.
  1963   "Japan's Contribution to Modern Anthropology." In J. Roggendorf, ed., *Studies in Japanese Culture*. Tokyo: Sophia University Press.
Gerholm, Tomas
  1995   "Sweden: Central Ethnology, Peripheral Anthropology." In Han F. Vermeulen and Arturo Alvarez Roldán, eds., *Fieldwork and Footnotes. Studies in the History of European Anthropology*. London: Routledge.
Gibbs, W. Wayt
  1995   "Lost Science in the Third World." *Scientific American* August:92-99.
Gieryn, Thomas F., and Richard F. Hirsh
  1983   "Marginality and Innovation in Science." *Social Studies of Science* 13:87-106.
Halstead, Beverly
  1985   "Anti-Darwinian Theory in Japan." *Nature* 317:587-589.
Hofer, Tamas
  1968   "Anthropologists and Native Ethnographers in Central European Villages: Comparative Notes on the Professional Personality of Two Disciplines." *Current Anthropology* 9(4):311-315.
Hultkrantz, Ake
  1968   "The Aims of Anthropology: A Scandinavian Point of View." *Current Anthropology* 9(4):289-309.
Ikeda, Kiyohiko, and Atuhiro Shibatani
  1995   "Kinji Imanishi's Biological Thought." In David Lambert and Hamish Spencer, eds., *Speciation and the Recognition Concept: Theory and Application*. Baltimore, MD: Johns Hopkins University Press.

Imanishi, Kinji
  1960   "Social Organization of Subhuman Primates in Their Natu-
          ral Habitat." *Current Anthropology* 1(5-6):393-407.
Ishida, Eiichiro
  1965   "European vs. American Anthropology." *Current Anthropo-
          logy* 6(3):303-318.
Kano, Takayoshi
  1983   "An Ecological Study of the Pygmy Chimpanzees (*Pan
          paniscus*) of Yalosodi, Republic of Zaire." *International
          Journal of Primatology* 4(1):1-32.
Kuwayama, Takami
  1997a   "Genchi no Jinrui Gakusha—Naigai no Nihon Kenkyû o
          Shushin to shite" (Native Anthropologists: With Special
          Reference to Japanese Studies Inside and Outside Japan).
          Minzokugaku Kenkyû (Japanese Journal of Ethnology) 61
          (4):517-542 (in Japanese).
  1997b   "Native Anthropologists: With Special Reference to
          Japanese Studies Inside and Outside Japan." *Japan Anthro-
          pology Workshop Newsletter* 26/27:52-56.
  1997c   "Response to Jan van Bremen." *Japan Anthropology Work-
          shop Newsletter* 26/27: 66-69.
Masataka, Nobuo
  1983   "Psycholinguistic Analysis of Alarm Calls of Japanese Mon-
          keys (*Macaca fuscata*)." *American Journal of Primatology*
          5(2):111-126.
  1986   "Rudimentary Representational Vocal Signaling of Fellow
          Group Members in Spider Monkeys." *Behaviour* 96:49-104.
  1988   "The Response of Red-Chested Moustached Tamarins to
          Long Calls from Their Natal and Alien Populations." *Ani-
          mal Behaviour* 36(1):55-61.
Matsuzawa, Tetsuro
  1985   "The Use of Numbers by a Chimpanzee." *Nature* 315:57.
Matsuzawa, Tetsuro, Y. Hasegawa, S. Gotoh, and K. Wada
  1983   "One Trial Long-Lasting Food Aversion Learning in Wild
          Japanese Monkeys (*Macaca fuscata*)." *Behavioral and
          Neural Biology* 39:155-159.
Miyadi, Denzaburo
  1964   "Social Life of Japanese Monkeys." *Science* 143:783-786.
Moore, Henrietta L., ed.
  1996   *The Future of Anthropological Knowledge.* London: Rout-
          ledge.

Mott, Luiz R. B.
  1982   "Indigenous Anthropology and Brazilian Indians." In Hussein Fahim, ed., *Indigenous Anthropology in Non-Western Countries*. Durham, NC: Carolina Academic Press.
Nakamichi, Masayuki, H. Fujii, and T. Koyama
  1983   Development of a Congenitally Malformed Japanese Monkey in a Free-Ranging Group during the First Four Years of Life." *American Journal of Primatology* 5(3):205-210.
Nakane, Chie
  1982   "The Effect of Cultural Tradition on Anthropologists." In Hussein Fahim, ed., *Indigenous Anthropology in Non-Western Countries*. Durham, NC: Carolina Academic Press.
Nakayama, Shigeru
  1995   "History of East Asian Science: Needs and Opportunities." *Osiris* 10:80-94.
Niessen, Sandra A.
  1994   "The Ainu in Minpaku: A Representation of Japan's Indigenous People at the National Museum of Ethnology." *Museum Anthropology* 18(3):18-25.
  1997   "Representing the Ainu Reconsidered." *Museum Anthropology* 20(3): 132-144.
Nishida, Toshisada
  1973   "The Ant-Gathering Behaviour by the Use of Tools among Wild Chimpanzees of the Mahali Mountains." *Journal of Human Evolution* 2:357-370.
  1976   "The Bark Eating Habits in Primates, with Special Reference to Their Status in the Diet of Wild Chimpanzees." *Folia Primatologica* 25(4):277-287.
Ohtsuka, Kazuyoshi
  1997   "Exhibiting Ainu culture at Minpaku: A Reply to Sandra A. Niessen." *Museum Anthropology* 20(3):108-119.
Reader, Ian
  1997   "Eurocentric Anthropology." *Anthropology Today* 13(5):20.
Sakura, Osamu, T. Sawaguchi, H. Kudo, and S. Yoshikubo
  1986   "Declining Support for Imanishi." *Nature* (323):586.
Shimizu, Akitoshi
  1997   "Cooperation, Not Domination; A Rejoinder to Niessen on the Ainu Exhibition at Minpaku." *Museum Anthropology* 20(3): 120-131.

van Bremen, Jan
    1988   "Indonesian Studies in Japanese Anthropology." *Bijdragen, Tot de Taal-, Land- en Volkenkunde* (Journal of the Royal Institute for Linguistics and Anthropology) 144(2 & 3):248-258.
    1997a   "Notes in the Margins of a Major Work." *Anthropology Today* 13(4):17-18.
    1997b   "Prompters Who Do Not Appear on the Stage: Japanese Anthropology and Japanese Studies in American and European Anthropology." *Japan Anthropology Workshop Newsletter* 26/27:57-65.
Yoshino, Kosaku
    1992   *Cultural Nationalism in Contemporary Japan.* London: Routledge.

MALADAPTATION:
A CHALLENGE TO RELATIVISM

Robert B. Edgerton

The concept of cultural relativism is one of our most venerable—and, many continue to say, most valuable—principles. This principle declares that there is no universally valid standard by which the traditional beliefs or practices of other cultures can be evaluated; they can only be judged relative to the cultural context in which they occur. This axiom did not originate in anthropology, although Franz Boas and his students at Columbia University did much to promote it. Rousseau, Montaigne, Hume and others espoused versions of cultural relativism. So did Herodotus and the fifth-century Sophists. But the first explicit formulation of the principle probably came, not from a Greek or an anthropologist, but from the American sociologist, William Graham Sumner, who wrote these still-famous words in 1906: "The mores can make anything right, and prevent condemnation of anything," and he meant exactly that (Sumner 1906).

As anthropologists described more and more of the world's diverse cultures, their assertions about cultural relativism grew in strength. In the 1920s and 1930s, thanks mainly to the work of Boas's students, Ruth Benedict, Margaret Mead, and Melville Herskovits, among others, cultural relativism became so fundamental to anthropological thinking that in 1939, Clyde Kluckhohn, already a prominent Harvard University anthropologist who would become even more influential, declared that cultural relativism was "probably the most meaningful contribution which anthropological studies have made to general knowledge" (Kluckhohn 1939:342). Without this principle, we would be left with arrogant ethnocentrism in which everything Western was superior to everything non-Western.

The rise of totalitarianism, the horrors of World War II, and the tensions of the Cold War weakened many scholars' faith in cultural relativism to such an extent that by the 1950s it came under fire (Hatch 1983). Around this time, several of the world's most respected anthropologists, all of whom had earlier endorsed the principle of cultural relativism, published critical evaluations of "primitive" societies, as folk societies were often referred to at that time. For example, in 1948 Alfred Kroeber, then the dean of American anthropology, not only rejected relativism, he wrote that as societies became more complex, they became more "humane." Furthermore, he defined "progress" not only as advances in technology and science, but as the abandonment of practices such as magic and superstition, ritual prostitution, segregating women at parturition or menstruation, torture, and human sacrifice (Kroeber 1948). In 1950 Ralph Linton, another leading anthropologist who possessed probably the most encyclopedic knowledge of world ethnography of anyone then alive, wrote that there could be universal ethical standards, a position that Clyde Kluck-hohn—no longer a committed relativist—endorsed five years later (Kluckhohn 1955; Linton 1952).

In 1953, Robert Redfield, a distinguished anthropologist at the University of Chicago, sided with Kroeber by writing that small-scale societies were less "decent" and "humane" than more "advanced civilizations" (Redfield 1953). And in a paper presented in 1965, George Peter Murdock, then the world's leading figure in cross-cultural comparative studies, wrote that Benedict's relativistic idea that a cultural element has no meaning except in its context was "nonsense," and that Herskovits's assertion that all cultures must be accorded equal dignity and value was "not only nonsense but sentimental nonsense" (Murdock 1965:146). He added that it was an "absurdity" to believe that practices such as slavery, magical therapy, cannibalism, and killing the aged should be accorded the same "dignity" or "validity" as old age security, scientific medicine, and metal artifacts. Murdock insisted that people everywhere prefer Western technology and would rather be able to feed their children and their elderly than kill them. Furthermore, he said, primitive peoples readily abandon such practices as cannibalism and headhunting "when colonial governments demonstrate the material advantages of peace" (Murdock 1965:149).

Despite potent anti-relativistic declarations by luminaries like Kroeber, Linton, Kluckhohn, Redfield, and Murdock the majority of anthropologists continued to reject the idea that civilized societies were ethically superior to primitive ones. Indeed, they deplored even the use of terms such as "civilized" or "primitive." And with relatively few exceptions, they continued to call for every culture to be respected in its own context. That was the consensual view in anthropology at the time, and it has continued to be.

In the 1970s a far more radical version of relativism came into vogue. Promoted by such distinguished anthropologists as Clifford Geertz and David M. Schneider, a new form of epistemological relativism came to challenge not only anyone's ability to evaluate other cultures, but to declare that cultures are incommensurable. Each one can only be understood—or more correctly, interpreted—in its own terms as a unique system of meanings. What is more, only someone enculturated in that system can fully comprehend it. As Renato Rosaldo put it: "My own group aside, *everything* human is alien to me" (Rosaldo 1984: 188).

Not only is each culture unique unto itself, but people's thoughts, feelings, and motivations are radically different from one culture to another. That being so, any attempt to generalize about either culture or human nature must be false or trivial (Schneider 1984). In this perspective, a person from another culture remains the "Other," forever incomprehensible. Physicist Charles Nissam-Sabat has chided epistemological relativists for adopting this extreme position because "they make the people they study falsely incomprehensible and thus dehumanized" (Nissam-Sabat 1987:935).

An earlier example of relativism might be taken from the famous Sapir-Whorf hypothesis. In its strong version, it asserted that the language a people spoke had such a profound effect on how they saw the world and thought about it, that people in different societies lived in radically different worlds of meaning. In the 1950s Benjamin Whorf, a student of Sapir, chose the Hopi language to illustrate this hypothesis asserting that the Hopi had no terms for time comparable to ours, and moreover that they had no tenses such as past, present, and future. As a result, he concluded, the Hopi conceived of time in a manner radically different from and, he added, scientifically more sophisticated than that of speakers of English. Subsequent research proved Whorf wrong on all counts: the Hopi did have tenses as well as various terms for time comparable to those used in English. Also, the Hopi had no difficulty thinking of time in the ways English speakers do (Malotki 1983). Attempts to show that language had a significant impact on thought in other societies also failed to confirm Whorf's ideas, and his relativistic hypothesis has been rejected in linguistics for at least fifteen years (Haugen 1977).

Even before the emergence of epistemological relativism, distinguished anthropologist Marvin Harris wrote: "As a result of the cultural relativistic critique, anthropologists no longer believe that the study of cultural evolution will provide a scientific basis for judging which cultures are aesthetically, ethically, or politically superior" (Harris 1971:448). Harris was right about the impact of relativism, but there is another reason why anthropologists have typically refused to evaluate the customs of other peoples. That reason is the long-held assumption that culture is an adaptive mechanism; therefore, traditional beliefs and practices must serve some useful purpose, a position that is explicitly stated in many contemporary introductory anthropology textbooks. Few contemporary anthropologists have made this assertion more often or more vigorously than Harris himself. In his book, *Good to Eat*, Harris insists that eating patterns that seem "impractical, irrational, useless or harmful" are in reality the utilitarian result of human attempts to maximize benefits and minimize costs, an argument he has previously advanced with regard to many other kinds of seemingly irrational beliefs and practices (Harris 1985:17).

The conviction that human practices and beliefs are adaptive is present in other scientific fields as well. For example, when Donald T. Campbell gave his presidential address to the American Psychological Association in 1975, he declared that culture should be regarded as adaptive. He noted that when an evolutionary biologist encounters some seemingly ludicrous or bizarre form of animal life, he approaches it with awe, "certain that behind the bizarre form lies a functional wisdom that he has yet to understand." Campbell urged psychologists and other social scientists to adopt the same sense of awe "when considering an apparently bizarre, incomprehensible feature of their own or another culture . . . expecting that when eventually understood, when our theories have caught up with it, that seemingly bizarre superstition will turn out to make adaptive sense." Campbell amended this comment by saying that instead of "awe," the proper approach should be "grudging, skeptical respect," but his belief in the adaptiveness of culture was unshaken (Campbell 1975:1104).

When the scholarly study of small-scale non-Western societies began in earnest in the late nineteenth century, many anthropologists accepted neither cultural relativism nor the belief that all customs are adaptive. E. B. Tylor, for example, perhaps the most influential of the nineteenth-century anthropologists, often referred to what he called "survivals," or customs that may once have served a useful social purpose but no longer do so, as "absurd" or "foolish" (Tylor 1871). Others agreed. But the idea that every custom had a positive function, whether manifest or latent, soon took hold in both anthropology and sociology (Eisenstadt 1990). Marvin Harris summarized the conventional wisdom as it existed in 1960: "Countless studies of extant socio-cultural systems and bio-organisms have been made to discover the functional status of socio-cultural and bio-morphic structures. In both realms the results of these studies indicate that bio-organisms and socio-cultural systems are largely if not exclusively composed of positive-functioned, that is, useful traits" (Harris 1960:60-61). Many scholars continue to agree with Harris. For example, in 1990, Richard A. Alexander, a leading evolutionary biologist wrote that "any human attribute that is too elaborate to be accidental should be considered adaptive" (Alexander 1990:249).

Despite such assertions, a few anthropologists have rejected this conclusion. To take one example, as a result of his ethnographic field research among the Tauade, a small population in Papua New Guinea, C. R. Hallpike concluded that their practice of warfare was not adaptive. Hallpike also believed that it was maladaptive for the Tauade to raise huge herds of pigs that "devastated" their gardens and led to "innumerable quarrels and even homicides," only to be slaughtered in such large numbers that they could not be eaten. He also saw no adaptive advantage to the Tauade in keeping rotting corpses in their villages. He observed that: "No doubt, the Tauade had survived to be studied, but their major institutions and practices seemed to have very little to do with this fact" (Hallpike 1986:iv). In an earlier ethnography of the Konso of Ethiopia, Hallpike concluded that the Konso did not need their elaborate age-grading system. "Primitive societies are not," he concluded, "beautifully adapted little organisms put together like watches, in which every component functions for the well-being and survival of the whole" (Hallpike 1972:372).

While a few cultural anthropologists like Hallpike were evaluating some cultural practices and beliefs in terms of dysfunction or pathology, parallel developments were taking place in evolutionary biology. Until quite recently, most evolutionary biologists also assumed that existing cultural practices were adaptive and attempted to explain these traits by matching them to reproductive fitness optimization models, but this assumption is no longer universally held (Boyd and Richerson 1985). Some scholars from fields such as ecology, biology, psychology, anthropology, and sociology have argued that there is no *a priori* reason to assume that any given cultural practice is adaptive (Lopreato

1984; Scott 1989). Moreover, various scholars have identified mechanisms that could lead to and perpetuate maladaptation (Barkow
1989).

The study of cultural adaptation is clouded by the fixed idea that
"primitive" societies were far more harmonious than societies caught
up in the modern world. We know that human misery, fear, loneli-
ness, pain, sickness, and premature death are typical of much of the
world today. We also know that people in contemporary societies are
often the hapless victims of such forces as racism, governmental
neglect, economic exploitation, corruption, ethnic, religious, and
political strife among other kinds of social, cultural, and environmental
pressures. However, many prominent scholars believe that this sort of
misery is not natural to the human condition, that people in smaller,
more homogeneous "folk" societies historically lived in greater
harmony and happiness, and that many small populations continue to
do so today. The belief that primitive societies are more harmonious
than modern ones, that life in the past was more idyllic than life today,
is not only reflected in the motion pictures and novels of our popular
culture, it is deeply entrenched in scholarly discourse as well. Once
we had a sense of "community," but it has been lost.

This view of history is based on the belief that the malaise and
mayhem of the modern world is not the natural human condition.
What we see today is thought to be the result of widespread social disorganization, divisive ethnic or religious diversity, class conflict, or
competing interests that plague large societies, particularly nation-
states. Because smaller and simpler societies, on the other hand,
developed their cultures in response to the demands of their immediate
and stable environments, their ways of life are said to have produced
far greater harmony and happiness for their populations. Robin Fox,
for example, vividly described the upper Paleolithic environment of
big-game hunters as one in which "there was a harmony of our evolved
attributes as a species, including our intelligence, our imagination, our
violence (and hence our violent imagination), our reason and our pas-
sions—a harmony that has been lost" (Fox 1990:3). If a small society
is found that lacks harmony, many social scientists have often concluded that this condition must be the result of the disorganizing effects
of culture contact, particularly urbanization. This belief, like cultural
relativism, has been deeply embedded in Western thought for centuries.

The belief that cities were characterized by crime, disorder, and
human suffering of all sorts while small, isolated, and homogeneous
folk societies were harmonious communities goes back to Aristo-

phanes, Tacitus, and the Old Testament. In the twentieth century, the contrast between folk "community" and urban "society" became one of the most fundamental ideas in all of social science. The conclusion that large urban societies lost the harmonious sense of community that was said to be characteristic of folk societies continues to be widespread among social philosophers, political scientists, sociologists, psychiatrists, theologians, novelists, poets, and the educated public in general. For example, Kirkpatrick Sale recently responded to criticism of his book, *The Conquest of Paradise* (about the European conquest of the native peoples of America), by insisting that compared to the cultures of Europe, the "primal communities" of preconquest America were more "harmonious, peaceful, benign and content" (Sale 1991).

Knowledge of life in folk societies—those small, traditional, and often less complex societies that existed all over the globe before the coming of states, industrialization, and world economic systems—comes primarily from the work of anthropologists. While theirs is usually the best available information about life as it has been lived in small-scale societies during the late nineteenth and twentieth centuries, this information is not always complete nor is it always entirely accurate. In the year or so that an anthropologist typically spends in a small society, he or she can learn only so much and, in the course of a professional career, will write only so much. This means that some aspects of life among small non-Western populations simply cannot be fully described. For a number of reason that we will discuss below, many anthropologists have chosen not to write about the darker side of life in folk societies, or at least not to write very much about it. This sometimes occurs because anthropologists believe that the cruel, harmful, or ineffective practices they see in a folk society are the result of social disorganization brought about by colonialism, something that, in fact, is often correct. And certain practices are sometimes not reported because doing so would offend the people being described or discredit them in the eyes of others. For these reasons along with other forms of personal bias, some anthropological monographs are idealized portraits. To take but one example, this is Jane Belo's report about the Balinese: "These babies do not cry, the small boys do not fight, the young girls bear themselves with decorum. . . . Everyone carries out his appointed task with respect for his equals and superiors, and gentleness and consideration for his dependents. The people adhere, apparently with ease, to the laws governing the actions, big and small, of their lives" (Belo 1935:141). Unfortunately for the authenticity of this idyllic vision, Belo went on—unwittingly, it would seem—to document instances in which men beat their wives, wives ran away from home, children defied their parents, and people rebelled against their customs and laws.

In addition to the personal idealism of anthropologists such as Belo and others, there has been a benevolent conspiracy on the part of some anthropologists not to betray the trust of the people with whom they have lived and worked (and whom they have often come to like and respect) by writing about their least likable or unreasonable practices. There is also the pervasive assumption among anthropologists that a population's long-standing beliefs and practices—their culture and their social institutions—must play a positive role in their lives or these beliefs and practices would not have persisted. As a result, when a society was encountered that seemed to lack a meaningful system of beliefs or effective institutions, it was usually assumed that the cause must lie in the baneful influence of other peoples—such as Western officials, soldiers, missionaries, or traders—who had almost always been on the scene before anthropologists were. When a society was encountered whose traditional beliefs and practices appeared to be meaningless or even harmful, the blame was often laid to external disruption. Thus, the conviction has persisted that before the social disorganization and cultural confusion brought about by foreign contact, the lives of traditional populations must have been harmonious and meaningful.

Therefore, rather than report the alienation, violence, or cruelty that sometimes dominated the lives of the people they came to study, some anthropologists tried to reconstruct the people's way of life as they believed it must have been before it was disrupted by the religious beliefs, taxes, laws, and economic interventions of the colonial powers. Few anthropologists believed that witchcraft, protest, suicide, rape, wife battering and feuding were unknown before folk societies were impacted by external forces, but most of them wrote their ethnographies as if such behaviors were either infrequent or somehow helped these people to adapt to their environmental circumstances. As a consequence, the myth of primitive harmony was inadvertently reinforced, even by anthropologists who knew better. The cumulative impact of relativistic and adaptivist assumptions has led generations of ethnographers to believe that there simply must be a good social or cultural reason why a long-established belief or practice exists.

To be sure, not everyone has made this assumption. Some ecologically oriented ethnographers, for example, have provided descriptions that carefully assess how adaptive a particular population's beliefs or institutions may be. Walter Goldschmidt's ethnography of the Sebei of Uganda is a good example. After analyzing the relatively positive social and cultural adaptations that the Sebei made during their recent history, he described what he referred to as "disequilibria and maladaptation," especially "the failure of the Sebei to establish a social order capable of maintaining their boundaries, and the failure to develop a commitment to a relevant set of moral principles" (Goldschmidt 1976: 353). His analysis went on to specify the changing socioeconomic circumstances that led to these "failures." Similarly, Klaus-Friedrich Koch, writing about the then-unacculturated Jalé who lived in the remote eastern Snow Mountains of Irian Jaya in the mid-1960s, concluded that the disputes and killing which were so common among them, and so divisive, resulted because Jalé methods of conflict management were "very few and very inefficient" (Koch 1974:159). However, for the most part, even ecologically oriented ethnographers have typically paid scant attention to maladaptation (Ellen 1982:195).

Humans in various societies, both urban or folk, are capable of empathy, kindness, even love, and they sometimes achieve astounding mastery of the challenges posed by their environments, but they are also capable of maintaining beliefs, values, and social institutions that result in senseless cruelty, needless suffering, and monumental folly in their relations among themselves, with other societies, and with the physical environment in which they live. People are not always wise, and the societies and cultures they create are not ideal adaptive mechanisms, perfectly designed to provide for human needs. It is mistaken to maintain, as many scholars do, that if a population has held to a traditional belief or practice for many years, then it must play a useful role in their lives. Traditional beliefs and practices may serve as important adaptive mechanisms, but they may also be inefficient, harmful, and even deadly.

Today, various scholars are beginning to agree that cultural practices can be maladaptive, and a few have gone so far as to say that entire societies can become pathogenic. This is not to suggest that most anthropologists share these views. It is impossible to be certain, but it seems likely that the majority of anthropologists would reject the idea that cultural maladaptation is common, and some vigorously reject the idea that it occurs at all. And it is almost certain that a large majority would not accept the assertion that entire societies can legitimately be thought of as "sick."

One reason why defining maladaptation is so difficult is that there are many levels at which it can be said to occur. It can involve a single gene or a number of linked genes, a single individual, a group of related individuals or cooperating groups of people. The focus can also legitimately fall on categories or corporate groups of people who share common interests and risks because of their age, gender, class, ethnicity, race, occupational specialty, or some other characteristic, or it can encompass an entire society, a kingdom, an empire, or a confederation. For some purposes, maladaptation may be conceptualized in terms of the well-being or survival of all people on earth.

Therefore, there are many potential criteria of maladaptation, each with a claim to legitimacy for certain purposes. I have chosen to rely on the most self-evident of these, because over the course of human evolution human breeding success has been a function of societal survival or growth; therefore, one measure of maladaptation is the failure of a society, or its culture, to survive due to the inadequacy of one or more of its beliefs or institutions. Second, maladaptation exists when enough members of a population are sufficiently dissatisfied with one or more of their social institutions or cultural beliefs that the viability of their society is threatened. Finally, it is maladaptive when a population maintains beliefs or practices that so seriously impair the physical or mental health of its members that they cannot adequately meet their own needs or maintain their social and cultural system. Defined in these three ways, I will contend that maladaptation is common among the world's societies, and what is more, that some degree of it is inevitable (see Edgerton 1992).

Many traditional societies have woefully inadequate health beliefs and practices, as their short life-expectancies dramatically illustrate. Some early urban populations were even less healthy. At its peak around A.D. 500, the Aztec city of Teotihuacan covered a larger area than imperial Rome and may have been the largest city in the world at that time. But its population was in dreadful health. Rates of malnutrition, stunted growth, deciduous tooth hypoplasia (a measure of stress), and infant and child mortality were higher than in any known population of that time or earlier. Life expectancy at birth ranged between 14 and 17 years, infant mortality was about 40 percent, and only 38 percent of everyone born lived to be as old as 15 (Story 1985).

Another maladaptive practice is the denial of colostrum to infants. Colostrum transfers specific immunoglobins to the infant during the earliest days of life when its own immune system is poorly developed. Colostrum contains macrophages that can kill bacteria and fungi, protecting the child against deadly enterocolitis. T-lymphocytes also occur in large numbers, with their highest activity in synthesizing immunoglobins and antibodies occurring immediately after the onset of lactation. For this reason, breast-feeding during the first week can be crucial in providing the infant with a high concentration of antibodies and in regulating the bacteria in its intestines. Colostrum also appears to contain antibodies against infectious agents specific to local environments. For example, colostrum from women in India contains antibodies against cholera; this is not the case among women in societies where cholera is not prevalent (Barkow 1989:304). To delay breast-feeding for several days until the colostrum is replaced by "true" milk is clearly harmful to the infant, yet this practice occurs widely. In societies that are over-populated this may be an adaptive practice, but for those experiencing severe population loss it would be maladaptive.

Some populations have failed to survive or have lost their culture, language, or social institutions because they were not able to cope with the demands that their environments made on them. This failure to thrive is the most calamitous form of maladaptation, but it is not the only one. A few people in all societies, and many people in others, feel alienated, become depressed, or attempt suicide. Others withdraw from social life or emigrate, and it is not uncommon for people to protest or rebel. Some populations are deeply committed to the beliefs and practices that make up their cultural world, but others are less so, and some are profoundly dissatisfied with their lives. This is true not only in urbanized societies like our own but in small-scale, folk societies throughout the world. Beliefs or practices that leave a population seriously discontented or rebellious are, under most circumstances, maladaptive because they threaten the survival of that sociocultural system and endanger the physical and emotional well-being of the people in it (Edgerton 1992).

For example, some people passionately dislike their society's customs or feel guilty about taking part in them. For example, although men among the Cheyenne Indians of the North American Plains sometimes gang-raped an errant wife as custom dictated, many said that they disliked doing so. Some Yanomamo Indians, whose culture exalted ferocity and perpetuated warfare, frankly admitted that they disliked having to live in fear of violent death (Johnson and Earle 1987), and Nisa, that outspoken !Kung San woman, found much to criticize about San culture. She even declared that the ways of the San god were "foul" (Shostak 1981:316).

Comparable examples can be drawn from the highlands of Papua New Guinea. Women among the Mae Enga said that they detested the frequent warfare that the men engaged in, no matter how just the cause of the violence might have been (Meggitt 1977:99), and according to Donald Tuzin, Ilahita Arapesh men openly admitted that they felt "deeply shamed" about their treatment of their sons during the physically painful and emotionally terrifying Tambaran initiation ritual (Tuzin 1982:349). Tuzin also quotes an Ilahita Arapesh man as follows: "It is true that sometimes men feel ashamed and guilty over eating good food while their wives go hungry" (Tuzin 1982:350). And FitzJohn Porter Poole reports this about the Bimin-Kuskusmin practice of cannibalism: "Many Bimin-Kuskusmin men and women whom I interviewed and who admitted to socially proper cannibalistic practices acknowledged considerable ambivalence, horror, and disgust at their own acts." He adds: "Many persons noted that they had been unable to engage in the act, had not completed it, had vomited or even fainted, or had hidden the prescribed morsel and had lied about consuming it" (Poole 1983:9). What is more, Poole observed that on the eleven occasions that he actually witnessed cannibalism among the Bimin-Kuskusmin, they exhibited "extreme reticence and ambivalence" about the act.

In some small, traditional societies, people frequently commit suicide. The loss of a friend, relative, or spouse to suicide can be deeply troubling to survivors and may lead to social conflict of various kinds, but the occurrence of a few suicides should not threaten a society's viability. However, it is not the case, as some anthropologists have declared, that suicide is always a rare event, nor one that offers no threat to a society's viability (Naroll 1969). Among the Bimin-Kuskusmin of highland Papua New Guinea, suicide occurs so often that, according to Poole, "its genesis, prevention, and ultimate social costs are of paramount concern to the Bimin-Kuskusmin" (Poole 1985:152). Ten percent of all deaths known to Poole during the six generations prior to his field research were due to suicide, and other suicides, such as those of children, may not have been reported. This suicide rate deeply troubled the Bimin-Kuskusmin. Perhaps even more remarkable, during the twenty-four months of Poole's field research in the early 1970s, thirty of the fifty-eight deaths that occurred—a startling 57 percent of the total—were suicides. In addition to these actual suicides, many people threatened suicide, and others attempted to kill themselves but failed.

It is not only small societies in economically marginal environments that have failed to maintain their population size, their culture, or their language because of military weakness or other factors. Great civilizations have collapsed, as millions of tourists who have been fascinated by abandoned pyramids, monuments, and cities can readily attest. The Aztec Empire, the Mayan civilization, and the great achievements of Peru came to an end. In North America, the less well-known but nevertheless complex horticulture societies of the Southwest, such as Hohokam and Chaco Canyon, collapsed too, as did the high cultures of the Mississippi Valley. So it was in Anatolia, Crete, China, Greece, Egypt, the Indus Valley, Mesopotamia, Rome, and other places. Whether over hundreds of years or quite suddenly, great urbanized societies, often with extensive empires, lost control over their populations and saw their political, religious, and social institutions shatter, their cultural forms fall into decay, and their complex economies collapse. Sometimes, there was great loss of life as well.

These collapses were not always due to maladaptive beliefs or practices, but that was sometimes the case. For example, if C. A. Burland is correct, Emperor Montezuma's religious beliefs played a vital role in the destruction of the Aztec Empire (Burland 1973). According to Burland, Montezuma believed that Cortes was the reincarnation of the Aztec god Quetzalcoatl. Disregarding the repeated advice of his council, Montezuma made no effort to stop the Spaniards' march on his capital. Instead, he showered them with gifts and welcomed them to his palace. His immense and well-armed army waited in vain for orders to destroy the white men who soon proved even to Montezuma that they were anything but godlike.

History also records numerous examples of prophets who led their followers to their deaths. For example, a belief in witchcraft and prophecy once led to such widespread famine that a society of over one hundred thousand people was decimated. This tragic example of the disastrous consequences of such beliefs took place among the Xhosa of southern Africa in the mid-nineteenth century. Like many other African societies of that time, the Xhosa believed in the existence of witches whom they blamed for all misfortune and evil. They also believed, although with less certainty and unanimity, in the powers of prophets.

When a Dutch ship brought cattle diseased with pleuropneumonia to a South African port in September 1853, the tragedy that was soon to envelop the Xhosa began. This fatal and highly contagious disease had already killed thousands of cattle in Europe, and it quickly began to ravage herds in southern Africa. At the same time, maize, the main crop of the Xhosa, was attacked by disease and then further damaged by torrential rain. The Xhosa believed that they knew the reason why. Witches were spreading death and destruction. Their king, Sarhili, promptly and righteously had twenty accused witches put to death, but cattle continued to die, and the maize crop failed. While the Xhosa continued to kill people who were said to be witches, lung sickness continued to kill their cattle. A new prophet, a teenage girl, insisted that only the slaughter of all Xhosa cattle and the total abandonment of cultivation could remove pollution from the land and destroy the evil power of the witches. She promised that if this were done and the Xhosa renounced witchcraft, new people would arrive in Xhosaland, bringing with them healthy new cattle and crops. Simultaneously, the Xhosa dead would rise, and there would be eternal youth and happiness for all. New cattle and corn would appear, and other food, clothing, and goods would emerge from the ground. The deaf, blind, and handicapped would all be cured of their afflictions, and the old would once again be young. Joy and plenty would reign in Xhosaland (Peires 1989:311-312).

King Sarhili finally made the painful decision to do as the prophet said, ordering that his own vast herds be slaughtered. Others followed his example, and soon most Xhosa had killed all their cattle. As the cattle were being slaughtered, the Xhosa sang, drank beer, and danced as they gorged themselves on beef, so much of it that it was impossible to eat more than a small portion. The rest was left to rot. During the months to follow the Xhosa ate nothing but roots, berries, bark, and even grass. Beginning with young children and elderly people, they died of starvation or disease. Dogs ate the dead bodies that lay everywhere. In 1855, before the starvation began, there were approximately 105,000 Xhosa in King Sarhili's domain. By 1858 there were only 25,916. In addition to the cattle that died of lung sickness, at least 400,000 others were slaughtered. British colonial officials promptly took advantage of the Xhosa's plight by permanently appropriating some 600,000 acres of their land, over two-thirds of Sarhili's entire kingdom. Xhosa political independence ended too, as they fell under British rule; their cultural and economic integrity would soon be lost as well. The expansion of white colonialism was inexorable, and Sarhili's people would have eventually succumbed to British dominion. But without the prophecy's terrible consequences, Xhosa independence would have lasted longer, and many thousands of lives would have been saved.

A number of small societies have destroyed themselves by their persistent feuding, usually killing one another to steal women. And thanks to their adherence to a counter-productive sexual practice one society in Irian Jaya probably would have done so, had not the Dutch intervened. The Marind-Anim knew they were severely underpopulated compared to their neighbors. In an effort to ensure the fertility of each new bride, every man in her husband's lineage had sexual intercourse with her on her wedding night, leaving her unable to walk the next morning. Rather than increasing her fertility, this practice produced pelvic inflammatory disease and with it, infertility. In an effort to compensate for this widespread infertility the Marind-Anim raided their neighbors to capture children, a practice that led to bloody retaliation and further population decrease (Van Baal 1984).

These few examples illustrate a widespread phenomenon. If maladaptive beliefs and practices are as common as they appear to be, their existence poses a challenge to the prevailing relativist and adaptivist paradigms. Subsistence activities must be reasonably efficient for a population to survive, but they need not be optimal (in the sense of providing the best possible nutrition for the least expenditure of time and energy). No population has yet devised an optimal means for exploiting its environment, and it is unlikely that all members of any society have agreed about what an optimal environmental exploitation should be. Moreover, no society yet described has met the needs of all its members to their own satisfaction. All societies, including those whose members are healthiest, happiest, and longest-lived, could do better. All could improve health and safety, all could enhance life satisfaction. There has been no perfect society, no ideal adaptation, only degrees of imperfection. Not only are humans capable of errors, of misjudging the ecological circumstances that they must learn to cope with, they are also given to pursuing their own interests at the expense of others and to preferring the retention of old customs to the development of new ones despite changing environmental circumstances. Culture, then, tends to be adaptive but is never perfectly so.

It should not be assumed, as it so commonly is, that any persistent, traditional beliefs or practices in a surviving society must be adaptive. It should be assumed instead that any belief or practice could fall anywhere along a continuum of adaptive value. It may simply be neutral or tolerable, or it may benefit some members of a society while harming others.

One important reason why maladaptive beliefs and practices are common has to do with the nature of human beings. Intelligent as humans are, people in many societies can provide no rational reason for clinging to certain beliefs or practices, and some of their most important decisions—when to raid an enemy, where to fish, whom to fear—are based on prophecies, dreams, divination, and other supernatural phenomena. And even when people attempt to make rational decisions, they often fail. For one thing, no population, especially no folk population, can ever possess all the relevant knowledge it needs to make fully informed decisions about its environment, its neighbors, or even itself (Kuran 1988). What is more, there is a large body of research involving human decision making both under experimental conditions and in naturally occurring situations showing that individuals frequently make quite poor decisions, especially when it comes to solving novel problems or ones requiring the calculation of the probability of outcomes, and these are the kinds of problems that often pose the greatest challenges for human adaptation (Douglas and Wildavsky 1982; Nisbet and Ross 1980). In general, humans are also not greatly skilled in assessing risk, especially when the threat is a novel one, and they tend to underestimate the future effects of warfare and technological or economic change. Even when disasters such as droughts, floods, windstorms, or volcanic eruptions recur periodically, people consistently misjudge their consequences (Lumsden and Wilson 1981). They also do not readily develop new technology, even when environmental stress makes technological change imperative (Cowgill 1975). Western economists use the concept of bounded rationality to refer to people's limited ability to receive, store, retrieve, and process information, and economic decision theory takes these limitations into account. Because of these cognitive limitations, along with imperfect knowledge of their environment, people commonly make imperfect decisions (Kuran 1988).

C. R. Hallpike, among others, has concluded that the thought processes of people in small-scale societies are incapable of comprehending causality, time, realism, space, introspection, and abstraction as these are utilized in Western science (Hallpike 1979). Whether so-called "primitive" thought is less abstract, more magical, or less able to assess marginal probabilities is an issue that continues to be debated, and in any event its resolution is largely irrelevant to the point I am attempting to make. I am asserting that most people in *all* societies, including those most familiar with Western science, sometimes make potentially harmful mistakes and tend to maintain them. It is quite possible that people in small-scale societies make more mistakes of this kind, but maladaptive decisions are made in all societies. So, too, all societies have fallen short of perfection in their attempts to harness the aggressive, envious, self-serving predispositions of humans everywhere (see Edgerton 1992).

Traditional solutions and long-standing beliefs and practices tend to persist not because they are optimally beneficial but because they generally work just well enough that changes in them are not self-evidently needed. Given all that we know about the sometimes astoundingly bad judgment of "rational" planners in modern nations, it seems unlikely that people in smaller and simpler societies that lack our scientific and technological sophistication would always make optimally adaptive decisions even should they try to do so. What is more, even if a population somehow managed to devise a near-perfect adaptation to its environment, it is unlikely that it could maintain it for any length of time.

The point of this argument is not that traditional beliefs and practices are never adaptive and that they never contribute to a population's well-being, nor is it that people never think rationally enough to make effective decisions about meeting the challenges posed by their environments. To do so would be absurd. Human behavior is not driven solely by the socially disruptive aspects of their biological predispositions although these are troublesome everywhere. People are also predisposed to cooperate, be kind to one another, and sometimes even sacrifice their interests for the well-being of others.

Much of what we have learned about human history and human nature suggests a picture of human accomplishments, not discord, failure, or pathology. Throughout the world, people have developed effective techniques of hunting, gathering, herding, and gardening. They have domesticated plants and animals, built houses, developed trade, established meaningful religions, and learned to govern themselves. They have also created moving forms of music and dance as well as dazzling works of art. Many advances in technology are dazzling too.

But humans can also be their own worst enemies by clinging to harmful beliefs and practices. If we are to understand the processes of cultural adaptation and maladaptation, relativism should be replaced by a form of evaluative analysis. One cannot study the relative success of human adaptation without making evaluative judgments. We would never countenance a relativistic prohibition against attempting to evaluate the conditions of life in our inner cities. We know that drug use, gang violence, child abuse, deteriorated housing, poor prenatal health care, rage, and hopelessness are not good for the impoverished and embattled people who live there, and these people know it far better than we do. Why then, should the principles of cultural relativism and adaptivism prevent us from evaluating comparable beliefs and practices that exist in many small, traditional societies?

References

Alexander, R. D.
    1990   "Epigenetic Rules and Darwinian Algorythms: The Adaptive Study of Learning and Development." *Ethology and Sociobiology* 11:241-303.
Barkow, J. H.
    1989   "The Elastic Between Genes and Culture." *Ethology and Sociobiology* 10:111-129.
Belo, J.
    1935   "The Balinese Temper." *Character and Personality* 4:120-146.
Boyd, R., and P. J. Richerson
    1985   *Culture and the Evolutionary Process.* Chicago, IL: University of Chicago Press.
Burland, C. A.
    1973   *Montezuma: Lord of the Aztecs.* New York: Putnam.
Campbell, D. T.
    1975   "On the Conflicts Between Biological and Social Evolution and Between Psychology and Moral Traditions." *American Psychologist* 30:1103-1126.
Cowgill, G. L.
    1975   "On Causes and Consequences of Ancient and Modern Population Changes." *American Anthropologist* 77:505-525.
Douglas, M., and A. Wildavsky
    1982   *Risk and Culture.* Berkeley: University of California Press.
Edgerton, R. B.
    1992   *Sick Societies: Challenging the Myth of Primitive Harmony.* New York: Free Press.
Eisenstadt, S. N.
    1990   "Functional Analysis in Anthropology and Sociology: An Interpretive Essay." *Annual Review of Anthropology* 19:243-260.
Ellen, R.
    1982   *Environment, Subsistence and System: The Ecology of Small-Scale Social Formations.* New York: Cambridge University Press.
Fox, R.
    1990   *The Violent Imagination.* New Brunswick, NJ: Rutgers University Press.

Goldschmidt, W. R.
1976 *The Culture and Behavior of the Sebei.* Berkeley: University of California Press.

Hallpike, C. R.
1972 *The Konso of Ethiopia. A Study of the Values of a Cushitic Society.* Oxford: Clarendon Press.
1979 *The Foundations of Primitive Thought.* Oxford: Clarendon Press.
1986 *The Principles of Social Evolution.* Oxford: Clarendon Press.

Harris, M.
1960 "Adaptation in Biological and Cultural Science." *Transactions of the New York Academy Science* 23:59-65.
1971 *Culture, Man and Nature.* New York: Thomas Y. Crowell.
1985 *Good to Eat: Riddles of Food and Culture.* New York: Simon & Schuster.

Hatch, E.
1983 *Culture and Morality: The Relativity of Values in Anthropology.* New York: Columbia University Press.

Haugen, E.
1977 "Linguistic Relativity: Myths and Methods." In W. C. McCormack and S. A. Wurm, eds., *Language and Thought: Anthropological Issues.* The Hague, Netherlands: Mouton.

Johnson, A. W., and T. Earle
1987 *The Evolution of Human Societies: From Foraging Group to Agrarian State.* Stanford, CA: Stanford University Press.

Kluckhohn, C.
1939 "The Place of Theory in Anthropological Studies." *The Philosophy of Science* 6:328-344.
1955 "Ethical Relativity: *Sic et Non.*" *Journal of Philosophy* 52: 663-677.

Koch, K-F.
1974 *War and Peace in Jalémo: The Management of Conflict in Highland New Guinea.* Cambridge, MA: Harvard University Press.

Kroeber, A. L.
1948 *Anthropology.* New York: Harcourt, Brace and Co.

Kuran, T.
1988 The Tenacious Past: Theories of Personal and Collective Conservation." *Journal of Economic Behavior and Organization* 10:143-171.

Linton, R.
   1952   "Universal Ethical Principles: An Anthropological View."
           In R. N. Anshen, ed., *Moral Principles of Action: Man's
           Ethical Imperative*. New York: Harper.
Lopreato, J.
   1984   *Human Nature and Biocultural Evolution*. Boston, MA:
           Allen and Unwin.
Lumsden, C. J., and E. O. Wilson
   1981   *Genes, Mind and Culture*. Cambridge, MA: Harvard Uni-
           versity Press.
Malotki, E.
   1983   *Hopi Time: A Linguistic Analysis of the Temporal Concepts
           in the Hopi Language*. Berlin, Germany: Mouton.
Meggitt, M. J.
   1977   *Blood Is Their Argument: Warfare Among the Mae Enga
           Tribesmen of the New Guinea Highlands*. Palo Alto, CA:
           Mayfield.
Murdock, G. P.
   1965   *Culture and Society*. Pittsburgh: University of Pittsburgh
           Press.
Naroll, R.
   1969   "Cultural Determinants and the Concept of the Sick
           Society." In S. C. Plog and R. B. Edgerton, eds., *Chang-
           ing Perspectives in Mental Illness*. New York: Holt, Rine-
           hart and Winston.
Nisbet, R., and L. Ross
   1980   *Human Inference: Strategies and Shortcomings of Social
           Judgement*. Englewood Cliffs, NJ: Prentice-Hall.
Nissam-Sabat, C.
   1987   "On Clifford Geertz and His 'Anti-Anti-Relativism.'" *Amer-
           ican Anthropologist* 89:935-943.
Peires, J. B.
   1989   *The Dead Will Arise: Nongqawuse and the Great Xhosa
           Cattle-Killing Movement of 1856-7*. London: James Curry.
Poole, F. P.
   1983   "Cannibals, Tricksters, and Witches: Anthropophagic
           Images Among Bimin-Kuskusmin." In P. Brown and D.
           Tuzin, eds., *The Ethnography of Cannibalism*. Washing-
           ton, DC: Society for Psychological Anthropology.
   1985   "Among the Boughs of the Hanging Tree: Male Suicide
           Among the Bimin-Kuskusmin of Papua New Guinea." In F.

X. Hezel, D. H. Rubenstein, and G. H. White, eds., *Culture, Youth and Suicide in the Pacific: Papers from the East-West Center Conference*. Honolulu, HI: East-West Center.

Redfield, R.
1953 *The Primitive World and Its Transformations*. Ithaca, NY: Cornell University Press.

Rosaldo, R.
1984 "Grief and a Headhunter's Rage: On the Cultural Force of Emotions." In E. Branner, ed., *Text, Play and Story*. Washington, DC: Proceedings of the American Ethnological Society.

Sale, K.
1991 "Letter to the Editor." *New York Times* July 25.

Schneider, D. M.
1984 *A Critique of the Study of Kinship*. Ann Arbor: University of Michigan Press.

Scott, J. P.
1989 *The Evolution of Social Systems*. New York: Gordon and Breach.

Shostak, M.
1981 *Nisa: The Life and Words of a !Kung Woman*. Cambridge, MA: Harvard University Press.

Story, R.
1985 "An Estimate of Mortality in a Pre-Columbian Urban Population." *American Anthropologist* 87:519-535.

Sumner, W. G.
1906 *Folkways*. Boston, MA: Ginn and Co.

Tuzin, D. F.
1982 "Ritual Violence among the Ilahita Arapesh: The Dynamics of Moral and Religious Uncertainty." In G. H. Herdt, ed., *Rituals of Manhood: Male Initiation in Papua New Guinea*. Berkeley: University of California Press.

Tylor, E. B.
1871 *Primitive Culture: Researches into the Development of Mythology, Philosophy, Religion, Language, Art and Custom*. London: J. Murray.

Van Baal, J.
1984 "The Dialectics of Sex in Marind-Anim Culture." In G. H. Herdt, ed., *Ritualized Homosexuality in Melanesia*. Berkeley: University of California Press.

SCIENCE,
OBJECTIVITY, MORALITY

Marvin Harris

Under the influence of postmodernist trends anthropologists have become increasingly preoccupied with the epistemological and moral-ethical impediments against the achievement of objectivity in their cultural accounts. Many anthropologists have abandoned what Roy D'Andrade (1995:399) has called an "objective model" and have adopted a "moral model" in its place. The objective model "tells about the thing being described" and is conducive to testing and replication by other observers, that is, it is science-oriented. The moral model on the other hand is subjective, tells how the agent who is doing the description reacts to the object described, and is aimed at identifying what is good and what is bad rather than what is true or false.

I share D'Andrade's general commitment to science-oriented anthropology, but cannot endorse some aspects of his argument. Specifically, I find the key dichotomies of objective versus subjective and science versus morality, to be misleading.

Putting the Observer in the Picture

The difference between objective and subjective lies in the methods used to describe the phenomena under investigation—methods in the one case that are public, replicable, and testable, and in the other case, private, idiosyncratic, and untestable. The current postmodern preoccupation with the observer's thoughts and feelings is subjective because it involves private, idiosyncratic, and untestable operations, not because it provides information about the observer's reaction to the observed.

This again is not an inconsequential quibble. Science-oriented, objective descriptions of cultures are not impaired by an examination of the observers' reactions and biases. On the contrary, objectivity actually requires some account of the relationship between the describing observer and the phenomena described in order to satisfy the rule that observers specify what they have done to gain the knowledge that they claim to possess. Postmodernists have a valid point when they complain that scientific descriptions conventionally remove all traces of the observer's personality in order to create what may very well be an illusory facade of objectivity. Science-oriented anthropologists need to put the observer in the picture. What we must resist are subjective accounts (as defined above) no matter whether they are about the observer or the observed. (Of course I'm not against novel-writing as long as the author does not attempt to make it the one and only form of ethnography.)

In scientific ethnography, putting the observer in the picture requires that we know such items as where and when and why the observer was in the field, who were the informants, what language was used, and what events took place that might have affected the research such as a personal illness, emotional stress, or the actions of hostile authorities. In D'Andrade's model, this kind of information would be subjective because it tells how the agent who is doing the describing reacted to the entities that are being described.

The Unity of Science and Morality

I turn to the second dichotomy: strict separation of the moral-subjective from scientific-objective models. D'Andrade denies that "one can blend together objectivity and morality in a single model" (1995:405). In my view this categorical distinction needlessly concedes the moral high ground to the science-bashing camp. I agree that scientific inquiry must be carried out in a manner that protects its findings from politico-moral bias to the greatest possible degree. But this does not mean that scientific inquiry should be (or can be) conducted in a politico-moral vacuum.

First of all there is strong empirical support for the position that morality in the form of culturally constructed values and preferences influences the definition and selection of researchable projects. What we choose to study or not to study in the name of anthropology is a politico-moral decision. The reason for this is that we are given

limited research funding. Therefore, the allocation of research effort is
a zero-sum game in which the commitment to one kind of study means
the neglect of alternative projects and problematics. The recent commitment to the study of gender roles and ethnicity to the neglect of
class stratification is an example of politico-moral choice. Another
example: when structural-functionalism held sway, many anthropological Africanists made the politico-moral choice to ignore conflict, labor
exploitation and the whole imperialist colonial context. This did not
necessarily lessen the objectivity of their analysis of corporate lineages
or puberty ceremonies.

I can illustrate the need to make a difficult moral-ethical choice concerning what to study and write about from my own experience in Portuguese Africa. As explained in the "Preface" to *Portugal's African
Wards*:

> This pamphlet contains a description of several alarming features of
> Portugal's present colonial policy in Africa. I have written it in
> order to discharge what I conceive to be a moral obligation. From
> June 1956 to May 1957 I was in Mozambique carrying out a
> research program. . . . In the course of my work I came to depend
> on a number of people, both Portuguese and Africans, for informa-
> tion and assistance. To these people I became more than a social
> anthropologist and even more than a friend. Many of them risked
> their jobs and their personal safety to tell me about the conditions
> under which they were forced to live, even though in their own
> minds they could never be entirely certain that I had not been sent
> to spy on them. . . . They knew that if I wanted to, I could at least
> "tell the world." Under these circumstances I cannot confine my
> writings to such "neutral" or purely technical subjects as would lead
> to no involvement in politically controversial issues (Harris
> 1958:1).

Despite this openly morally, ethical commitment, I argued that my
findings about the colonial system (the "Indigenato") were objective
(and hence scientific). One of the main points supporting the objectivity of my account was that my preconceptions weighed against the
belief that the Portuguese colonial system was as oppressive as it
turned out to be. I expected to find race relations that contrasted
markedly with those of the Union of South Africa and could not be
accused of finding in Mozambique only what I wanted to find.

The Importance of "Getting It Right"

Morality blends with science in another very important way. Moral-ethical decisions need to be based on the best available knowledge of what the world is like. Science-bashers condemn science as an obstacle to the making of morally, ethically correct political decisions. But the shoe is on the other foot. It is a lack of scientific knowledge that places our politico-moral decisions in greatest jeopardy. To claim the moral high ground, one must have reliable knowledge. We have to know what the world is like; who is doing or has done what to whom; who and what are responsible for the suffering and injustice we condemn and seek to remedy. If this be so, then science-minded anthropologists may plausibly claim that their model is not only moral but morally superior to those that reject science as a source of reliable knowledge about the human condition. Fantasies, intuitions, interpretations, and reflections may make for good poems and novels, but if you want to know what to do about the AIDS time bomb in Africa, or landlessness in Mexico, neglect of objective data is reprehensible.

Let me underscore the point that the blended model applies only to the extent that the blending takes place without violating the distinctive rules of scientific-objective inquiry. Distorting the data-gathering process in order to make the findings concur with a desired politico-moral outcome must be vigilantly excluded. It is in this sense and only in this sense that the call for the rigid separation of the moral and science models is an ineluctable imperative.

Of course, merely following the rules of scientific inquiry does not guarantee the achievement of reliable knowledge. Scientists make mistakes and some even cook their data. But given its many successes (in anthropology as well as in the harder sciences), science is the best available system for providing a factual foundation for politico-moral decision-making. Anti-science paradigms—such as ethnopoetics, interpretationism, hermeneutics, and phenomenology—provide no such foundation and therefore cannot be regarded as morally superior to neo-positivist paradigms.

Critical Anthropology

Disturbed by what they conceive to be anthropology's continuing support of colonial and neo-colonial policies and other repressive and exploitative relationships, many anthropologists have turned toward the support and practice of what they call "critical anthropology" (Marcus and Fischer 1986). Critical anthropologists aim to expose injustice and exploitation as a new departure that supplants the false pretensions of politically free or neutral positivist approaches. But a politically engaged anthropology is no novelty. It has roots that go back at least as far as E. B. Tylor and his identification of anthropology as "essentially a reformer's science . . . active at once in aiding progress and in removing hindrance" (quoted in Lowie 1937:83).

Throughout the entire course of the twentieth century, a battle has raged over the relative contributions of nature and nurture to the evolution of sociocultural systems. If we take this battle into consideration, anthropology has never ceased to be "a reformer's science," or in postmodern times, what is being called critical anthropology. It is true that much of the political thrust of anthropology in the nineteenth and early twentieth centuries was colonialist, racist, and sexist. But not liking a particular political formula does not diminish its criticality. Moreover, science-oriented anthropologists have scarcely all been hereditarians and raciologists. On the contrary, science-oriented anthropologists have a long history of contributing to the struggle against racism, antisemitism, colonialism, and sexism; and like it or not, to military and civilian intelligence gathering during World War II; and to the anti-Vietnam War movement (especially through the invention and spread of the Teach-In). And all this before the generation of the critical anthropologist had gotten out of graduate school.

So there is nothing very new, let alone startling, when critical anthropologist Nancy Scheper-Hughes writes that "if we cannot begin to think about social institutions and practices in moral or ethical terms, then anthropology strikes me as quite weak and useless" (1995:410). I agree, but only if we add the proviso that if we cannot begin to think about social institutions and practices in scientific-objective terms then anthropology will be even weaker and more useless.

Scheper-Hughes is justly famous for her commitment to the well-being of the people she has studied (in Ireland, Brazil, South Africa), and for her unflinching determination to foreground the crippling effects of poverty and inequality. But I see no necessary contradiction between her indignation at the "medicalization" of hunger in Brazil (where the effects of hunger and chronic malnutrition are treated with tranquilizer pills) and the requirements of D'Andrade's objective model.

Scheper-Hughes herself almost reaches the same conclusion. She states that "those who question the truth claims of objectivist science do not deny that there are discoverable 'facts' in the world. . . . Some things are incontestably 'factual' and these need to be studied empirically." If one is concerned with the number of infant deaths in rural Brazil for example, or the incidence of "necklacing" in South Africa, "the researcher has a strong scientific and a moral imperative to get it right." But she is quick to qualify this imperative with a disclaimer: "Crucial empirical work of this kind . . . need not entail a philosophical commitment to Enlightenment notions of reason and truth." Instead of being guided by such notions which lead one to positivism and false certainties, the new brand of empirical studies "can be guided by critical-interpretive concerns about the inevitable partiality of truth and about the various meanings that 'facts' and 'events' have in the existential, cultural, and political sense" (Scheper-Hughes 1995:436).

These do not appear to be a coherent set of principles adequate for guiding the conduct of politically responsible research. If there are some things that we need to get right, then there must be other things that we don't need to worry about getting wrong. But just what are the things we need to get right and what are the things we can get wrong? Without a coherent set of methodological principles for distinguishing between research that requires empirical data and research that is free of such a requirement, we would obviously be better off sticking to the maligned "Enlightenment notions of reason and truth," since we have no way of knowing that the "inevitable partiality" will be less partial for the critical anthropologist than for those who follow different approaches. Merely telling us that facts and events have different meanings is of little use. Why should we attend to some meanings and not to others?

Unlike postmodernists whom she felicitously excoriates for their relativism and obscurantism, Scheper-Hughes intends to "speak truth to power." This is a noble ambition. But I cannot see how she expects to do this and at the same time accept the Foucauldian mantra that "the objectivity of science and of medicine is always a phantom objectivity" (see Miller 1992). I would argue to the contrary: without science, morality is always a phantom morality. Without science, critical anthropology will dissolves back into the postmodernist mainstream where radical skepticism, relativism, and nihilism are the order of the day (Gross and Levitt 1994; Rosenau 1992).

There is more than a little irony in the critical stance Scheper-Hughes and other critical theorists take toward the Enlightenment. For activists interested in defying the powerful and defending the poor and the weak, what better source of inspiration can be found than the works of Rousseau, Condorcet, and Thomas Paine?   Prominent conservative voices, namely the authors of the notorious *The Bell Curve* (Herrnstein and Murray 1994), also decry the influence of the Enlightenment precisely in order to have America learn to live with more inequality.

References

D'Andrade, Roy
   1995   "Moral Models in Anthropology." *Current Anthropology* 36:399-408, 433-436.
Gross, Paul, and Norman Levitt
   1994   *Higher Superstition: The Academic Left and Its Quarrels With Science.* Baltimore, MD: Johns Hopkins University Press.
Harris, Marvin
   1958   *Portugal's African Wards.* New York: American Committee on Africa.
   1995   "Comment on the 'Objectivity and Militancy Debate.'" *Current Anthropology* 36:423-424.
Herrnstein Richard, and Charles Murray
   1994   *The Bell Curve.* New York: Free Press.
Lowie, R. H.
   1937   *The History of Ethnological Theory.* New York: Holt, Rinehart and Winston.
Marcus, George E., and Michael M. J. Fischer
   1986   *Anthropology as Cultural Critique.* Chicago, IL: University of Chicago Press.
Miller, James
   1992   *The Passion of Michel Foucault.* New York: Simon & Schuster.
Rosenau, Pauline
   1992   *Post-Modernism and the Social Sciences.* Princeton, NJ: Princeton University Press.
Scheper-Hughes, Nancy
   1995   "The Primacy of the Ethical: Propositions for a Militant Anthropology." *Current Anthropology* 36:409-420, 436-438.

CULTURE
IS NOT EVERYTHING

Roy D'Andrade

There is a notion widespread among American cultural anthropologists which holds that "culture is everything." According to this view, culture is the dominant *causal* force in human life. This chapter will present a short historical account and a critique of the unfortunate consequences of this notion. An attempt will be made to describe more exactly what culture typically does and does not cause. Some comments will be made about the recent shift in anthropology to a concern with power and how this is related both to the notion that culture is everything and to the psychological alienation of major figures in current cultural theory. Finally, possible alternative directions will be briefly mentioned.

Definitions

To begin: The standard definition of culture in the world outside anthropology is something like:

> The totality of socially transmitted behavior patterns, arts, beliefs, institutions, and all other products of human work and thought considered as the expression of a particular period, class, community, or population: Edwardian culture; Japanese culture; the culture of poverty (*The American Heritage Dictionary of the English Language*, 3rd edition).

In anthropology, the term has been widely discussed and debated.

Kroeber and Kluckhohn's 1952 book, *Culture*, presents an analysis of over 150 definitions of the word culture. For example:

Tylor (1871) Culture, or civilization . . . is the complex whole which includes knowledge, belief, art, law, morals, custom, and any other capabilities and habits acquired by man as a member of society.

Benedict (1931) . . . that complex whole which includes all the habits acquired by man as a member of society.

Boas (1930) Culture embraces all the manifestations of social habits of a community, the reactions of the individual as affected by the habits of the group in which he lives, and the products of human activities as determined by these habits.

Kroeber (1948) . . . the mass of learned and transmitted motor reactions, habits, techniques, ideas, and values—and the behavior they induce—is what constitutes culture.

Kroeber and Kluckhohn (1952) Culture consists of patterns, explicit and implicit, of and for behavior acquired and transmitted by symbols, constituting the distinctive achievement of human groups, including their embodiment in artifacts.

Notice that in these definitions, culture is just about everything but the physical environment. Culture is defined as the *totality of behaviors* acquired by members of a group.

There is a well-known problem with this type of omnibus definition. The problem is this: if we define culture in such a way that it consists of the behavior acquired and transmitted by a society, we then cannot properly use the idea of culture to *explain* this behavior. Such an explanation is nothing more than word magic—we call what they do culture, and then we say we have explained why they do what they do by calling it culture.

In the decade after the Kroeber and Kluckhohn book was published, anthropologists began to move away from the omnibus definition, restricting the term to just the *ideas* acquired and transmitted by members of a social group. The phrase "patterns *of* and *for* behavior" used by Kroeber and Kluckhohn nicely straddles the fence between idea and act—"patterns *for* behavior" refers to ideas people have about what should be done, while "patterns *of* behavior" refers to actual behaviors.

In the 1950s, a shift took place in the social sciences from a former behaviorist paradigm to a more cognitive paradigm. Noam Chomsky, George Miller, Jerome Bruner, and others in psychology and linguistics rejected the major tenets of behaviorism and began to develop theories which dealt directly with mental processes. In anthropology, both Clifford Geertz and David Schneider came out strongly against an omnibus definition of culture. Schneider says "cultural constructs, the cultural symbols, are different from any systematic, regular, verifiable pattern of actual, observed behavior. That is, the pattern of observed behavior is different from culture" (1968:5). Schneider in a later paper continues the same line of reasoning:

> Culture is not that Tylorian inventory of pots, pans, rocks, and crocks which must of necessity end with the phrase "et cetera," . . . All such definitions of culture lead to a difficulty which may be called "naive cultural determinism," the sort where when one asks "why do the Nuer practice the levirate?" and the answer is given, "Because it is their culture" (1976:203).

Geertz makes the same point:

> The conceptual morass into which the Tylorean kind of *pot-au-feu* theorizing can lead, is evident in what is still one of the better general introductions to anthropology, Clyde Kluckhohn's *Mirror for Man*. In some twenty-seven pages of his chapter on the concept, Kluckhohn managed to define culture in turn as: (1) "the total way of life of a people"; (2) "the social legacy the individual acquires from his group"; (3) "a way of thinking, feeling, and believing"; (4) "an abstraction from behavior"; (5) a theory on the part of the anthropologist about the way in which a group of people in fact behave; (6) a "storehouse of pooled learning"; (7) "a set of standardized orientations to recurrent problems"; (8) "learned behavior"; (9) a mechanism for the normative regulation of behavior; (10) "a set of techniques for adjusting both to the external environment and to other men"; (11) "a precipitate of history" (1973:4-5).

Geertz contrasts Kluckhohn's position with his own: "The concept of culture I espouse . . . is essentially a semiotic one. Believing, with Max Weber, that man is an animal suspended in webs of significance he himself has spun, I take culture to be those webs" (1973:5). Ward

Goodenough's earlier definition of culture was also very influential: "A society's culture consists of whatever it is one has to know or believe in order to operate in a manner acceptable to its members" (1957).

Most anthropologists have come to follow Goodenough, Geertz and Schneider in treating culture as knowledge, meaning, symbol, construct, model, etc. However, as indicated by the dictionary definition given above, this shift has not yet changed the popular conception of culture, which is still Tylorean.

Once the term "culture" was limited to ideas-meanings-symbols-knowledge-understandings, it then became theoretically possible to claim that people did things *because* of their culture. We would all agree that someone's understandings or interpretations or knowledge about the world affect that person's behavior. This is a central part of the folk model of the mind—what one thinks and believes affects how one acts. If one wants to buy ice cream, one goes to a store where one believes ice cream is sold. And if one believes the stock market is about to crash, and one wants to keep one's wealth, one sells one's stock. When understandings or interpretations are "cultural"—that is, are shared and learned as part of being a member of a group—it is eminently reasonable to say that culture influences what people do. But anthropologists' claims have gone far beyond just saying that what people do is affected by their culture. There has been a stream of claims in anthropology to the effect that culture *determines* or *constitutes* or *constructs* things. To say that culture determines or constructs something is to say, by definition, that culture, by itself, causes something to be the way it is. This is a claim that culture is both the *necessary* and *sufficient* cause of this thing.

With regard to this issue of cultural constructionism, I wish to briefly discuss one more point. The claim that many anthropologists make is that "reality is culturally constructed." There is certainly some truth to this. Cultural objects such as money, rights, marriage, names, etc., have a special kind of reality—they exist not just as ideas, but as "things" in the sense that we agree that we will act as if these things are real, and in so acting these things become real to us. Thus we agree to treat certain kinds of printed paper as if it had value, and people as if they had rights, and certain sounds as if they were the names of people, and so on. And in so doing, certain kinds of printed paper, people, and certain sounds do have value, rights, and become names.

There is another type of cultural object which is like the "we agree-to-treat-them-as-real" objects. This is the category of gods, ghosts, witches, etc., which can be very real to members of some society, even though you or I may think they are not real. The category of things like gods, ghosts, and witches has weaker causal properties than the category of things like money, rights, and names, because although many people in a society may believe that the gods are real, for those people who do not believe the gods are real, the gods are *not* real. However, a society can institutionalize the norm that something will be treated as if it were something else, and if certain pieces of paper are institutionalized as having value, the fact that some individual does not believe that these papers have value does not take the value from these pieces of paper—even that individual must still take other people's money as if it were valuable.

These culturally constructed objects are both striking and important. Talcott Parsons (1951) called this part of culture "constitutive culture." But constitutive culture is only one part of culture. In my experience as a cognitive anthropologist, I have found that many cultural models are simply descriptive and are strongly shaped by the ordinary world of normal perception.

Folk taxonomies in botany and zoology, the folk model of the mind, the categorization of colors, and numerous other cultural classification schemes seem to be strongly influenced by the structure of the world as normally perceived. So, the statement that reality is culturally constructed is another of these partial truth arguments, in which a claim is made as if "culture is everything," and only on closer inspection does one find out that the claim is much exaggerated—one part of culture is made to stand for the whole. I believe that people in other cultures most of the time inhabit the same reality you or I do. Cultural reality is more often reality-shaped than culturally constituted.

Culture and the Psyche

The object that anthropologists most typically claim is culturally constituted is some part of the human psyche (by the psyche I mean the contents and processes of the human mind, including perception, cognition, emotion, motivation, and intention). Thus the self, subjectivity, emotions, sex differences, etc., are all said to be culturally constituted (or socially constructed—the two phrases mean the same thing in most contexts). The idea that the human psyche is culturally constituted has penetrated deeply into anthropology and it is now more or less doctrine.

The arguments that are used to support this position typically use a simple conceptual trick. The trick is to conflate the *representation* of something with that *something*. Thus, one's *representation* of one's *self* is considered to be the same as one's *self*, one's *representations* of one's *feelings* is considered to be the same as one's *feelings*, etc. Once this conflation is made, then evidence that culture strongly affects the *representation* of something can be said to be evidence that culture constructs that *thing*. So, since culture affects ideas about the self and ideas about the self are the same as the self, then it must be true that culture constructs the self (see Spiro 1994 for a critique of this tactic). The same trick can be used to show that any aspect of the human psyche is culturally constructed.

If one really wanted to prove the claim that culture constructs or determines the self, emotions, sex differences, subjectivities, and so on, one would have to demonstrate that *nothing* but culture makes the self, emotions, and so on. If something other than culture has some role in "making" the self, emotions, etc., one can only claim that the self, emotions, etc. are *partially* constructed (that is, "shaped") by culture. This is a much weaker claim. And as soon as one says it, the question immediately arises "how much of the 'shaping?'. . . 80%? 10%?" The wonderful feeling of having explained *all* evaporates into pale and inaccurate percentages.

The conceptual trick of claiming that the representation of something is the same as that something works especially well for things like the self and emotions because while the self and emotions are not *just* symbolic constructs, it is generally recognized that symbolic constructs do make up a *part* of the self (e.g. self-representations make up a part of the self), and that symbolic constructs are *part* of what makes up emotions (e.g. the cognitive appraisal part of the emotions). So it is easy to slide from part to whole, and to claim that since symbolic constructs are *important* in the making of self and emotion, then the self and emotion are *nothing but* symbolic constructs. Given the assumption that the human psyche is made up of nothing but symbolic constructs, and given that culture determines symbolic constructs, then it logically follows that culture determines the content of the human psyche. The logic is sound but the premise is wrong.

I am not aware of any anthropologist who has explicitly presented the claim that the human psyche is made up of nothing but symbolic constructs. It is too counterintuitive. The self cannot be nothing but a symbolic construct if the self has agency, because symbolic constructs do not have agency (for a related argument about the autonomy of the self see Parish 1994). Emotions cannot be nothing but symbolic constructs if emotions consist in part of sensations because sensations are not themselves symbolic constructs. So what one reads are skillfully hedged claims. The following example is taken from the "Introduction" to *Language and the Politics of Emotion*, edited by Abu-Lughod and Lutz:

> Emotion can be said to be created in, rather than shaped by, speech. . . . To say this is not to reduce the concept of emotion to the concept of speech, even though a discourse-centered approach might be construed as a rejection or obscuring of the body.
>
> Although in this volume we focus on emotions as discourse, working to pry emotions loose from psychobiology, that does not mean that we do not recognize the possibility that emotions are also framed in most contexts as experiences that involve the whole person, including the body. Here Bourdieu's thoughts on "body hexis" are suggestive, providing ways of thinking about the fact that emotion is embodied without being forced to concede that it must be "natural" and not shaped by social interaction. [Bourdieu] defines body hexis as a set of body techniques or postures that are learned habits or ingrained dispositions that both reflect and reproduce the social relations that surround and constitute them. . . . Extending this definition to the emotions enables us to grasp how they, as cultural products, are reproduced in individuals in the form of embodied experience (1990:12).

In this quote we encounter such phrases as "emotions can be said to be created in . . . speech," "emotion as discourse" and emotions as "cultural products . . . reproduced in individuals." In these phrases the authors come close to the explicit "emotion as symbolic construct" position. But emotions are not entirely liberated from the body, since the authors say "emotions are also framed in most contexts as experiences that involve the whole person, including the body." Thus the role of internal sensation is not exactly denied, although the authors say they want "ways of thinking about the fact that emotion is embodied without being forced to concede that it must be 'natural' and not shaped by social interaction."

One is struck with the complexity of this dance of assertions and denials about the causal role of the body and the "natural." Hedged claims to be sure, but the intent is clear—"to pry emotion loose from psychobiology." And the spirit is not ecumenical; the authors do not seem to want culture and the psychobiological to both share causal roles in producing emotions. Rather, they appear to want the psychobiological exorcized. But if the exorcism is successful then emotion becomes something without sensation and without a body, and this is too counter-intuitive to be presentable. So the role of the body must be brought back, but denied as a causal force and treated as the passive vehicle of learned social habits.

Culture and the Social System

Culture is not only said to construct the human psyche, it is also said to completely control the workings of society. The idea that culture is the dominant cause of most things in human life has almost erased the idea that society, or the social system, also has causal powers. I was especially struck with this when reading the late Ernest Gellner's book, *Conditions of Liberty*, in which he discusses the fall of the Soviet Union. Because Gellner is a British social anthropologist, I was quite surprised that he presents in his book a purely idea-driven explanation for the fall of the Soviet Union. Basically, he argues the Soviet Union fell because its social system depended on a religion and this religion failed. Gellner says:

> The unification of the political, economic, and ideological hierar-chies into one single bureaucratic pyramid is not only disastrous for practical performance, it also seems to be catastrophic for the social soul. By sacralizing this world, and above all the most mundane aspects of the world, it deprived men of that necessary contrast between the elevated and the earthy. . . . The world cannot bear the burden of so much sacredness. . . . Marxism appears to have no viable vulgar, corrupted folk variant. So perhaps it was its deifica-tion of the current and concrete historical process which was its undoing (1994:42).

According to Gellner, this religion failed because it lacked the divi-sion between profane and sacred. Here we have, from someone whose work I generally admire, a completely "culturalist" explanation of the fall of the Soviet Union. (However, it is quite possible Gellner made these claims tongue in cheek, or at least twinkle in eye.)

Rather than invoking culture as an explanation of the fall of the Soviet Union, a more social system-based explanation might invoke the fact that the Soviet social system performed miserably. The failure of the Soviet system to deliver goods and services and to make reasonable decisions about matters great and small was notorious. And because the system was inefficient and frustrating, and because the ideals which had made great frustrations bearable had eroded, the regime *had* to be ruthless. However, replacement of executive leadership over time moved toward safe bureaucratic choices. The secretariat did not want another Stalin, but unfortunately that is what they needed to stay in power. All the myth makers, spin doctors, discourse formulators, and ideology constructors could not keep the system going when the regime lost both credibility and the will to use effective violence. Some people may think that if ideologists create the proper discourse, then even very punitive systems can remain in power. But this did not happen—the discourse of the Soviet professional apologists was contradicted by everyday lived experience and the Russian people had egos autonomous enough to notice and act on such facts.

Gellner's mistake, if one may call it that, is the assumption that a society's social system is primarily a creation of the culture. Then if the social system collapses, it must be because there is something wrong with the culture. This means the fall of the Soviet system must be due to a flaw in ideology. Of course, the causes of the fall of the Soviet Union are undoubtedly complex and my comment addresses just one of many possible contributing factors (see Verdery 1996 for a detailed analysis of the fall of socialist systems in Eastern Europe). The point is that when a very eminent social anthropologist gives an explanation of the fall of the Soviet Union totally in terms of "culture" it seems to me that one can reasonably wonder whether anthropology has any explanation for anything except that "the culture did it."

Consider the following illustrative fable:

Once upon a time a single, relatively homogeneous society which tended to migrate hither and yon, split into two groups, one which went east, the other which went west. Each settled in their new areas and became farmers. But conditions were quite different in the east and the west. The east was relatively lush, with lots of water and good soil. The west was much harsher and farming was harder, and more emphasis was placed on care of large animals. In the west, a system of segmentary lineages developed, with constant splitting and fusion among lineages. The westerners were also bedeviled by plundering bands of mountain people. Political organization in the west was centered on various war leaders, while in the east, which had little outside threat, leadership was centered on the production of series of agricultural rituals. The east was also fortunate in being on the edge of an ancient trade route, and found that specialization in crafts allowed exchange with traders for new kinds of tools, spices, and craft objects. Over time, the socialization of children in the east began to differ considerably from the socialization of children in the west, with the western children being socialized to be independent and tough, while the children in the east were socialized to be responsible and sociable. And, not surprisingly, the religious systems of the two became very different, with the west specializing in a variety of initiation rituals and spirit possession, while in the east religion centered more on seasonal rituals and the propitiation of ancestors. Eventually, both the east and west societies came to be studied by anthropologists. Both had superb ethnographies written about them which became part of the disciplinary canon. And, lo and behold, to this very day students are taught that the differences between the easterners and westerners are due to the fact that they have different cultures. After all, what else could they be due to?

In a sense, the generalization is true—the east and west have different cultures, and these cultures orient, guide and instigate the very different behaviors to be observed in the east and west. So in that sense, the differences in behavior can be said to be due to the fact that easterners and westerners learn different cultures, are expected to act in different ways, and have internalized different values and goals. But, in another sense, it is like a bad joke to ascribe the differences between east and west to culture. This is a trivial explanation, like the man who explained that he wore his pajamas outside of street clothes "because he wanted to." Certainly the two cultures are different. But that is exactly what needs to be explained, not what explains the differences. One can invoke culture as one immediate cause of much of what people do, but in this example the more significant question is *why* each culture is the way it is. Culture is both a cause of certain things and something which itself is caused. Because it causes some things does not mean *it* is not caused. And often the interesting question is—"what caused some piece of culture to be the way it is?"

It is clear—at least in the fable—that the events that changed things were various exigencies that effected family, systems of production, the exercise of power, contacts with other societies, etc. To say that the two communities are different because they have different cultures does not really explain anything. What explains the differences are various events which created *experiences* which affected the culture directly or indirectly.

Culture as a Guidance System

While culture has important causal effects, these effects often tend to keep things as they are rather than to create new forms of action. As has been frequently pointed out, cultural values and norms and beliefs tend to be conservative—they primarily direct people in ways which reproduce what was done before. Most cultural learnings are like this—they are inheritances of past experience and they make preferential or obligatory the enactment of past solutions. But although culture tends to be inertial, this does not mean that it cannot be changed. The experiences of the westerners and easterners in the fable were different because of environmental and economic and social factors, and these differences were large enough and lasted long enough for these experiences to become new definitions of how the world is, to produce new adaptations to these new definitions of the situation, to organize "interests" into different configurations, and to eventuate in new institutions.

Another way of saying this is to say that culture tends to be selective. New experiences are understood in the light of past experiences, and past experience is what culture codifies. This selectivity does not normally initiate change, but it can. Some parts of the collection of cultural models we call "culture" do initiate change. Scientific knowledge, for example, grows rapidly because the norms of science, while themselves quite conservative, are directed toward the discovery of new facts and theories. The new knowledge produced by science can have strong social and cultural effects when they combine with economic and social motivations, as we all have experienced (Adams 1996). Similarly, moral geniuses have, in the historical past, formed new systems of belief and value which have radically altered both psyches and social systems.

But the general point is that culture, far from being the great uncaused causer, *has a particular place in the great causal scheme of things* (Spiro 1994). Anthropologists have relatively well-formed ideas about what one can expect to find in this guidance system, and it is a very rich and extensive variety of things. Every culture is a wonder, but it is typically on the back side rather than the leading edge of the causal arrow. Culture is a good place to look to understand a good deal about *what* people are doing, but not such a good place to look to understand why people started to do something in the first place, or even why they continue to do it.

Even with respect to being an inertial force, different parts of the culture vary in how inertial they are (Strauss and Quinn 1997). The prices of commodities are norms and are just as "cultural" as anything else. But prices change quickly with conditions of supply and demand, which are part of the economic system, not culture per se. Would anyone argue that prices are *determined* by the culture? In contrast to the market, religious rituals typically change slowly, and it makes more sense to say that ritual performance is culturally determined. But even the performance of ritual can be responsive to external forces, as the shift of the Catholic Mass from Latin to the vernacular illustrates.

Using Strauss and Quinn's terms, any part of culture can be either "hard" or "soft" (or in between). To say that a cultural schema is "hard" is to say that it resists change, either because it is deeply inter-nalized within individuals, or because it is strongly institutionalized in a system of statues and roles. It is "incontestable" or "uncontested" culture. To say that a cultural schema is "soft" is to say that a cultural schema can be easily changed. It is "contestable" culture. Prices are contestable soft cultural schemas. I know the 1998 price of a 7300 Power MacIntosh and this is a shared understanding, as cultural as any-thing else. But it is very likely this price will change in the next year. It is a piece of soft culture, constantly being modified. However, I doubt that our belief that medical doctors need extensive technical training will change much in the next century. This belief is a piece of hard culture. It has been "institutionalized" in that having this techni-cal training is part of the role of a doctor, backed by serious sanctions and a deeply internalized cultural model concerning the need for com-petence in dealing with life-threatening problems. Hard culture is often called "structure."

Power and Culture

The current emphasis on culture as the dominant cause in human life has a very "idealistic" or Hegelian bias. It is interesting that critical social theory has moved from the anti-Hegelian materialism of Marx back to the philosophical idealism of Hegel. The Frankfurt School opened the materialist theory of Marx to the possibility of psychologi-cal and cultural forces. The structuralist Marxism of Althusser moved Marxism even further toward idealism, and post-structuralists have moved the cycle full circle.

In fact, it appears to have moved more than full circle. One of the major things that has been happening in anthropology is that, little by little, the god term "culture" is being eclipsed by the new god term "power."   One can speculate that something like this had to happen, since as it began to be clear that the concept of culture has become over-extended, some contrasting causal entity has to be brought into the theoretical system to make anything happen.   And "power" sounds like a hard contrast to "culture."   One might expect that this would lead to a greater concern with economic systems as a source of power, or with the study of the operation of the state, or with any of a number of sources of "power."   But, in the main, anthropology has followed Foucault's lead in theorizing about power.   Foucault says:

> By power, I do not mean "Power" as a group of institutions and mechanisms that insure the subservience of the citizens of a given state. . . . I do not mean, either, a mode of subjugation which, in contrast to violence, has the form of the rule.   Finally, I do not have in mind a general system of domination exerted by one group over another (1980:2).

What then, *is* the stuff of power?   Foucault is elusive on this point, but perhaps the following quotes will give his sense: "power relations are rooted in the system of social networks" (1980:224); "power and knowledge directly imply one another . . . there is no power relation without the correlative constitution of a field of knowledge, nor any knowledge that does not presuppose and constitute at the same time power relations" (1979:27-28); "it is in discourse that power and knowledge are joined together" (1980:100).

For Foucault power and knowledge and discourse are so intertwined that they cannot be separated.   In practical terms, Foucault's analysis of power turns out to be primarily an analysis of discourse.   And what Foucault describes as power/discourse/knowledge is just what most anthropologists would call culture.   It is rooted in social networks; it is a system of ideas which is represented in talk, practices, institutions; it defines what is true; it is pervasive, systematic, inescapable, and can be used in controlling others.   The major thing that Foucault adds to older conceptions of culture is an emphasis on coercion, on the disciplining and punitive character of culture.

The general point here is that in following Foucault, anthropologists did not really turn to any new concepts outside culture, they merely found culture again in a different vocabulary—one that told them that culture was power itself.   But if culture is power itself, what should we call the kinds of power that Foucault says are not power, such as institutional power, subjugation by rule, or group domination?   Where is the social system? In following Foucault, anthropology continued to ignore causal forces outside culture.

Culture and Metaphysical Idealism

Although both his supporters and detractors often talk about Foucault as if he were a metaphysical idealist who believes that the facts about human beings are created through our discourse about them, this is probably incorrect. Dreyfus and Rabinow (1982) have an excellent analysis of Foucault's strategy of "bracketing" truth claims and looking at discursive practice as an isolated phenomenon. They argue that, for Foucault, the truth of discourse about humans is unknowable—the only thing one can do is trace the history of power relations embodied in discourse and institutions. But from this position it is easy to draw the conclusion that since all we can know is discourse, that discourse is all there is. Although Foucault may not say this, many of his supporters seem to think he did and agree with what they think he said.

Clifford Geertz has a position which is similar to Foucault's, expressed in his well known account of the Indian story about turtles:

> There is an Indian story—at least I heard it as an Indian story—about an Englishman who, having been told that the world rested on a platform which rested on the back of an elephant which rested in turn on the back of a turtle, asked . . . what did the turtle rest on? Another turtle. And that turtle? "Ah, Sahib, after that it is turtles all the way down" (1973:28-29).

Geertz continues: "Such, indeed, is the condition of things. . . . Cultural analysis is intrinsically incomplete. And, worse than that, the more deeply it goes the less complete it is" (1973:29).

Like Foucault, Geertz holds that we will never know any real or complete truth about our cultural lives; not that there is no truth, just that we can never reach it. This brings to mind the joke that David Schneider liked so well about the three baseball umpires. Asked by a rookie umpire how they made their decisions about balls and strikes, the first and most junior umpire said "I calls them as they are." The second umpire said "I calls them as I sees them." The third and most senior umpire said "They ain't nothing till I calls them." The point of this joke is a bit more complex than the point of the turtles story, but the generalization remains the same—in cultural analysis, reality in the ordinary sense is unknowable or irrelevant.

Perhaps it is worthwhile to point out that Schneider, Foucault and Geertz have all used the trick of substitution of a partial truth for an absolute truth discussed above. Certainly it is the case many claims made in the human sciences are not true, and it is the case that it is difficult to know which claims are true and which are not. But there is no reason to believe that we can never know that *any* of these claims are true or false. Because some things may never be known does not mean that *all* things will never be known. And in fact, many social science claims already have considerable empirical support. They may not be the exact truth, but the betting is that they are reasonable approximations. And that is no different in principle than the situation in physics. The assertion that human realities or cultural meanings or causal relations *cannot* be known is fantasy, and there is no more reason to believe such fantasy than there is to believe Hegel's speculation that history is controlled by the *geist* of pure reason. Such speculations are often supported by metaphysical arguments, moral appeals, rhetorical put-downs, and clever stories, but there is no *evidence* that human realities or cultural meanings cannot be known. It may sound deep and wise to say such things but it is rhetorical drivel nonetheless.

Culture and Alienation

Part of the attraction of Foucault and other postmodernists is said to be that they connect power with history, or criticize the sexism, racism and colonialism of the West. But not all of the major theoretical figures are exemplars of political correctness. Especially impressive in this regard is the rise in prominence within culturalist circles of Nietzsche. Nietzsche, it is fair to say, was enormously elitist, admiring an aristocratic minority and saying that the majority of people, "bungled and botched" as they are, should have *no* claim to happiness or well being, since they are fit only as means for the great to show their excellence. Nietzsche was also very sexist—Bertrand Russell once quipped that while Nietzsche said that if one was going to visit a woman one should not forget to bring one's whip, he, Nietzsche, who had never had *any* kind of relationship with any woman but his sister, knew that if he did try to have relationships with women, nine out of ten of them would quickly get the whip away from him. But, Nietzsche as joke aside, why should a dead white male, flamboyantly promoting the mistreatment of women and justifying the misery of the masses by the presence of a hero, become an "in" figure? Other important intellectual figures are bitterly attacked exactly because they are thought to be sexist elitist dead white males.

This paradox is not limited to Nietzsche. Many of the figures often cited by postmodernists and cultural critics were also—to say the least— politically incorrect. De Man and Heidegger have backgrounds as Nazi sympathizers. Althusser murdered his wife. Hegel thought local wars a good way for the state to stay in shape. Given the strong tendency to moral rectitude of postmodernism and cultural criticism, what accounts for the fact that these figures are not taken to task for their ethical lapses? Why is there a lack of accountability for *these* people?

My speculative answer involves the fact that Foucault and others in this group were deeply alienated from Western culture. With respect to Foucault, I find his alienation reflected in his sense that culture is a pervasive, oppressive, constraining, intrusive force. Psychological anthropologists have noted that culture, when not internalized by the individual, is not experienced as rewarding or valuable, but rather comes to be experienced as an *external* constraint and an *imposed* discipline, arbitrary, punitive and systematic (Spiro 1994). Foucault's writings express this alienated experience, and those who are similarly alienated may find such a perspective personally validating. The attraction of these "nihilist" figures in general seems to be that they express an alienation from Western culture and society which is consonant with the alienation felt by many intellectuals. Because of the centrality of their disaffection, Foucault, de Man, Heiddeger, Nietzsche and others can be forgiven their lapses and be uncritically accepted; the important thing is that they hated and attacked what is felt to be the real enemy—the bourgeois, sexist, racist, homophobic, colonialist, religious culture which is supposed to be "ours" but which is not really "us." Once one's culture loses meaning, one sees only power.

Culture Is Related to What, How?

A final note. If this analysis that the concept of culture has been over-extended is right, then anthropology needs something more than the concept of culture. Viewed not as everything, but as an important force in its own right, the concept of culture will continue to be indispensable. But more is needed in anthropology than just the culture concept. A suspicion of this type is discussed by Clifford Geertz, who states:

The danger that cultural analysis, in search of all-too-deep-lying turtles, will lose touch with the hard surfaces of life—with the political, economic, stratificatory realities within which men are everywhere contained—and with the biological and physical necessities on which these surfaces rest, is an ever present one. The only defense against it . . . is to train such analysis on such realities and such necessities in the first place (1973:30).

Geertz is right about the danger—this chapter is primarily about exactly this. But the solution is not to continue to do cultural analysis. This just adds to the stack of turtles. Cultural meanings, social exigencies, cognitive capacities, emotional proclivities, etc., are not unrelated causal forces which can be studied each in isolation from the other. Cultural norms, beliefs and values, the social system, the economic system, different psychobiological processes, etc., all interact in complex ways to affect action. Rather than continuing to make interpretations forever, anthropology should turn to working on the way these causal systems interact with each other.

There has already been good progress in the study of some of these causal relationships. There is a long history of work on the relationship between culture and the psyche. However, integration of this work into the mainstream of anthropology has been blocked by the pervasive cultural constructionist position that holds that everything that needs to be understood about subjectivity, the self, emotions, sex differences, etc., can be found out by cultural analysis alone, and that use of explicit psychological theory is reductive and morally suspect.

A different problem exists in understanding the relationship between culture and social systems. At present, anthropology is in a theoretical muddle regarding this. There is a growing literature of good empirical work on a number of issues but there is not yet any consensus on an integrated theory. If one asks one's anthropologist colleagues "What is your theory about how culture and social systems are related to each other?" one does not usually receive a clear and well worked out answer. It is not like the case of anthropology and psychology where answers have been worked out and many anthropologists just do not want to listen. Rather, it seems that the issue fell into confusion back in the late 1950s and early 1960s over the key question of how behavior is related to social structure (Kuper 1983). With the turn of British social anthropology toward Lévi-Strauss and purely mental structures, the issue was never clarified.

In current anthropology there is a basic lack of recognition about the need for work on the relation of culture to psyche to social system. An obvious reason for this lack of recognition is the belief that culture is everything, which makes those who believe it blind to any such need. But, hopefully, more and more anthropologists will come to recognize that culture is not all, and as they do, they will become more interested in exploring how culture is related to other forces. The concept of culture has become over-extended, flabby, over-weight. It needs not replacement, nor more puffery, but some good, healthy, theoretical and empirical exercise.

References

Abu-Lughod, Lila, and Catherine Lutz
    1990   "Introduction." In L. Abu-Lughod and C. Lutz, eds., *Language and the Politics of Emotion*. Cambridge: Cambridge University Press.
Adams, Robert McCormick
    1996   *Paths of Fire*. Princeton, NJ: Princeton University Press.
Benedict, Ruth
    1931   *The Science of Custom in The Making of Man*. New York: Morrow.
Boas, Franz
    1930   "Anthropology." *Encyclopedia of the Social Sciences*. Vol. 2.
Dreyfus, Herbert L., and Paul Rabinow
    1982   *Michel Foucault: Beyond Structuralism and Hermeneutics*. Chicago, IL: University of Chicago Press.
Foucault, Michel
    1979   *Discipline and Punish: The Birth of the Prison*, A. Sheridan, trans. New York: Random House.
    1980   *The History of Sexuality*, R. Hurley, trans. New York: Random House.
Geertz, Clifford
    1973   *The Interpretation of Cultures*. New York: Basic Books.
Gellner, Ernest
    1994   *Conditions of Liberty*. London: Penguin Books.
Goodenough, Ward
    1957   "Cultural Anthropology and Linguistics." In (n.e.) *Language and Linguistics 9*. Washington, DC: Georgetown University.

Kroeber, A. L.
  1948   *Anthropology.* New York: Harcourt, Brace, and Co.
Kroeber, A. L., and Clyde Kluckhohn
  1952   *Culture: A Critical Review of Concepts and Definitions.*
          Papers of the Peabody Museum of American Archaeology
          and Ethnology 47(1).
Kuper, Adam
  1983   *Anthropology and Anthropologists: The Modern British
          School.* London: Routledge & Kegan Paul.
Parish, Steven
  1994   *Moral Knowing in a Hindu Sacred City: An Exploration of
          Minds, Emotion, and Self.* New York: Columbia University Press.
Parsons, Talcott
  1951   *The Social System.* New York: Free Press.
Schneider, David
  1968   *American Kinship: A Cultural Account.* Englewood Cliffs,
          NJ: Prentice-Hall.
  1976   "Notes toward a Theory of Meaning." In K. Basso and H.
          Selby, eds., *Meaning in Anthropology.* Albuquerque: University of New Mexico Press.
Spiro, Melford
  1994   *Culture and Human Nature.* New Brunswick, NJ: Transaction Press.
Strauss, Claudia, and Naomi Quinn
  1997   *A Cognitive Theory of Cultural Meaning.* Cambridge: Cambridge University Press.
Tylor, E. B.
  1871   *Primitive Culture.* London: John Murray.
Verdery, Katherine
  1996   *What Was Socialism, and What Comes Next?* Princeton,
          NJ: Princeton University Press.

Theoretical Perspectives

CAUSAL INDIVIDUALISM
AND THE UNIFICATION OF ANTHROPOLOGY

Tim O'Meara

How can anthropologists claim that their unique contribution to understanding human affairs is their holistic approach when anthropology itself is so fragmented?

From the inception of our discipline, most researchers have taken anthropology's holistic approach to mean some approach to understanding patterns or systems of thought and behavior conceived as holistic entities. According to E. B. Tylor's classic definition of culture (1871), for example, an open-ended laundry list of traits becomes "that complex whole," and the task of our discipline becomes discovering the properties, operation, structure, nature, or meaning of that whole. Anthropology ("the study of people") becomes culturology ("the study of culture"), or perhaps sociology ("the study of society") or semiology ("the study of meaning"). While anthropology shares with other disciplines the goals of describing, explaining, and appreciating the characteristics and behaviors of people, most anthropologists thus claim a proprietary interest in the study of "superorganic" systems or entities.

Over the years researchers have taken various systems as their phenomena of interest; they have conceived those systems as composed of different elements in various kinds of relations; and they have viewed their systems as essentially integrated or as things of shreds and patches, as essentially static or dynamic, real or abstract, unique or universal, with boundaries sharp or ill-defined (a recent vogue has been to "see culture as composed of seriously contested codes and representations" [Clifford 1986:2]). This focus on holistic systems, together with entrenched disagreement over what they consist of and how they operate, has resulted in the alienation of sociocultural anthropology from biological anthropology and in the fragmentation of sociocultural anthropology itself into numerous and often contradictory or incommensurable schools. Seeing no substantive way to overcome this fragmentation, anthropologists commonly advance moral and political arguments to the effect that unification can be achieved if we would only exercise more tolerance for opposing views—as if the way to advance our knowledge of human affairs was to paper over substantive disagreements with the cultural relativist creed of "different but equally valid," which itself is under dispute.[1]

My purpose here is to suggest that substantive unification of all five fields of anthropology, including their properly scientific and humanistic sides, can be forged by taking organic human beings rather than superorganic systems as our subject matter. Anthropologists might then describe what people think, believe, and otherwise do, and describe what they are in their physical natures, individually and in statistical aggregate, and anthropologists might also explain why people do what they do and why they are physically the way they are, appreciate people in their goodness or wickedness, evoke the personal meanings of their daily lives, moralize over their conditions, and do what we can to help those people who want and deserve our help. The "holism" of this vision of anthropology comes not from carrying out our profession as if people actually constructed and are in turn constructed by some superorganic whole, but from recognizing that people's decisions and actions influence and are in turn influenced by the whole range of motives, ideas, and conditions studied more narrowly by our sister disciplines.

My justification for taking organic humans rather than superorganic systems as the subject matter of anthropology is my previous argument to the effect that causation in social contexts (as elsewhere) is solely a matter of the physical properties and attendant causal-mechanical operations of and interactions among physical entities, notably including individual humans and their constituent parts (see O'Meara 1997). According to this argument, the so-called "relational properties" described in "social facts" are not causal properties and the "superorganic" social entities that are said to emerge with them are not causal entities. Consequently, "group properties" are not causal properties, and the supra-individual or otherwise supra-physical groups or systems that are said to emerge with them have no causal efficacy in themselves. The event correlations commonly presented as behavioral laws or as evidence of supra-individual causation are just statistical sum-maries of what numerous individuals do as they go about operating and interacting by means of the constituent physical mechanisms and their respective states that biological evolution, individual development, and accumulated experience have provided them.

If the physical causation argument is generally correct, then supra-physical properties and entities have no direct effect on anything, and therefore they have no direct explanatory import for anything—regard-less of whether supra-physical or superorganic properties or entities might be said to "exist" in some sense, and regardless of whether some people believe them to exist, and to have causal efficacy, and then act according to those mistaken beliefs. The physical causation argument implies further that event-laws, which are correlations among types of events, are not causal laws that "govern" and therefore explain the behavior of human beings and other physical entities. Explanatory laws should be conceptualized instead as being of two kinds, the first stating that a physical entity is of a certain kind if it has a certain con-stellation of physical properties, and the second stating that types of physical properties or entities interact in certain ways (see O'Meara 1997, n.d.). The implications of this "physical account" for under-standing human affairs might be referred to as "causal individualism" in order to distinguish it from "methodological individualism," which incorrectly allows mind/brain and society/individual causal dualism, and which incorrectly takes correlations among events as causal or (at least) explanatory laws, and then vainly strives to show how the sup-posedly causal terms referring to supra-physical properties and entities could be reduced to causal terms referring only to physical individuals. Consequently, it would be a mistake to assume, as Harris does (1997: 411), that causal individualism is just a terminological variant of meth-odological individualism, and therefore subject to the same time-worn criticisms. Causal individualism flatly denies the two major premises of methodological individualism: (1) the empirical premise that supra-physical properties and entities are causal properties and entities, and (2) the conceptual premise that correlations among types of events are causal laws.

Causal individualism is fundamentally the empirical claim that understanding why human affairs occur as they do requires and is limited to causal-mechanical explanations of the operations of and interactions among individual human beings and other physical entities, and conversely that explanations of human affairs are necessarily faulty if they assert or imply that supra-individual or otherwise supra-physical properties or entities have causal efficacy in themselves (O'Meara 1997). As a general theory, causal individualism thus renders super-fluous any claim that supra-physical forces or entities also operate in human affairs as well as rendering superfluous the claim that correla-tions among types of events govern any aspect of those affairs (O'Meara n.d.).

Anthropology's Holistic Approaches

Anthropologists generally agree that culture, society, and meaning would have no existence without individual people. Nevertheless, researchers have long claimed some kind of superorganic reality for the systems they study. Harris insists that even though "sociocultural systems are abstractions," they are nevertheless "physically real" (1997:413). Radcliffe-Brown is not so bold, stating obliquely that "social structures are just as real as are individual organisms" (1952: 190). Lakoff denies them physical reality, but claims some other kind of reality: "Cultural categories are real and they are made real by human action. Governments are real. They exist. . . . Physical objects are, no doubt, the best examples of things that exist, but they are by no means the only examples. An enormous number of the products of the human mind exist, though not in the way that trees and rocks exist" (1987:207).

Most anthropologists practice or condone some form of "meth-odological holism . . . [where] one starts with the fact that men are social beings, that is, one takes society as a global fact irreducible to its parts" (Dumont 1986:2), which depends in turn on what might be called "causal holism." The only alternative has formerly appeared to be "methodological individualism," which begins "by positing individ-ual human beings, who are then seen as living in society; sometimes one even attempts to show society as arising from the interaction of individuals" (Dumont 1986:1). Dumont claims, however, that "when-ever one declares that, in the final count, and beyond all abstraction, one is concerned with living men, i.e., living individuals, all I can see there . . . is a protest of modern ideology against a true sociological perspective" (1979:799, cited with approval by Varenne 1984:283). The empirical evidence and logical arguments that underlie causal indi-vidualism imply, however, that the "true sociological perspective" is false—regardless of how anyone chooses to "view" or "represent" human affairs, and regardless of whether it or any competing theory correlates with any "ideology," "cultural bias," or "sacred value" of any Americans or of any anthropologists, as Dumont (1986), Varenne (1984), Moffatt (1984), and Rosaldo (1984) charge.

Three Great Theoretical Questions of Holistic Anthropology

Most researchers would agree that culture guides or controls human behavior in some way. Ortner observes that "Anthropologists—American ones, anyway—have for the most part long agreed that culture shapes, guides, and even to some extent dictates behavior" (1984:152). Varenne is just able to concede that "The cultural structure is of course not absolutely deterministic" (1984:297). The question of how super-organic entities could guide individuals or determine their behavior is just one of holistic anthropology's three great theoretical questions, the other two being how parts of the whole "influence" each other and how individuals "construct" those wholes. Ortner argues, for example, that anthropology's theoretical problems "can be subsumed within Peter Berger and Thomas Luckmann's [1967] little epigram: 'Society is a human product. Society is an objective reality. Man is a social product'" (1984:158). Ortner argues that rival theoretical schools emphasize one or two sides of the triangle, while "modern versions of practice theory . . . appear unique in accepting all three sides" (1984:159).

Practice theory may have the virtue of putting "human agency back in the picture," but Ortner criticizes other models for assuming "too much rationality on the part of actors" and "too much active-ness" (1984:159, 151). In spite of individualism being "at the heart of much of practice theory," an "insistence upon holism" remains, and the goal remains to understand "why the system as a whole has a certain configuration" or to explain "the relationship(s) that obtain between human action . . . and some global entity which we may call 'the system'" (1984:144, 149, 157, 153). Citing Bourdieu and Sahlins, Ortner defines "the system" as "patterns of relations between categories, and of relations between relations," which "behave in many ways like the American concept of culture" (1984:148). Practice theory thus contends that holistic patterns "behave" and that they "govern" individuals:

> society and history are not simply sums of *ad hoc* responses and adaptations to particular stimuli, but are governed by organizational and evaluative schemes. It is these (embodied, of course, within institutional, symbolic, and material forms), that constitute the system . . . the analytic effort is . . . to explain the system as an

integral whole (which is not to say a harmoniously integrated one) by referring it to practice. . . . What a practice theory seeks to explain . . . is the genesis, reproduction, and change of form and meaning of a given social/cultural whole, defined in—more or less—this sense (Ortner 1984: 148-149).

It may be, however, that a century of wrangling has failed to yield a consensus on how holistic patterns and people enter into mutual relations, not because those problems are "so difficult and complex" or because "the discipline is actually still in its beginnings" (Dumont 1986:7, see also Watson et al. 1984:45), but because there are no such causal relations within or among holistic entities or between holistic entities and humans.

Nevertheless, holism was so popular that by 1932 Murdock could rightly claim "practical unanimity" among social anthropologists in their acceptance "that culture, a uniquely human phenomenon independent of the laws of biology and psychology, constitutes the proper subject of the social sciences" (1932:200). Nor has the allure of holism faded over the decades. Surveying anthropological theory since the 1960s, Ortner observes that "society (or culture) has been regarded as an objective reality in some form or another, with its own dynamics" (1984:158). Dumont argues that "every time we confront a foreign society the holistic approach is called for, and the ethnologist or anthropologist cannot do without it" (1986:2). Recently, a host of revitalization books and commentaries assures us of the irreducibility of culture and the unity of vision this affords the discipline (e.g. Winthrop 1990).

A Proprietary Interest in Disunity

Contrary to public rhetoric, a fundamental objection to unification runs deep within the discipline. Rather than fostering a unity of vision, supra-physical or "holistic" concepts were originally seized upon and elaborated by Durkheim and the Boasians in order to isolate the nascent social sciences from psychology and biology, and later from economics. As Gumperz and Levinson note: "The social sciences were founded on Durkheim's argument that the irreducibility of social facts made psychological reductionism impossible" (1991:615). Since every aspect of *people* was already studied by rival disciplines, the new social, cultural, and semiotic "sciences" were founded on and justified by taking *emergent patterns* as their phenomena of study—phenomena that literally transcend individual people. Thus, Lévi-Strauss presumed to divorce anthropology from the "natural" sciences by imagining that:

> in both anthropological and linguistic research, we are dealing strictly with symbolism. And although it may be legitimate or even inevitable to fall back upon a naturalistic interpretation in order to understand the emergence of symbolic thinking, once the latter is given, the nature of the explanation must change as radically as the newly appeared phenomenon differs from those which have preceded and prepared it. Hence, any concession to naturalism might jeopardize the immense progress already made . . . and might drive the sociology of the family toward a sterile empiricism, devoid of inspiration (1963:51).

Gumperz and Levinson note further that: "Anthropology is . . . a generalizing discipline. . . . It is simply hard to compete with the specialists" (1991:622). Cognitive anthropologists, for example, are in competition with cognitive scientists and linguists. In response, cognitive anthropologists appear at times to have engaged in a self-protective labeling exercise, where even ordinary knowledge of the world, such as "cut fingers bleed" and "rain makes the roof wet," is styled as "cultural knowledge" or "cultural models" simply by virtue of being "shared" among two or more people (D'Andrade 1989:810, 824). With proliferation, we get "cultural authority," "cultural renditions," "cultural thematicity," "cultural understandings," and even the redundant "shared cultural understandings" (Quinn and Holland 1987:9-11), as if putting a cultural spin on human cognition increased its transparency to anthropologists.

Over the years, such re-definitions have provided a tactical advantage inside and outside the discipline. The history of anthropology is replete with attempts to carve out turf by applying new terms or new analogies that "reconceptualize" the patterning of human affairs. After the first half-century, Malinowski opined that "unless the anthropologist and his fellow humanists agree on what is the definite isolate in the concrete cultural reality, there will never be any science of civilization" (1960[1944]:39). He would have been disappointed with the next half century of conceptual infighting, however, for as Rabinow observed recently:

> The first move in legitimating a new approach is to claim it has an object of study, preferably an important one, that has previously

escaped notice . . . it is still not clear whether the deconstructive-semiotic turn (an admittedly vague label) is a salutary loosening up, an opening for exciting new work of major import, or a tactic in the field of cultural politics to be understood primarily in sociological terms (1986:242).

Ortner (1984:132) notes that "the idea that culture was embodied in public, observable symbols was the key to the liberation of symbolic anthropology from earlier American cultural anthropology," so society is "less and less represented as an elaborate machine or a quasi-organism than as a serious game, a sidewalk drama, or a behavioral text" (Geertz 1980:168; see also Kaplan and Manners 1972:164, 171, 187; LeVine 1984:76; Sangren 1988).

The sub-disciplines of anthropology have allied themselves substantively with virtually every other discipline. Substantive unification inside anthropology would therefore presuppose a similar unification outside anthropology. But if those other disciplines were unified on their own accounts, what niche would anthropology occupy? Faced with that question, many anthropologists shy away from a substantive unification that might disenfranchise them, preferring a superficial rally round the totemic concept of culture, which provides them with a proprietary object of study. Attempts to "reduce" that holistic entity—or more properly to demote it to its prior position as a subjectively identified, supra-individual or otherwise supra-physical pattern that has no causal efficacy in itself—are seen as job threatening. As Brodbeck noted long ago, "those concerned with group sciences . . . are darkly suspicious that the proponents of reductionism aim primarily to put them out of business by denying them any real subject matter" (1958:8). Similarly, Gumperz and Levinson decry what they see as the "tendency to reductionism in opposite directions towards the psychological or the social" (1991:615). They advocate "the recognition of a middle ground, this domain of externalized cognition, which partakes of both the psychological and the social," which they claim "promises to overcome a dichotomy that has always left 'social facts' in an ontological limbo" (1991:615). In matters of fact, however, the middle ground is not always the firmest.

Defenses against "Reductionism"

Holists concede that superorganic entities cannot exist apart from people, and they usually deny the existence of a "collective unconscious or group mind" (Nadel 1951:276). Nevertheless, they argue that "macro-social entities and qualities are, to an important degree, *sui generis* entities not reducible to individual facts" (Luke 1987:350). Eight arguments are commonly employed as defenses against reductionism:

1. Argument by Definition

Reduction of any holistic entity to its elements is logically impossible because the entities are defined as consisting of a pattern, structure, or global configuration of those elements. Varenne, following Schneider, claims, for example, that: "Culture is integrated. This is an observational fact" (1984:289). But as Varenne implicitly acknowledges on the following page, this is not an "observational fact" at all, but a restatement of Schneider's definition: "Schneider conceives of culture . . . as a *system* of consistencies" (1984:290). Conceived as a system, culture is irreducible by definition—hence the incredulity in Harris's retort that "The reductionists would have us believe that individual behavior *is* culture" (1964:172).

2. Reductio ad Absurdum *Argument*

Since sociocultural anthropology is generally equated with the study of holistic entities, many anthropologists see the reduction of those entities as so disabling that it must be rejected out of hand. For Nadel, transition to a holistic level "gives at least the illusion of stepping into another order of existence governed by regularities peculiar to it and only there established" (1951:212). Nadel then employs a curious *reductio ad absurdum* argument to reject any premise that would imply the holistic "illusion" actually to be an illusion: "the fact that man's . . . culture and society, broken down to psycho-physical entities, disappear as phenomenal entities, means that the subject matter of these disciplines itself disappears" (1951:12). Durkheim pioneered the argument, noting that: "This conception of the social milieu, as the determining factor of collective evolution, is of the highest importance. For, if we reject it, sociology cannot establish any relations of causality" (1938:247). Douglas (1989) employs the same argument against micro-economics, as Sahlins (1976) does against Malinowski. Sahlins charges that Malinowski's "elimination of symbol and system from cultural practices . . . constitutes an epistemology for the elimination of culture itself as the proper anthropological object. Without distinctive properties in its own right, culture has no title to analysis as a thing-in-itself" (1976:83), which is precisely the conclusion reached by causal individualism.

3. Pragmatic Argument

Kaplan and Manners argue that: "if individuals are the only reality, then it follows that statements about sociocultural institutions ought to be reduced to or explained by statements about the psychological functioning of individuals . . . [but such attempts] have invariably foundered" (1972:131). This argument begs the question of the reality of institutions, however. The argument states in effect that even if sociocultural institutions are not real, statements about "them" should be reducible to statements about individuals, which are real. But if institutions are not real, then success in describing and explaining "them" is no test of a theory that deals with reality. Instead, the shoe is on the other foot, for the better a theory describes and explains the properties and operation of things that do not exist, the worse we should judge it. Arguments concerning the reduction of holistic entities thus depend upon prior arguments concerning their reality. If the physical account is generally correct, however, then existential claims about so-called intentional entities and their relational properties can always be restated as claims about the physical properties of individuals who do the intending and the physical entities (if any) toward which they have those intentions. Like a theory that explains the behavior of people in the presence of ghosts, we should entertain theories that attribute reality to people's beliefs and attitudes about ghosts, as those beliefs and attitudes occur in the physical states of peoples' brains, rather than entertaining theories that attribute reality to ghosts themselves.

4. Mental Construction of Reality Argument

Lakoff notes that: "One of the cornerstones of the objectivist paradigm is the independence of metaphysics from epistemology. The world is as it is, independent of any concept, belief, or knowledge. . . . Minds, in other words, cannot create reality." Lakoff argues, however, that "this is false and that it is contradicted by just about everything known in cultural anthropology." "Is there," he asks, "a real category *nehcihäshA* that includes not just maternal uncles but all the relations characterized by the rules formulated by Lounsbury? Fox culture is real. And such a category is real in Fox culture. . . . In such cases human minds have produced such realities. This is the case for institutional facts of all kinds" (Lakoff 1987:207). We all recognize that people's actions depend on what they know of other people's thoughts, words, and deeds, and we know that patterns can be abstracted from those thoughts, words, and deeds. If Lakoff's claim that minds can "create reality" intends more than these obvious points, it must be that the *patterns* are phenomenal realities in themselves. Since virtually everyone acknowledges that institutions have no physical existence in themselves, we might wonder what sort of real existence Lakoff claims for them. Exegesis is unnecessary, however, for Lakoff immediately contradicts his reality-of-institutional-facts argument with the more candid observation that: "We create cognitive models of the world, and we have a natural tendency to attribute real existence to the categories in those cognitive models" (1987:209). Thus, Lakoff himself recognizes that attributing reality to cognitive models does not actually make them real.

5. Behavioral Argument

Having attributed reality to something they have conceptualized, people may then act *as if* it were real. Searle describes this attribution process as the "construction of social reality," which is quite different from Lakoff's social or mental construction of reality argument. Searle shows that people "construct" social institutions through iterations of the argument *X counts as Y in context C* (1995:80). Acting as if these constructions were real usually involves a social contract, not all aspects of which need be understood by all actors. Gellner notes that "individuals do have holistic concepts and often act in terms of them" (1959:493), but as Keesing argues, the fact "that members of our species subjectively perceive (or at least in conventional metaphor . . . talk about) the societal and cultural as thinglike is a phenomenon to be explicated, but not . . . necessarily replicated, by the social theorist" (1984:293).

Ignoring the possibility of false consciousness, Harris argues against causal individualism by noting that "the participants themselves carry with them emic models of the institutions, organizations, and behavioral patterns that define their social lives" (1997:412). Seizing on a common turn of phrase, Harris then claims that "if people can become members of social groups, then social groups must have an existence separate from and prior to the individuals that join them, which is exactly the ontological condition that O'Meara is trying to avoid" (1997:413). His opening claim is circular, however, for it is the existence of "social groups" that Harris wishes to demonstrate, and he cannot claim that people "become members of social groups" without first assuming their existence. Bloch supplied the appropriate rebuttal twenty years ago in noting that one of the most salient aspects of human affairs is that "people may be extensively mystified by the static and organic imaginary models of their society which gain a shadowy phenomenological reality in ritual communication" (1977:287). Anthropologists have not advanced their understanding of those affairs, nor demonstrated their moral virtue, by agreeing with participants that their imaginary models are real (or as Jackson [1989] would say, "true"). Instead, they have merely "confounded the systems by which we know the world with the systems by which we hide it" (Bloch 1977:290). In the second part of his claim, Harris distorts the causal individualism argument by insisting that the critical question is to determine the "ontological condition." I argued, however, that regardless of what ontologies we choose to employ as conceptual tools for any particular purpose, "our *causal* ontologies must include only those entities that have causal efficacy in themselves" (O'Meara 1997:400). It is thus irrelevant whether terms such as "social group" are common or useful in certain contexts (they are both). Neither demonstrates the causal efficacy of their referents.

6. Actual Procedure Argument

Anthropologists share the human tendency to attribute reality to categories in their cognitive models and then to act (or at least in conventional metaphor talk) accordingly. Gellner has "little doubt that actual procedure in historical and social explanation often is holistic" (1959:496), while Varenne observes that the holistically conceived event or custom is "the basic unit of anthropological fieldwork and constitutes the bulk of all ethnography" (1984:288). They take this descriptive evidence as supporting "the contention that this must be so" (Gellner 1959:496). As Gellner once argued, to do otherwise might lead us to question the sensibility of both participants and observers:

> It is true that the fact that X acts and thinks in terms of an holistic idea—e.g., he treats the totem as if it were his tribe, and the tribe as if it were more than the tribesmen—is itself a fact about an individual. On the other hand, though the holistic term as used by the observer may be eliminable, as used by the participant it is not. Are we to say that a logical [sic] impeccable explanation of a social situation is committed to crediting its subjects with nonsensical thoughts? (1959:493).

Gellner himself later answered that question in the affirmative, however, giving detailed examples of "social control through the employment of absurd, ambiguous, inconsistent or unintelligible doctrines" (1962:43).

7. Argument by Assertion

Many critics have questioned the status of anthropology's holistic entities. Bidney describes them as "metaphysical" and "transcendental" (1944). Spiro challenges their "ontological reality" (1961). At the end of a career in the holistic mainstream, Murdock famously confessed that such concepts are reifications, or "Anthropology's Mythology" (1972). Foucault criticizes "groupings that purport to be natural, immediate, universal unities" (1972:29). Bourdieu condemns the "scientific objectification" of Lévi-Strauss, Saussure, and others as an attempt to "reify abstractions" (1977:26; see also pp. 73, 203). In spite of such criticisms, anthropologists have continued to assert the reality of holistic entities. Harris states that "culture is as real as our genes" (1977). Ortner states that systems and structural approaches have "established the reality of the thinglike nature of society" (1984:159). Freilich headlines culture as a "Real Base for a Hard Social Science" (1989:27). But whether we call holistic patterns "real" or "transcendental" is irrelevant. All parties agree that we can abstract various patterns from the thoughts, words, and deeds of humans. Virtually everyone also agrees that the abstracted patterns do not enjoy physical reality in themselves. Thus, debate over the "reality" or "existence" of these holistic patterns is a pointless debate over the use of those terms. What matters is not how we choose to conceive or label them, but whether they have causal efficacy.

8. Causal Efficacy Argument

Individuals do act differently when they group together and when they are isolated, and patterns abstracted from the behavior of several individuals are different from patterns abstracted from the behavior of any one individual—if only because individuals differ somewhat in their properties and circumstances. Therefore, new patterns of behavior may be said to "emerge" when people group together. The relevant issue, however, is whether that conceptual patterning of elements produces a causally efficacious thing-in-itself as the physical patterning of elements in a physical entity does. Harris claims as much when he defines culture as "patterns of bodily activity as well as of thought" and then urges students to "understand how culture controls what we think and do" (1991:23, 65).

Bourdieu argues, however, that it is a fallacy to treat "the objects constructed by science, whether culture, structure, or modes of production, as realities endowed with a social efficacy, capable of acting as agents responsible for historical actions or as a power capable of constraining practices" (1977:26). Foucault argues against the notion that holistic "unities" have "influence . . . which refers to an apparently causal entity (but with neither rigorous delimitation nor theoretical definition) the phenomenon of resemblance or repetition; which links, at a distance and through time" and he concludes that "we must out those forms and obscure forces" (1972:21-22). Holists nevertheless assume that a patterning of cultural elements is itself a causal property by virtue of which a holistic cultural entity emerges, or they assume that a patterning of cultural event types constitutes an autonomous causal law or principle that "governs" or "generates" human affairs (see O'Meara 1997). Anthropology's existential claims of holism thus ultimately rest on a claim of *causal holism.*

I have argued, however, that the only ostensibly scientific warrant for claiming that supra-physical entities such as social institutions, minds, and species have causal efficacy in themselves by virtue of the relational or otherwise supra-physical properties ascribed to them by observers is the faulty event-based regularity theory of causation, together with its attendant accounts of causal properties, entities, laws, and explanations (O'Meara 1997, n.d.). Progress is now being made in formalizing a physical account of causation and its attendant accounts of causal properties, entities, laws, and explanations within the more general empiricist tradition and within the long-standing physicalist tradition in science.[2] According to this "physical account," it is an empirical fact that *causation* is exclusively a matter of the physical properties of, and the resulting mechanical operations of and interactions among, what can be characterized as physical entities (Dowe 1992, 1995, n.d.; Salmon 1984, 1989, 1994).

Causal Entities and Pseudo-Causal Entities

Identifying causal entities is an essential precursor to understanding how the world works. Our understanding is deficient to the extent that we ascribe causal efficacy to things that we may conceive of and refer to as entities, but which have no causal efficacy in themselves—that is, when we ascribe causal efficacy to what might be called "pseudo-causal entities."[3] Developing an idea proposed by Dowe (1992), Salmon (1994) argues that a causal entity transmits a nonzero amount of at least one conserved quantity, so it can always be marked in some way by interacting with another causal entity such that the conserved quantity is altered in some way and the resulting mark is then transmitted through space-time. This "test of mark transmission," originally proposed by Reichenbach, is the direct empirical test of causal efficacy. It thus provides a "useful experimental method" for distinguishing causal entities from pseudo-causal entities (Salmon 1994:303) as well as for identifying causal properties and distinguishing them from pseudo-causal properties. Before applying this analysis further to anthropology's superorganic holism, we need to make two additional distinctions not mentioned by Salmon or Dowe: first, between different conceptual levels or (more properly) physical length-scales at which causal entities might be designated; and, second, between two different analytical types of pseudo-causal entities.

1. Designating Causal Entities at Different Length-Scales
A quick look around tells us that causal entities come in different sizes and complexities of internal organization. A large-scale, complex entity such as a planet or a human being might be called a "macro-entity," which consists of and operates by numerous smaller entities, or "mini-entities," such as the earth's tectonic plates or a person's organs. The causal properties and operating characteristics of any mini-entity is determined in turn by its constituent "micro-entities" (molecules, atoms, and so on), by their organization, and by the energy that maintains that organization. The larger entity is literally bound together at the level of micro-entities by ionic and co-valent bonds (Ashcroft and Mermin 1976:379). Since electromagnetic fields are physically real causal entities, those bonds are as well. At each length-scale, the smaller constituent units arrange themselves physically according to their own respective shapes or forms and their electromagnetic or gravitational fields, creating larger scale causal entities with one or more new causal properties and characteristics of operation. Thus, a physical macro-entity does have "emergent" causal properties of its own, which the mini or micro-entities alone would not have even if they were somehow aggregated into the same physical pattern, but not physically bound together in the same way.

At any one length-scale, our designation of causal entities is constrained by significant differences in causal properties among different entities that might be so designated (e.g., ice cubes floating in water, or different types of adjacent tissues in a human). As we proceed from micro to larger and larger length-scales, however, we can also identify causal entities of a larger size and complexity as appropriate units of observation, analysis, and explanation—quantum particles, atoms, molecules, and so on up to planets, solar systems, and galaxies. The choice of length-scale (and hence the choice of causal ontology) depends partly on the pragmatic considerations of our research questions, but that choice is constrained by empirical evidence showing significant differences in the strength of physical bonding between causal entities at different length-scales.

A table and the air around it are both composed partly of widely spaced, fast-moving molecules, with no line or shell to be found that would separate what we call the table from what we call the air. There is more to tables and air than just particles in motion, however. Diffuse electromagnetic fields interconnect all the molecules—within the table and the air and between the table-molecules and the air-molecules. What makes it useful to distinguish the table as a separate causal entity from the air around it is the dramatic difference in the kind and strength of bonding among the table-molecules compared with those of the air surrounding it. Even though electro-magnetic causal bonds also operate between air-molecules and table-molecules, such bonds are insignificant at the length-scale of tables. Thus, for research questions at that length-scale, we rightly consider the table to be a causal entity in itself. At the length-scale of planets, however, none of the inter-molecular bonds is significant compared to the massive gravitational force of the earth, which binds them all together into what at the length-scale of planets is pragmatic to consider as a single causal entity. Just the opposite holds at the length-scale of the molecules themselves.

At any length-scale, energy would have to be applied from some source in order to "mark" the larger causal entity—that is, in order to add to or otherwise rearrange the smaller causal entities that are its constituent parts. It is partly the relative significance of these interconnecting causal bonds at different length-scales, considered in light of the explanatory question at hand, by which we make the pragmatic choice of saying whether such a causal interaction has marked the smaller scale entity (e.g. a person's skin) or the larger scale entity (e.g. the person).[4]

As we proceed from smaller length-scales right up to the scale of the universe, we never encounter a scale at which causal entities are united by *supra-physical* properties to form larger scale, *supra-physical* causal entities—no length-scale at which culture, *conscience collective*, or other *supra-physical* entities emerge with their own supra-physical causal properties and efficacy. Honderich puts the matter succinctly: "causes and effects are all . . . physical. What is not physical is not cause or effect" (1988:16). While electromagnetic or gravitational fields undoubtedly operate between people, such inter-personal causal "relations" are never strong enough to significantly affect the operation of those individuals for any research question that anthropologists are likely to pursue. Thus, contrary to Murdock (1932:207), the super-organic does not rest upon the organic precisely as the latter rests upon the inorganic.

2. Types of Pseudo-Causal Entities

Now consider two analytical types of pseudo-causal entities. The first type, exemplified by a shadow, has no parts at all, and it has no causal properties or efficacy in itself. Its apparent properties are entirely the result of our interpretation of the configurations made by causal entities. The second type of pseudo-causal entity, exemplified by a spot of light, is most relevant for anthropology. A spot-type pseudo-causal entity *is* a patterning of individual entities (quanta of light), *similar* to the way a person is a patterning of mini- and micro-entities, but with one critical difference. Unlike the parts of a person, the parts of a spot-type pseudo-causal entity are, to use Hume's phrase, "conjoined but never connected." Because of our mental "habits" of pattern recognition and induction, and because our eyes cannot distinguish the individual quanta, we may think or conceive of a spot of light as an entity, but it is not a causal entity in itself (see Salmon 1984).[5]

At a greater length-scale, a load of buckshot fired at a target may appear to be a single entity and may even make a single hole. Lacking significant physical bonds between them at that scale, however, the individual pellets do not constitute a larger causal entity, or thing-in-itself. Even when individual entities are quite large, an inductive error may lead to the conclusion that a patterning of individual causal entities is itself a causal entity. When small fish swim in tightly packed synchrony, a shark may mistake *them* for a much larger *it*. By a similar inductive error, we may conclude that a mob or an institution is a causal entity in itself, having its own attributes, behavior, efficacy, and laws. But while we may say that people are "bound" together by gift-giving and other social relationships, such bonds are metaphorical, not physical, and therefore no social "whole" emerges from them as a causal entity in itself.

Individuals in a social group may interact directly with each other and with other causal entities such as plants and animals in their immediate environment, and still other causal entities such as air and light may transmit information between those entities—all of which can be conceptualized together as a holistic entity such as a society or an ecosystem in which the causal individuals interact but never become fused into a larger causal entity. Their aggregate behaviors will be patterned as a result, but only because each individual responds, not because any collective responds. As fish swim, for example, their bodies "mark" the water, creating pulses or waves that are transmitted through space-time to nearby fish, which sense the waves with an organ called the "lateral line." The water in effect transmits signals between schooling fish (not "fish in a school"). When the waves conform to a certain pattern, each fish responds with a certain movement according to the evolved characteristics of its nervous system. Depending on the species and the patterning of waves, the fish may turn in synchrony or scatter. In neither case does the "school" become a causal thing-in-itself with its own causal properties and efficacy. Similarly, sound and light waves transmit information through the air between rioting people (not people "in a mob"), though the pattern-production, pattern-recognition, decision-making, and response capabilities of people are obviously far greater and more complex than those of fish. Rioting people may, like schooling fish, either synchronize or disperse by their individual actions. Thus, individuals who engage in social relations do act differently than they otherwise would, but it is a logical error to conclude that they do so because social groups are causal things-in-themselves or because the individuals or their groups are governed by group laws.

Practice theorists base their explanatory programs on the assertion that individual actors are not "wholly autonomous"—their actions instead being partly determined by some vast, supra-individual patterning called "structure" that actively "shapes" social action (e.g. Roscoe 1993a:113, 1993b:136; citing Bourdieu, Giddens, and Cohen).[6] Interpersonal power is said to operate through a "multiple and mobile field of force relations," which "operates independent of conscious subjects" (Foucault 1980:102, cited in Best and Kellner 1991:51). As a causal argument, this is false. At any length-scale and for any research question in the human sciences, humans operate as autonomous causal entities. To argue otherwise is to falsely imply that some mysterious, supra-physical, pseudo-causal entity is actively fiddling with the stuff inside people's heads. I suspect the assertion that individual actors are not "wholly autonomous" should be read instead as not "wholly isolated," in the sense that people gather or receive information from the outside world and then act on that information. While true, such an assertion is commonplace.

Intentionality and Indeterministic Causal Entities

Anthropologists and other social scientists have long been perplexed by the apparent incompatibility of universal or "deterministic" laws of human behavior with intentional choice and with the relative unpredictability of some human affairs. Under the event account, causal determinism does appear to preclude intentional choice. Following that account, Toulmin equates cause with "compulsion" (1970:5, 15-16, 21), Harré and Secord equate cause with "external stimuli" (1972:27, 29), and Giddens argues that determinism leaves "no place for a conception of the actor as a reasoning agent, capable of using knowledge in a calculated fashion so as to achieve intended outcomes" (1977:85). A common attempt to surmount this problem is to claim that human affairs are inherently indeterministic (e.g. Aberle 1987:551; Bohman 1991; Evans 1977:593; Garfinkel 1981:155; Little 1991:227; Roscoe 1995:499). Harris claims specifically that "An understanding of cultural evolution requires . . . probabilistic versions of causality," which he justifies by reference to quantum mechanics (1968:424, 282, 428; see also 1979:244).

No such problem arises under the physical account. We have the subjective feeling of acting by our "free will" precisely because, in whatever circumstances we find ourselves, we choose and carry out our actions by the operation of our own brain mechanisms. Nothing is achieved by claiming that these mechanisms operate in the manner of, or because of, quantum indeterminism. As Neils Bohr pointed out long ago in an invited lecture to the Royal Anthropological Society, choice is nonrandom by definition, so quantum indeterminism can provide no foundation for choice or free will (1958:22; see also Carnap 1966:216-222; Russell 1981 [1917]:149-151). Honderich points out that so-called indeterminist theories of the mind, instead:

> have as their fundamental proposition that an originator somehow *controls* decisions and actions. More particularly . . . it *controls* relevant neural events. . . . Proponents of the indeterminist theories take Quantum Theory as leaving it perfectly open whether or not the synaptic event is subject to another kind of determination, non-neural determination (1988:332-333).

As an example, Honderich (1988:304) cites Popper and Eccles, who argue for "the active influence of the self-conscious mind upon neural machinery" (1977:476). Such brain/mind dualism involves a contradiction: "A defender of indeterminist pictures of the mind . . . must embrace and deny a certain interpretation of Quantum Theory at the same time. He embraces it to escape physical determination, and denies it by introducing mental determination" (Honderich 1988:332-333).

Indeterminist theories of the mind are actually hidden-variable theories. They assert that "what may be taken to be a purely random event, from the point of view of Quantum Theory most favorable to them, is in fact in some way absolutely and precisely determined by the hidden variable which is an originator" (Honderich 1988:333). In anthropology, that originator becomes the "structure," the "culture," the "system," or the *conscience collective*.

Instead, anthropologists could conclude that thinking occurs in the operation of deterministic neural mechanisms. Any particular outcome of these operations depends not only on laws of universal or "deterministic" form, which describe the characteristic causal properties of the types of entities involved, but also on the particular states in which those properties occur, which are the unique result of the individual's life experiences. Young emphasizes that these particulars may be "either inherited or learned" and that the "large computational powers of the brain depend on the presence of large numbers of units operating in parallel . . . not in a hierarchy leading up to a dominant command neuron" (1987:197, 128). He concludes that: "Although we do not know how the brain computes intentions we now know for certain that it does compute them" (Young 1987:74). Salmon argues that at least some causal entities may operate indeterministically (1984:184-205). His argument directly concerns only quantum phenomena, but he generalizes to other kinds of incompletely predictable events, including suicide and car theft (1984:109, 116-119; see also 1982). His apparent conclusion that humans operate as indeterministic mechanisms would no doubt be supported by many anthropologists (e.g. Harris 1997:412). Indeed, Salmon's own arguments in this regard closely parallel those of standard social science. In discussing probabilistic causality and statistical explanation, Salmon shifts back to an implicit event ontology (1984:24-47, 113-120, 184-205). This shift is apparently justified by his argument that it may be possible to demonstrate the objective homogeneity of certain classes of quantum particles, tokens of which spontaneously produce different kinds of events (1984:48-83). Regardless of the possible acceptability of this argument for quantum particles, Salmon does nothing to justify its extension to humans, where a demonstration of the objective homogeneity of classes is impossible. Salmon's extension of quantum indeterminism to human affairs is based instead on the observation that some types of social events are relatively unpredictable. The apparent unpredictability of social events is prejudiced by the form of his analysis, however, which is borrowed uncritically from standard sociology.

Salmon (1984:38-39, citing Greeno 1971) does not distinguish proxy variables such as "race," "class," and "income," which sociologists (justifiably) use in trying to *predict* an occurrence of social acts such as "car theft," from the underlying physical mechanisms by which a person operates in deciding to and then stealing a car. Such proxy variables are "societal facts" (Mandelbaum 1973[1955]), which may appear to be causal properties under the faulty event account, but not under Salmon's own physical account. Regardless of how astutely we sort juvenile delinquents into classes according to such proxy variables, we can never be sure that the individuals in a class are homogeneous with respect to the brain and other physical properties that together might lead them to carry out a "car theft." Individual differences in motivational and other relevant causal factors remain among individuals of any such class. Correlations based on classifying individuals according to social facts are reduced accordingly, but without having any bearing on the determinacy of the underlying psychological mechanisms.

Salmon also overlooks the point that behavioral events we class together for some purpose may have been caused by significantly different sets of conditions. This further reduces our ability to predict that type of event, but again without having any bearing on the determinacy of the causal mechanisms involved. Rosenberg goes further, asserting that "like effects must have like causes" (1988:120). This is a misapplication of Newton and Einstein's "Identity Principle" to social events and other supra-physical patterns, where actions that fulfill the paradigm *X counts as Y in context C* may result from different sets of causes (e.g. different sets of causes can lead people to engage in "car theft"). Similar problems underlie the so-called "indeterminacy of social entities" (Little 1991:227, see also Bohman 1991:232-234). Boas (1896) recognized long ago, however, that it is a logical error to argue from a similarity of behavioral patterns back to a similarity of causes.

In addition, the relevance of quantum indeterminism to human affairs remains obscure. The behavior of any one quantum particle is *absolutely unpredictable*, while the pattern produced by a very large number of particles is *almost precisely predictable*. The *relative unpredictability* of some human affairs bears little or no resemblance to such "indeterminism." Nevertheless, Penrose invokes "a probabilistic aspect of neuron firing," claiming that "the same stimulus does not *always* produce the same result" (1989:396, emphasis added). Even if this were true, it would imply that the "same stimulus" *usually* does produce the "same result," and only *sometimes* does not, which implies the operation of some hidden variable(s), not the random firing of quantum particles. Penrose finally drops the argument and accepts that both conscious and unconscious thought are probably deterministic (1989:431).

To make matters worse for the indeterministic view of mind, it is entirely possible that quantum entities themselves operate deterministically, as Salmon recognizes. Albert reports that: "Although the [indeterministic] Copenhagen interpretation probably remains the guiding dogma of the average working physicist, serious students of the foundations of quantum mechanics rarely defend the standard formulation anymore" (1994:67). Albert argues instead for David Bohm's quantum theory, which "describes a real, concrete and deterministic physical entity" (1994:63).[7] Albert concludes that "the possibilities that the laws of physics are fully deterministic and that what they describe are the motions of particles (or some analogue of those motions in relativistic quantum field theory) are both, finally and definitively, back on the table" (1994:67).

Unification and the "Ideal Explanatory Text"

Following Salmon, a scientific explanation of why a particular behavior occurred would include a description of the causal entities and interactions that produced it, beginning with the first antecedent set. Each of those antecedent entities and states was produced in turn by a prior set of entities and states, however, and each of those by another. The properties and behavior of any particular entity thus result from an infinitely long and expanding series of antecedent causal entities and their interactions. Each causal entity in that series can be said to belong to a certain class or type, tokens of which each have the same characteristic causal properties, as described by generalizations or "laws," and so operate and interact in characteristic ways. Railton calls a complete description of that infinite causal series (and its laws) the "ideal causal text" or "ideal explanatory text" (1981:241-242, 247-248; see also Salmon 1984:159-164). Explaining why something occurred might thus involve recounting the history of causal interactions (e.g. who did or said what to whom) that led to the physical properties of one or more entities being in their given states at a given time, all of which might be characterized as etiological or historical explanation.[8]

In addition to tracing causal interactions back in time, as described by Railton, an explanatory text could also proceed by mechanical reduction in length-scale, showing that the type of physical entities in question have their characteristic constellations of causal properties because at successively "reduced" length-scales they consist of certain other types of physical entities (e.g. humans consist of certain kinds of organs, which consist of tissues, cells, molecules, and so on), each with its own lawful constellation of characteristic causal-mechanical properties. Explanation by reduction in length-scale thus complements etiological explanation.[9]

Since the historical part of an ideal text describes a potentially infinite series of causal interactions, it is impossible to produce an entire "ideal text." All actual explanations fill in only one or more items from that infinite series. In addition, most actual explanations examine causal entities at only one or two length-scales. Researchers might help explain the properties and behavior of individual people, for example, by discussing (explicitly or implicitly) some of the causal properties, operations, and interactions of some of their constituent organs, tissues, or genetic materials, while leaving the constituent entities at smaller length-scales for other researchers. No one has to present even a sizable part of the ideal text in order to explain something adequately in a specific context. Increasing (not "achieving") understanding depends instead on producing one or more relevant parts of the ideal text. Explaining something thus consists of presenting relevant "explanatory information" (Railton 1981:240-247). What parts of the ideal text are relevant in a given explanatory context depends on pragmatic considerations, including the interests of researchers and audience, what parts of the ideal text are already known to them, what aspects of the phenomenon are to be explained, how the phenomenon might be controlled, or who might be blamed for its occurrence. Explanations from different disciplines can thus complement each other in two ways:

1. by filling in different parts of the history or etiology that resulted

in one or more entities being in their given states (the common distinction in evolutionary studies between "proximate" and "ultimate" explanations is a case in point), and

2. by filling in the characteristic or particular causal properties and operations of causal entities identified at different length-scales—organic chemistry complements neurology, for example, which complements psychology, which (among other things) complements sociocultural anthropology.

Researchers from different disciplines may thus present complementary parts of a larger "ideal explanatory text" that fit together to form a more complete—but never totally complete—explanation. No distinct segment of the etiology of causal interactions might be labelled "cultural," however, and no length-scale is found where autonomous "cultural" properties or entities emerge with causal efficacy. Assuming that a common idea behind various definitions of "culture" is that of learning something from other people, then *specifically "cultural" explanations would consist of specifying those parts of the etiology or those causal properties or entities at any length-scale that resulted in part from social learning.*

In the now classic case of Kuru, for example, causal states that resulted from social learning combined with other causal states that did not result from social learning to produce the occurrences and epidemiology of that viral disease (see Gajdusek 1977; Lindenbaum 1979). Since the ideal causal text of even the clinical symptoms of the disease includes the learned supernatural beliefs of the Foré people, the Kuru disease can legitimately be said to result partly from "cultural" causes, and so can be given a "cultural" explanation. The adjective *cultural* here signifies states that resulted partly from social learning, while the noun *culture* signifies a subjectively defined patterning among those causal states. While various patterns may be found among the causal states that derive in part from social learning, and while such patterns may differ from one social grouping of people to another, no "cultural pattern" as such actively "guides," "directs," "generates," or "probabilistically determines" Foré behavior. Instead, individual Foré people direct their own actions by the neural mechanisms of intentional choice, which in this case unfortunately employed a combination of incorrect and incomplete knowledge of how the world works, most of which they acquired through social learning.

The ready unification of "cultural" and "biological" explanations in the case of Kuru is not due to any "interaction" between biology and culture, as is sometimes said metaphorically. Instead, the relevant causal interactions by which people choose and direct their actions literally occur within a person's own physical brain mechanisms, not between a biological brain, a holistic psyche or self, and a holistic culture or society. Thus, biology, psychology, and cultural anthropology do not explain different kinds of phenomena requiring different kinds of analysis, as Sperber (1986) argues. Instead, those disciplines commonly specify complementary parts of a larger explanatory text. The substantive and theoretical unification of anthropology and related disciplines can and should proceed by unifying those complementary explanations.

Causal Primacy

Much acrimony arises in anthropology over competing claims of causal "primacy" or "priority" for certain types of explanations. The analysis presented above suggests that this debate has gone unresolved because the claims are not empirically testable as commonly stated. Harris's claim for the causal primacy of infrastructure (e.g. 1992:297), for example, as well as competing claims by Sahlins (1976), Rappaport (1982, 1984), and others are untestable for at least three reasons (there are more).

First, the claim is protected from contradiction by the recognition of "feedback" (e.g. Harris 1979:71-72). The feedback is said to occur, moreover, between structures or institutions that are abstract patterns, which have no causal efficacy (primary or otherwise). Rappaport tries to deflect criticism of his functional analysis of Maring ritual ecology by asserting that "as for pig demography's regulating the ritual cycle rather than the other way around, the same argument could be made about the relationship between a thermostat and a furnace" (1982:303). Such analogies err by imbuing conceptual entities such as "pig demography" and "ritual cycle" with the causal efficacy of physical entities such as thermostats and furnaces. As Peoples (1982) argues, neither pig demography nor the ritual cycle regulates the other. Instead, people produce both of those patterns (and hence the correlation between them) by their individual decisions and cooperative actions. The feedback occurs between individual people, pigs, sweet potatoes, and other causal entities—not between holistic structures, institutions, or other such pseudo-causal entities.

Second, in spite of vigorous attempts to clarify Marx's terminology, Harris (1968:232-234, 1979:51-54) cannot provide objective criteria for identifying which conditions belong to the "infrastructure," which to the "structure," and which to the "superstructure." Rappaport's analysis suffers from the same ambiguity. Pigs, for example, simultaneously have a demography and a part in ritual. Ambiguity arises because the various structures, modes, and institutions are all subjectively abstracted patterns. Unlike causal entities, which have a *physical structure* of their own that is identifiable by any competent observer, these pseudo-causal entities depend for their *logical structure* on the cognitive operations of individual researchers, who are notoriously likely to "conceive of" them differently.

Third, claims of causal priority are immune to empirical refutation because the claims are protected by the qualification that the causation involved is "probabilistic" (e.g. Harris 1979:72-73, 1992:297). Under the faulty event account, such a qualifier appeared to be an unremarkable part of statistical explanations (e.g. Hempel 1965). With a physical account of causation, however, probabilistic causality mistakenly implies that human beings themselves operate indeterministically. The qualifier is more appropriately taken to imply that conforming cases are more *essential* than nonconforming cases. A holistic "law" is just a correlation among event types, however, and the addition of new test cases cannot refute a correlation, they can only adjust its statistical probability. Harris argues that "as a nomothetic research strategy, cultural materialism does not predict the behavior of individuals; it predicts (or retrodicts) the behavior of aggregates of individuals" (1984:649). Using correlations to predict aggregate patterns is of great value, but it does not constitute explanation. The aggregates themselves have no causal efficacy, and correlations among them do not describe laws that "govern" either individuals or their aggregates.

Explaining why individuals act as they do in statistical aggregate is a tractable problem for which claims of supra-physical causation and reference to event-laws are entirely superfluous. If the material desires of capitalists inspire them to create an ideology that helps control laborers, for example, then those material desires constitute a relevant part of the causal explanation of the capitalists' actions. If that ideology in turn mystifies laborers into compromising their own material interests, then ideological factors constitute a relevant part of the causal explanation of the laborers' actions. Going beyond that to claim that either material or ideological factors are "primary" in structuring the social whole is an unscientific quest for essence, which in other contexts Harris rightly criticizes (e.g. 1979:11-12). Finally, Harris himself reveals that the causal primacy of infrastructure is not an empirical claim. Instead, it is a moral claim to the effect that "responsibility for the system as a whole cannot be prorated equally among the superordinate and subordinate classes" (1979:303).

Unifying Science and Humanism

Anthropology's legitimate charter as a holistic discipline includes the unification of scientific explanations of human affairs together with their humanistic understanding and appreciation. I am told, however, that "humanism" refers to the "deep understanding of complex meaning," and so is the antithesis of science. Genuine humanism need not conflict with causal explanations as described here, however, though it does conflict with the supposed operation of supra-physical properties and entities and with the operation of event-laws. According to Webster, the meaning of the term "humanism" includes an "individualistic and critical spirit, and emphasis on secular concerns . . . [a] doctrine, attitude, or way of life centered on human interests or values . . . that asserts the dignity or worth of man and his capacity for self-realization through reason and that often rejects supernaturalism."

Thus, by definition humanism is antithetical to any form of supernaturalism or transcendentalism (O'Meara 1990a:751, see also Lett 1997: 116-122). Humanism as a doctrine, attitude, or way of life is viable only if human affairs consist of and operate by physical human beings and their actions—and no more. Explanations of human affairs are humanistic in this traditional sense precisely when they are causal-mechanical explanations of individual actions rather than logical-subsumption explanations of holistic patterns. In particular, causal individualism is humanistic because: (1) it explains the behavior of humans rather than the pseudo-behavior of superorganic entities; (2) it explains that behavior by reference to the causal properties of humans and other physical entities rather than the supra-physical properties of pseudo-causal entities; (3) it shows that the central causal mechanisms directing human affairs are the minds/brains of human beings rather than the disembodied structures of mindless and brainless holistic patterns or the *conscience collectives* of superorganic groups; and (4) it shows how people's desires, values, emotions, knowledge, and even belief in the causal efficacy of non-existent or superorganic entities all help to produce their actions through the individual operations of forethought and intentional choice. As Lett argues:

Anthropology is a *humanistic science* in every sense of the term,

. . . its subject matter involves the whole of human phenomena, and . . . its epistemological, ethical, and aesthetic principles are entirely congruent with the philosophy of humanism. Anthropology is also humanistic in the sense that its interest in the cultural expressions of human creativity overlaps with the central focus of the humanities (1997:121).

The ideal explanatory text is strictly limited to the "scientific" goals of providing descriptions and causal explanations, and the various branches of the human sciences are together legitimately engaged in describing everything that humans do and explaining why they do it. This scientific endeavor does not compete against, but instead is complemented by "humanistic" accounts aimed at appreciating, evoking, empathizing with, moralizing over, or excoriating humans and what they do. Knowledge of the life and times of people adds greatly to our understanding and appreciation of them as people. Such evocative information helps to humanize ethnographic figures, it helps us to empathize with them, and it is interesting in its own right. By including both kinds of information (perhaps with evaluative judgments), anthropologists may unite both a scientific description and explanation of people's actions with a wider humanistic appreciation of those people and their way of life. Thus, anthropology is humanistic precisely when it concerns the conditions and behaviors of organic humans, not when it concerns the logical permutations of superorganic concepts. Concerning my own early attempt at such unification in a problem-oriented ethnography (1990b), one reviewer (a semiotic holist of the Chicago school) commented with apparent surprise that the book "somehow manages to be *both* analytically sophisticated and narratively evocative." No special skill was involved, however, just a determined interest in understanding people.

Notes

The author gratefully acknowledges the support of the Obermann Center for Advanced Studies of the University of Iowa.

1. Harris (1997:414-415) imputes some devious motive to my use of the term "human affairs," but I chose it merely because it is so general that it does not prejudge arguments by *a priori* ruling out any phenomenon of interest to anthropologists.

2. Harris (1997:411) misrepresents my claim in this regard. Like several other anthropologists who have attempted to develop a supra-physical science, Harris believes (1997:411) that the event account of Hempel and others not only fits, but is responsible for the great success of the physical sciences. I contend, however, that the success of the physical sciences is due primarily to its long-standing tradition of physicalism, and that the "physical account" is a formalization of that tradition (O'Meara 1997:400). Physicalism only appears superficially to accord with the event account in some respects when investigating very simple physical entities (O'Meara 1997:406). The event account supports transcendentalism or phenomenalism, however, which is directly contrary to physicalism. As I noted before (1997:400), phenomenalism was characteristic of many early positivists such as Mach (1914), but has now been discredited in the physical sciences. It remains dominant, however, in the supra-physical or "special sciences."

3. Salmon uses the technical terms "causal process" and "pseudo causal process," which confuses many readers, so I have substituted the conceptually simpler terms "causal entity" and "pseudo-causal entity."

4. Note that in some cases, such as when dealing with a gas or a liquid at equilibrium, where the between-particle fields are relatively strong and homogeneous, it may not be useful for many purposes to divide the larger entity conceptually into its smaller causal units.

5. Boyer cites Michotte's (1963) "famous experiments showing that subjects spontaneously put forward causal interpretations of the move-ments of spots and geometrical patterns on a screen . . . people 'see' the passage of one spot *causing* another spot's change of direction" (1992:192).

6. Thanks to Paul Roscoe for his friendly discussions of these mat-ters.

7. Bohm's theory takes not only quantum particles, but also quantum fields to be physically real, and so appears to be entirely con-gruent with the physical account.

8. Vayda's "eventamental" explanation is generally of this type, except that he follows Lewis (1986) in holding to the regularity theory

of causation, denying the relevance of any form of causal laws, and speaking of causal histories as occurring "in the form of causally connected events" (1997, see also 1996).

9. Causal explanation also involves two other aspects (as developed in O'Meara 1997, and O'Meara n.d.) that are not so directly relevant to the unification argument presented here. These include explanation by:

1. *Classification and Identification of Natural Kinds.* Arguing from observation that a particular physical entity appears to be of a certain natural kind (e.g. a normal human being) and therefore can be presumed to have the constellation of causal-mechanical properties known to be characteristic of entities of that kind (e.g. the physical attributes of human nature).
2. *Mechanical Interaction.* Arguing that as long as the entity retains the causal properties characteristic of its type, it will interact with another type of property or entity in a certain mechanical way, and a certain state of affairs can therefore be expected to result when they interact from given initial states.

References

Aberle, David
    1987   "Distinguished Lecture: What Kind of Science is Anthropology?" *American Anthropologist* 89(3):551-566.
Albert, David Z.
    1994   "Bohm's Alternative to Quantum Mechanics." *Scientific American* May:58-67.
Ashcroft, Neil W., and N. David Mermin
    1976   *Solid State Physics.* New York: Holt, Rinehart, and Winston.
Berger, Peter, and Thomas Luckmann
    1967   *The Social Construction of Reality.* Garden City, NY: Doubleday.
Best, Steven, and Douglas Kellner
    1991   *Postmodern Theory: Critical Interrogations.* London: Macmillan.
Bidney, David
    1944   "On the Concept of Culture and Some Cultural Fallacies."

American Anthropologist 46:30-44.

Bloch, Maurice
    1977   "The Past and the Present in the Present." *Man* 12:278-292.
Boas, Franz
    1896   *Race, Language and Culture.* New York: Macmillan.
Bohman, James
    1991   *New Philosophy of Social Science: Problems of Indeter-
            minacy.* Cambridge: Polity Press and Blackwell.
Bohr, Niels
    1958   *Atomic Physics and Human Knowledge.* New York: John
            Wiley & Sons.
Bourdieu, Pierre
    1977   *Outline of a Theory of Practice*, R. Nice, trans. Cambridge:
            Cambridge University Press.
Boyer, Pascal
    1992   "Causal Thinking and Its Anthropological Misrepresenta-
            tion." *Philosophy of the Social Sciences* 22(2):187-213.
Brodbeck, May
    1958   "Methodological Individualism: Definition and Reduction."
            Philosophy of Science 25(1):1-22.
Carnap, Rudolf
    1966   "Determinism and Free Will." In Martin Gardner, ed.,
            Philosophical Foundations of Physics. New York: Basic
            Books.
Clifford, James
    1986   "Introduction: Partial Truths." In J. Clifford and G. E.
            Marcus, eds., *Writing Culture.* Berkeley: University of
            California Press.
D'Andrade, Roy G.
    1989   "Cultural Cognition." In Michael I. Posner, ed., *Founda-
            tions of Cognitive Science.* Cambridge, MA: MIT Press.
Douglas, Mary
    1989   "Culture and Collective Action." In Morris Freilich, ed.,
            The Relevance of Culture. New York: Bergin & Garvey.
Dowe, Phil
    1992   "Wesley Salmon's Process Theory of Causality and the
            Conserved Quantity Theory." *Philosophy of Science* 59:
            195-216.
    1995   "Causality and Conserved Quantities: A Reply to Salmon."
            Philosophy of Science 62:321-333.
    n.d.   *Physical Causation* (manuscript, forthcoming).

Dumont, Louis
    1979   "The Anthropological Community and Ideology." *Social Science Information* 18(6):785-817.
    1986   *Essays on Individualism.* Chicago, IL: University of Chicago Press.
Durkheim, Emile
    1938   *Rules of Sociological Method.* New York: Free Press.
Evans, T. M. S.
    1977   "The Predication of the Individual in Anthropological Interactionism." *American Anthropologist* 79(3):579-597.
Foucault, Michel
    1972   *The Archaeology of Knowledge.* London: Tavistock Publications.
    1980   *The History of Sexuality.* New York: Vintage Books.
Freilich, Morris, ed.
    1989   *The Relevance of Culture.* New York: Bergin & Garvey.
Gajdusek, D. C.
    1977   "Unconventional Viruses and the Origin and Disappearance of Kuru." *Science* 197:943-960.
Garfinkel, Alan
    1981   *Forms of Explanation: Rethinking the Questions in Social Theory.* New Haven, CT: Yale University Press.
Geertz, Clifford
    1980   "Blurred Genres: The Refiguration of Social Thought." *The American Scholar* 49(2):165-179.
Gellner, Ernest
    1959   "Holism Versus Individualism in History and Sociology." In Patrick Gardner, ed., *Theories of History.* New York: Free Press.
    1962   "Concepts and Society." Reprinted in Bryan R. Wilson, ed., *Rationality.* (1979) Oxford: Basil Blackwell.
Giddens, Anthony
    1977   *Studies in Social and Political Theory.* New York: Basic Books.
Greeno, James G.
    1971   "Theoretical Entities in Statistical Explanation." In Roger C. Buck and Robert S. Cohen, eds., *PSA 1970.* Dordrecht, Netherlands: Reidel.
Gumperz, John J., and Stephen C. Levinson
    1991   "Rethinking Linguistic Relativity." *Current Anthropology* 32(5):613-623.

Harré, R., and P. F. Secord
  1972   *The Explanation of Social Behavior.* Oxford: Basil Black-
         well.
Harris, Marvin
  1964   *The Nature of Cultural Things.* New York: Random House.
  1968   *The Rise of Anthropological Theory.* New York: Thomas
         Y. Crowell.
  1977   Interview comments in the NOVA documentary "Sociobiol-
         ogy: The Human Animal." WGBH and BBC Television,
         New York: Time-Life Films.
  1979   *Cultural Materialism: The Struggle for a Science of Culture.*
         New York: Vintage Books.
  1984   "Comment on Westen's Cultural Materialism." *Current
         Anthropology* 25(5):648-649.
  1991   *Cultural Anthropology.* 3rd edition. New York: Harper
         Collins.
  1992   "Distinguished Lecture: Anthropology and the Theoretical
         and Paradigmatic Significance of the Collapse of Soviet and
         East European Communism." *American Anthropologist* 94
         (2):295-305.
  1997   "Comment on O'Meara's Causation and the Struggle for a
         Science of Culture." *Current Anthropology* 38(3):410-415.
Hempel, Carl G.
  1965   *Aspects of Scientific Explanation and Other Essays in the
         Philosophy of Science.* New York: Free Press.
Honderich, Ted
  1988   *Mind and Brain: A Theory of Determinism.* Vol. 1. Ox-
         ford: Clarendon Press.
Jackson, Michael
  1989   *Paths Toward a Clearing: Radical Empiricism and Eth-
         nographic Inquiry.* Bloomington: Indiana University Press
Kaplan, David, and Robert A. Manners
  1972   *Culture Theory.* Prospect Heights, IL: Waveland Press.
Keesing, Roger M.
  1984   "Comment on Varenne." *Current Anthropology* 25(3):292-
         293.
Lakoff, George
  1987   *Women, Fire, and Dangerous Things: What Categories
         Reveal about the Mind.* Chicago, IL: University of Chicago
         Press.

Lett, James
   1997   *Science, Reason and Anthropology: The Principles of Rational Inquiry.* Lanham, MD: Rowman & Littlefield.
LeVine, Robert A.
   1984   "Properties of Culture: An Ethnographic View." In R. Shweder and R. LeVine, eds., *Culture Theory: Essays on Mind, Self, and Emotion.* Cambridge: Cambridge University Press.
Lévi-Strauss, Claude
   1963   *Structural Anthropology.* New York: Basic Books.
Lewis, David
   1986   *Philosophical Papers* Vol. 2. New York: Oxford University Press.
Lindenbaum, Shirley
   1979   *Kuru Sorcery: Disease and Danger in the New Guinea Highlands.* Mountain View, CA: Mayfield Publishing.
Little, Daniel
   1991   *Varieties of Social Explanation.* Boulder, CO: Westview Press.
Luke, Timothy W.
   1987   "Methodological Individualism: The Essential Ellipsis of Rational Choice Theory." *Philosophy of Social Science* 17: 341-355.
Mach, Ernst
   1914   *The Analysis of Sensations.* Chicago, IL: Open Court.
Malinowski, Bronislaw
   1960   *A Scientific Theory of Culture.* 1944. Reprint, Oxford: Oxford University Press.
Mandelbaum, Maurice
   1973   "Societal Facts." In J. O'Neill, ed., *Modes of Individualism and Collectivism.* London: Heineman.
Michotte, A.
   1963   *The Perception of Causality.* New York: Basic Books.
Moffatt, Michael
   1984   "Comment on Varenne." *Current Anthropology* 25(3):293.
Murdock, George Peter
   1932   "The Science of Culture." *American Anthropologist* 34:200-215.
   1972   "Anthropology's Mythology." Proceedings of the Royal Anthropological Institute of Great Britain and Ireland, 1971.

Nadel, S. F.
    1951   *The Foundations of Social Anthropology*. London: Cohen
            and West.
O'Meara, J. Tim
    1990a   "Anthropology as Metaphysics: Reply to Shore." *American
            Anthropologist* 92(3):751-753.
    1990b   *Samoan Planters: Tradition and Economic Development in
            Polynesia*. Ft. Worth, TX: Holt, Rinehart, and Winston.
    1997   "Causation and the Struggle for a Science of Culture." *Cur-
            rent Anthropology* 38(3):399-410, 415-418.
    n.d.   "Causation and the Application of Darwinian Thinking to
            the Explanation of Human Behavior" (article under review).
Ortner, Sherry B.
    1984   "Theory in Anthropology Since the Sixties." *Comparative
            Studies in Society and History* 26(1):126-166.
Penrose, Roger
    1989   *The Emperor's New Mind: Concerning Computers, Minds,
            and the Laws of Physics*. Oxford: Oxford University Press.
Peoples, James G.
    1982   "Individual or Group Advantage? A Reinterpretation of the
            Maring Ritual Cycle." *Current Anthropology* 23(3):291-
            310.
Popper, Karl R., and J. C. Eccles
    1977   *The Self and Its Brain*. Berlin, Germany: Springer.
Quinn, Naomi and Dorothy Holland
    1987   "Culture and Cognition." In Dorothy Holland and Naomi
            Quinn, eds., *Cultural Models in Language and Thought*.
            Cambridge: Cambridge University Press.
Rabinow, Paul
    1986   "Representations Are Social Facts: Modernity and Post-
            Modernity in Anthropology." In J. Clifford and G. Mar-
            cus, eds., *Writing Culture*. Berkeley: University of Cali-
            fornia Press.
Radcliffe-Brown, A. R.
    1952   *Structure and Function in Primitive Society*. New York:
            Free Press.
Railton, Peter
    1981   "Probability, Explanation, and Information." *Synthese*
            48:233-256.
Rappaport, Roy A.
    1982   "Comment on Individual or Group Advantage? A Reinter-

pretation of the Maring Ritual Cycle, by James A. Peoples."
Current Anthropology 23(3):303-305.

1984 *Pigs for the Ancestors*. 3rd edition. New Haven, CT: Yale University Press.

Rosaldo, Renato

1984 "Comment on Varenne." *Current Anthropology* 25(3):293-294.

Roscoe, Paul

1993a "Practice and Political Centralisation." *Current Anthropology* 34(2):111-124.

1993b "Reply." *Current Anthropology* 34(2):133-140.

1995 "The Perils of 'Positivism' in Cultural Anthropology." *American Anthropologist* 97(3):492-504.

Rosenberg, Alexander

1988 *Philosophy of Social Science*. Boulder, CO: Westview.

Russell, Bertrand

1981 "On the Notion of Cause." *Mysticism and Logic*. 1917. Reprint, Totowa, NJ: Barnes & Noble Books.

Sahlins, Marshall

1976 *Culture and Practical Reason*. Chicago, IL: University of Chicago Press.

Salmon, Wesley C.

1982 "Causality in Archaeological Explanation." In Colin Renfrew, Michael J. Rowlands, and Barbara Abbott Segraves, eds., *Theory and Explanation in Archaeology*. New York: Academic Press.

1984 *Scientific Explanation and the Causal Structure of the World*. Princeton, NJ: Princeton University Press.

1989 "Four Decades of Scientific Explanation." In P. Kitcher and W. Salmon, eds., *Scientific Explanation*. Minneapolis: University of Minnesota Press.

1994 "Causality without Counterfactuals." *Philosophy of Science* 61:297-312.

Sangren, P. Steven

1988 "Rhetoric and the Authority of Ethnography: 'Post-Modernism' and the Social Reproduction of Texts." *Current Anthropology* 29:405-435.

Searle, John R.

1995 *The Construction of Social Reality*. New York: Free Press.

Sperber, Dan

1986 "Issues in the Ontology of Culture." In Barcan Marcus et al., eds., *Logic, Methodology and Philosophy of Science VII*. New York: Elsevier.

Spiro, Melford E.
   1961   "Social Systems, Personality, and Functional Analysis." In B. Kaplan, ed., *Studying Personality Cross-Culturally*. Evanston, IL: Row and Peterson.

Toulmin, Stephen
   1970   "Reasons and Causes." In Robert Borger and Frank Cioffi, eds., *Explanation in the Behavioral Sciences*. Cambridge: Cambridge University Press.

Tylor, E. B.
   1871   *Primitive Culture*. London: John Murray.

Varenne, Hervé
   1984   "Collective Representation in American Anthropological Conversations: Individual and Culture." *Current Anthropology* 25(3):281-291, 295-299.

Vayda, Andrew P.
   1996   *Methods and Explanations in the Study of Human Actions and their Environmental Effects*. Jakarta, Indonesia: Center for International Forestry Research/World Wildlife Fund Special Publication.
   1997   "Rappaport and Causal Explanations of Events." Paper presented at the American Anthropological Association Annual Meeting, Washington, DC.

Watson, Patty Jo, Steven A. LeBlanc, and Charles L. Redman
   1984   *Archeological Explanation: The Scientific Method in Archeology*. New York: Columbia University Press.

Winthrop, Robert H., ed.
   1990   *Culture and the Anthropological Tradition*. Lanham, MD: University Press of America.

Young, J. Zed
   1987   *Philosophy and the Brain*. Oxford: Oxford University Press.

A REALIST/POSTMODERN
CONCEPT OF CULTURE

Joseph A. Maxwell

For many people, the combination of "realist" and "postmodern" in the title of this chapter is an oxymoron. Realism, with its implication of a single "real" world, is in some ways antithetical to the whole intent of postmodernism, which repudiates the urge toward "totalizing metanarratives" (Rosenau 1992:6). In attempting to join these two perspectives, I want to argue that a realist concept of culture is, in important ways, compatible with, and indeed supports, many of the insights and claims of postmodernism.

My goal is not to *reconcile* realism and postmodernism—to attempt this would be a profoundly modernist approach. Instead, I want to put the two perspectives in dialogue with one another, and to show that they have important and mutually supporting implications for the concept of culture. To some extent, I am attempting to do what Bernstein does in his analysis of Habermas and Derrida. Using Adorno's concept of "force-field," he tries to demonstrate that, while these two thinkers cannot be reconciled, they do supplement each other, and constitute "two intertwined strands" of the modern/postmodern condition:

I do not think there is a theoretical position from which we can reconcile their differences, their otherness to each other—nor do I think we should smooth out their "aversions and attractions." The nasty questions that they raise about each other's "project" need to be relentlessly pursued. One of the primary lessons of "modernity/postmodernity" is a radical skepticism about the possibility of a reconciliation—an *aufhebung*, without gaps, fissures, and ruptures.

However, *together*, Habermas/Derrida provide us with a force-field that constitutes the "dynamic, transmutational structure of a complex phenomenon"—the phenomenon I have labeled "modernity/ postmodernity" (Bernstein 1992:225).

I will begin by discussing contemporary philosophic realism, and then present some of realism's implications for the conceptualization of culture. Many of these implications challenge aspects of the traditional anthropological concept of culture, and while none of these challenges are completely new, I think that all of them are strengthened, and some are significantly reframed, by a realist perspective. Finally, I will take up the relationship of some of these implications to postmodernism, and try to show how postmodernism both supports, and is supported by, some of these same challenges.

Realism

Philosophic realism is defined by Phillips (1987:205) as "the view that entities exist independently of being perceived, or independently of our theories about them." More specifically, Lakoff lists the following characteristics of what he terms "experiential realism": (a) a commitment to the existence of a real world; (b) a recognition that reality places constraints on concepts; (c) a conception of truth that goes beyond mere internal coherence; and (d) a commitment to the existence of stable knowledge of the world (1987:xv). Such views, which during much of the twentieth century were ignored or disparaged, first by positivists and empiricists and later by constructivists and other antipositivists, have emerged, in modified form, as a serious position in current philosophical discussion (Feyerabend 1981; Leplin 1984; Levine 1993; Phillips 1987; Putnam 1981, 1987, 1990; Salmon 1984, 1989; Strawson 1989; Suppe 1977). The idea that there is a real world with which we interact, and to which our concepts and theories refer, has proved to be a resilient and powerful one which, following the demise of positivism, has attracted an increasing amount of philosophic attention.

Realist approaches have become so prevalent that Kleinman, for example, can refer in passing, with no sense that this claim needs to be explicitly defended, to the "consensus on neorealism that characterizes the contemporary discourse in the history and philosophy of science" (1986:225). While the term "consensus" is somewhat of an exaggeration (cf., for example, Levine 1993), it is clear that realism is a legiti-

mate and respected stance in philosophy. There are philosophic problems with realist approaches that remain unresolved, and realist
philosophers themselves disagree about many of these issues; one advocate of realist views has claimed that "scientific realism is a majority
position whose advocates are so divided as to appear a minority"
(Leplin 1984:1). However, equally serious problems confront alternative positions, and realism promises to successfully address many of
the difficulties with the latter approaches.

Realism has begun to have a substantial influence on the philosophy
and methodology of the social sciences (e.g. Bhaskar 1989; Campbell
1988; Cook and Campbell 1979; Hammersley 1992; Hawthorn 1987;
House 1991; Huberman and Miles 1985; Lakoff 1987; Manicas 1987;
Maxwell 1992; Pateman 1987; Sayer 1992; Secord 1986; Shweder
1991). However, contemporary realist views have so far had little
influence on cultural theory. This chapter is intended to address this
neglect, and to propose a realist approach to the concept of culture and
to some of the issues pertaining to culture which are currently being
debated.

There are three main features that distinguish most contemporary
realist approaches from positivism and empiricism. The most important of these is that realists reject the theoretical instrumentalism that
was one of the main characteristics of positivism (Feyerabend 1981:
176-202; Norris 1983; Phillips 1987:40). Realists see theoretical terms
as referring to actual features and properties of a real world, rather
than being (as many positivists argued) simply useful logical constructions based on observational data, "fictions" which are valuable in
making predictions but which have no claim to any "reality." The latter view, generally termed "instrumentalism," although largely discredited in philosophy, is still influential in psychology and the social
sciences (Salmon 1984:5-7).

Second, and closely connected to the first point, most contemporary
realists accept the validity of the concept of "cause" in scientific
explanation, a concept that was one of the main targets of both positivism and its antipositivist critics. While many positivists rejected
causality as a metaphysical notion that should have no role in science,
most realists see causality as intrinsic to either the nature of the world
(Strawson 1989) or to our understanding of it (Putnam 1990; Salmon
1984). As Putnam puts it:

whether causation "really exists" or not, it certainly exists in our
"life world." What makes it real in a *phenomenological* sense is the

possibility of asking "Is that really the cause?" that is, of *checking* causal statements, of bringing new data and new theories to bear on them. . . . The world of ordinary language (the world in which we actually live) is full of causes and effects. It is only when we insist that the world of ordinary language (or the *Lebenswelt*) is defective . . . and look for a "true" world . . . that we end up feeling forced to choose between the picture of "a physical universe with a built-in structure" and "a physical universe with a structure imposed by the mind" (1990:89).

Third, most contemporary realists deny that we can have any unmediated, "objective" knowledge of this real world, and argue that all theories are grounded in a particular perspective and worldview. This is a key tenet of many versions of contemporary realism: "critical" realism (Bhaskar 1989; Cook and Campbell 1979), "internal" (or "pragmatic") realism (Putnam 1987, 1990), "experiential" realism (Lakoff 1987), "constructive" realism (Howard 1991), "artful" realism (Shweder 1991), and "subtle" realism (Hammersley 1992). These different views all agree that there is no possibility of attaining a single, "correct" understanding of the world, what Putnam describes as the "God's eye view"—all knowledge is partial, incomplete, and fallible. Lakoff states this distinction between "objectivist" and "realist" views as follows:

> Scientific objectivism claims that there is only one fully correct way in which reality can be divided up into objects, properties, and relations. . . . Scientific realism, on the other hand, assumes that "the world is the way it is," while acknowledging that there can be more than one scientifically correct way of understanding reality in terms of conceptual schemes with different objects and categories of objects (1987:265).

One of the major implications of realism for anthropology and the other social sciences is that it re-legitimates ontological questions about the phenomena we study. If our concepts refer to real phenomena, rather than to abstractions from sense data or to our own constructions, it makes sense to ask, to what phenomena or domains of phenomena do particular concepts refer, and what is the nature of these phenomena? At one time, such entities as atoms (cf. Salmon 1984) and genes (cf. Keller 1983) were generally believed to be artificial constructs, abstractions that were theoretically useful, but which had no actual existence;

a characteristic instrumentalist view. For both of these entities, a realist stance is now prevalent.

One of the ontological problems that has recurrently occupied social scientists is the relationship among culture, society or social structure, mind or personality, and the biological or behavioral organism. Cole (1991), for example, has recently argued that much of what psychologists call "social" is really cultural, and that we need a more psychologically useful concept of culture. D'Andrade states that:

> Such terminological quarreling might seem to be academic foolishness. However, most of the battles about the nature of culture have been enlightening, perhaps because they make explicit our assumptions about what is out there, and perhaps because as our assumptions become more explicit, we find that there are more kinds of things out there than we had thought (1984:114).

Rather than review the different approaches to these issues and their relative advantages and difficulties, I will present a position that I see as particularly compatible with the realist approach that I am taking here. This position is based on the brief but influential formulation by Kroeber and Parsons (1958) of the distinctions between culture, social system, personality, and biological organism. Although I find their distinctions particularly useful, I believe that the grounds on which they made these distinctions are philosophically outdated, and I propose a different way of conceptualizing these distinctions. I then develop the implications of their model for a number of key issues in current debates over culture. Finally, I will argue that the conception of culture embodied in their model is surprisingly compatible with aspects of postmodernism, and that this approach to culture facilitates the application of some postmodern insights to cultural theory.

Kroeber and Parsons's Model

Kroeber and Parsons interpreted the relationships among the four concepts of culture, society, personality, and the biological organism as the historical product of two analytic distinctions. The first of these distinctions was an attempt to separate a sociocultural sphere of investigation from that of the biological sciences, basically along the lines of the heredity-environment distinction. The organism belonged to the biological sphere, but society and culture (at first more or less undifferentiated) were seen as independent of the biological characteristics of the organism, and as transmitted by learning rather than heredity.

The second distinction, a much later one, restricted culture to systems of symbolic-meaningful entities such as ideas and values, while using "society" to refer to systems of interactions among individuals and collectivities. This distinction was stated more fully by Parsons:

> The social-system focus is on the conditions involved in the interaction of actual human individuals who constitute concrete collectivities with determinate membership. The cultural-system focus, on the other hand, is on "patterns" of meaning, e.g., of values, of norms, of organized knowledge and beliefs, of expressive "form" (1961:34).

Kroeber and Parsons noted that a similar distinction had taken place at the biological level, separating a specifically psychological component, usually termed "personality," from the biological organism.

These two distinctions generated a fourfold model of the relationships among these concepts:

culture	society or social system
personality	biological organism

While I want to retain this fourfold model, I think the particular grounds on which Kroeber and Parsons made these two distinctions are outdated and no longer plausible. First, basing the separation of the biological and social sciences on the heredity-environment distinction leads to serious conceptual difficulties. As is now generally recognized, it makes no sense to speak of any characteristic of an individual as being due to hereditary rather than environmental causes, or vice versa; every phenotypic trait of an organism is the result of the interaction of genetic and environmental factors, and "relative importance" is meaningless as applied to the cause of any characteristic considered by itself (Dobzhansky 1962:42-46; Lewontin 1974). It *is* meaningful to ask about the relative importance of genetic and environmental factors in producing the *differences* with respect to a particular trait among individuals *in a specified population*, but such differences are almost never due exclusively to hereditary or environmental factors. Consequently, it is futile to attempt to distinguish sociocultural from biological phenomena on the basis of whether the characteristics of the individual are innate or acquired.

A more satisfactory separation of sociocultural from biological phenomena employs the distinction between the individual and the system or collectivity of individuals; in fact, Kroeber and Parsons's analysis is more consistent with this distinction than with the heredity-environment distinction (cf. Parsons 1961:33-34). "Organism" and "personality" refer to properties of individuals; "society" and "culture," to properties of systems or collectivities of individuals. This distinction, employing the concept of level of organization or complexity (Pattee 1973; Simon 1969), avoids incorporating causal assumptions into the distinctions among these concepts. However, as Kroeber (1949:120) clearly saw, levels of organization should not be confused with levels of abstraction; culture and society pertain to a higher level of organization (the collectivity level) than do individual minds or behavior, but are not thereby more abstract.

The basis for Kroeber and Parsons's second distinction, that between culture and society, and also between personality and the biological organism, was not explicitly presented in their paper. I argue that this distinction is best seen as that between physical phenomena and ideational or mental phenomena. To justify this position fully would require a lengthy presentation of recent work on the philosophy of mind and the relevance of this work to the concept of culture. Here, I will present only a brief sketch of an approach to mind, and an account of how this view of mind can be employed in developing a model of culture and its relationship to society, personality, and organism.

My use of the mind/body distinction does not entail the existence of separate substances or entities, but only that there is what William James called a "double aspect" to our understanding of the world, a view that Putnam (who, remember, is a major proponent of contemporary realism) traces to Kant. Conant, commenting on Putnam's views, says that:

> Kant does not say that there are two "substances"—mind and body (as Descartes did). Kant says, instead, that there are "dualities in our experience" (a striking phrase!) that refuse to go away. . . . What is of permanent significance here is Kant's idea that the relation between mind and body should not be pictured as a binary opposition, a dualism of two incommensurable kinds of entity, but rather as a *duality*: two complementary poles of a single field of activity—the field of human experience (1990:xxii).

The approach to culture that I take here is not based on or derived from any particular philosophy of mind, other than accepting this duality of experience. However, the distinction between mind and body as involving two perspectives rather than two different "substances" is incorporated in one particular approach to mind known as "functionalism" (Fodor 1980, 1981; Putnam 1975), and a further investigation of this approach can be illuminating. Putnam explains functionalism as follows:

> According to functionalism, the behavior of, say, a computing machine is not explained by the physics and chemistry of the computing machine. It is explained by the machine's *program*. Of course, that program is realized in a particular physics and chemistry, and could, perhaps, be deduced from that physics and chemistry. But that does not make the program a physical or chemical property of the machine; it is an abstract property of the machine. Similarly, I believe that the psychological properties of human beings are not physical and chemical properties of human beings, although they may be realized by physical and chemical properties of human beings. Although any behavior of a computing machine that can be explained by the program of that computing machine can, in principle, be predicted on the basis of the physics and chemistry of the machine, the latter prediction may be highly unexplanatory. Understanding why the machine, say, computes the decimal expansion of pi, may require reference to the abstract or functional properties of the machine, to the machine's program and not to its physical and chemical make up (1975:xiii).

Functionalism is thus compatible with realism and even with materialism, but not with reductionism or behaviorism. It is an attempt to provide a philosophical justification for our everyday use of mental terms to refer to inner, unobserved causes of behavior, and not an attempt to eliminate such terms either by reducing them to neurophysiology or by interpreting them as referring to behavior or behavioral dispositions. "Mind" is a concept used in understanding the inner phenomena that are, among other things, important causes of behavior. It refers to phenomena that can also be conceptualized in physical terms, but provides a useful perspective on these phenomena that physical theories currently lack, and for which the latter may never be able to substitute.

In this view, "consciousness," in the subjective sense, is not implied by the use of mental terms. Mental states and processes can legitimately be ascribed whenever doing so increases our understanding of an individual's behavior (Bruner, Goodnow, and Austin 1956:54-55). This stance is implicit in the approach of ethologists such as von Uexkuell (von Bertalanffy 1968:227), Portmann (1961), and Tinbergen (1961), who use concepts such as "image" and "mood" to represent the minds of animals. The general applicability of such a "mentalistic" perspective, even to entities that are well understood in physical terms, is shown by Boulding's discussion (1956:20-22) of the value system and image of the outside world that a thermostat possesses. Bateson similarly argues that: "We can assert that *any* ongoing ensemble of events and objects which has the appropriate complexity of causal circuits and the appropriate energy relations will surely show mental characteristics" (1971:315).

The importance of these arguments is that the use of "mind" in theory or description commits one neither to the existence of mysterious non-material entities—the "ghost in the machine" (Ryle 1949:15-16)—nor to an ultimate reliance on introspection and subjectivism. Statements about entities that belong to this "mental" framework are in principle as testable by scientific methods as statements about any other hypothesized entities that are not subject to direct observation, with the added advantage that through introspection we can often gain additional information about mental processes.

The definition of culture as "mental" does not imply that culture is necessarily "in people's heads." As implied above, the "mental" perspective is applicable to a wider range of phenomena than people's (or other organism's) brains, and the view of culture that I present here is quite compatible with seeing culture as located in artifacts as well as in individuals, providing that these constitute part of a social system (see Hutchins 1995).

A common misunderstanding of realism as it pertains to the social sciences is that it applies only to *physical* entities, and that "mental" phenomena are outside its reach. For example, Hawthorn argues that: "The more cautious agree that what we say about the world is internal to our scheme and so indeterminate. But they nevertheless insist that there are contents of the world, roughly speaking, those contents of the world that are not the contents of consciousness, for which realism is true" (1987:271).

This view seeks to partition the world into one domain in which realism is valid, and a separate domain in which constructivism or relativism can still be maintained. However, the types of realism that I am presenting here do not attempt such a separation; they hold that while our *knowledge* of the world is inherently a construction from a particular perspective, there is nonetheless a real world, which can be understood in both mental and physical terms, about which our constructions can be more or less correct. As Frazer and Lacey put it: "Even if one is a realist at the ontological level, one *could* be an epistemological interpretivist . . . our knowledge of the real world is inevitably interpretive and provisional rather than straightforwardly representational" (1993:182). Thus, while realism rejects the idea of "multiple realities" in the sense of independent and incommensurable *worlds* in which different individuals or societies live, it is quite compatible, not only with the idea that there are different valid *perspectives* on the world, but also with the point that these perspectives, as held by the people we study, are *part of* the world that we want to understand, and that our understanding of these perspectives can be more or less correct (Phillips 1987).

In my reformulation of Kroeber and Parsons's model, the culture-society distinction is based on the same criterion as the body-mind distinction: that is, that cultural and social concepts belong to the mental and physical frameworks, respectively. They are distinguished from those concepts referring to mind and the biological organism, respectively, by the fact that they pertain to collectivities rather than to individuals. As a society can be seen as consisting of a group of individuals and the behavioral relationships among them, so a culture can be conceived of as the associated set of minds of these individuals and the communicative relationships among them.

My interpretation of Kroeber and Parsons's fourfold distinction among these concepts can be represented as a 2 x 2 matrix:

	mental	*physical*
collectivity	culture	society or social system
individual	mind or personality	organism

This formulation of the concept of culture conflicts with some other influential views of culture. I will deal with some of the most important of these alternative theories, briefly explaining why I think they are untenable. In particular, I will argue that culture is not behavior, that it is not a "level" in a hierarchical relationship with society or personality, and that it is not necessarily shared. I will devote most of my argument to the third of these points, because it is the one that is currently most controversial, and is the one where the juxtaposition of realism and postmodernism is the most productive. I will also try to show what difference these differences make: how the concept of culture that one employs has important methodological consequences for one's fieldwork and analysis.

However, to modify the predominantly negative tone of what follows, I want to emphasize what I think culture *is*: a domain of phenomena that is both symbolic-meaningful (i.e., part of the mental rather than physical perspective) and collective, that cannot be reduced to individual behavior or thought or subsumed in social structure, but that is causally connected to both behavior and social structure. Stated baldly, this may seem to be little more than common sense, but I think its implications are worth investigating, because many formulations of culture have incorporated different assumptions that I think are unwarranted and unproductive.

Culture Is Not Behavior

In the model I present here, culture is not behavior, nor is it an aspect or quality of behavior. Culture, like mind, belongs to the symbolic-meaningful framework, and cannot be reduced to the overt behavior of individuals. Behavior (in the broad sense of "observations of individuals") constitutes the *evidence for* culture; but to see culture as *consisting* of behavior (e.g. Harris 1964) ignores the fact that people's mental activities are the immediate *causes* of their behavior, not simply an aspect of that behavior. By collapsing culture into behavior, such theories abandon the use of culture as a powerful concept for *explaining* behavior. (It is not coincidental that many of the theorists who took this approach to culture employed environmental adaptation as the major concept for explaining behavior.) Additional difficulties with this so-called "materialist" definition of culture are presented by Werner and Schoepfle (1987: 69-71), who contrast this with what they call the "cognitivist" viewpoint.

While probably no one still holds that culture consists in a straightforward way of people's actual behavior, rather than of their ideas and concepts (cf. Harris 1979), some still-influential approaches understood culture as ideational, but saw the ideational realm as itself pertaining to propensities for, or abstractions from, behavior. Two prominent theorists who took such an approach are Geertz (1973), in his use of the idea of "thick description," and Schneider (1980).

Geertz borrowed his concept of "thick description" from Ryle's influential analysis of "mind." Ryle maintained that "mental" terms denote a person's propensity to act in certain ways. He argued that:

> when we characterise people by mental predicates, we are not making untestable inferences to any ghostly processes occurring in streams of consciousness which we are debarred from visiting; we are describing the ways in which those people conduct parts of their predominantly public behavior. True, we go beyond what we see them do and hear them say, but this going beyond is not a going behind, in the sense of making inferences to occult causes; it is going beyond in the sense of considering, in the first instance, the powers and propensities of which their actions are exercises (1949:51).

The advantages of this approach are obvious: it removes mental activities from "the secret grotto in the skull" and locates them in the public, social world. Furthermore, it accomplishes this without resorting to the cruder forms of mechanism or behaviorism, which attempted either to do away with mind altogether or to identify it as an epiphenomenal "aspect" of behavior.

However, there are substantial philosophic difficulties with Ryle's position. His theory was one example (although an unacknowledged one) of the instrumentalist tendency in positivism (described above), which held that the meaning of every scientific term must ultimately be specifiable in terms of direct and public observational data. Theoretical terms, those that do not refer directly to observation, were construed as dispositional terms that are based upon, and are ultimately reducible to, observational terms. This position was seen as necessary in order to insure objectivity for all scientific statements and to avoid untestable and therefore meaningless theoretical concepts.

However, this formulation of scientific meaning was shown to be untenable (Carnap 1956; Hempel 1952, 1956; Phillips 1987). Not only are there apparently insuperable logical difficulties in the way of the proposed reduction of theoretical to observational terms, but, as Hempel pointed out, "it is precisely these "fictitious" concepts rather than those fully definable by observables which enable science to interpret and organize the data of direct observation by means of a coherent and comprehensive system which permits explanation and prediction"

(1952:31).

Both Geertz's use of "thick description" and Schneider's definition of culture as an abstraction from behavior (1980:126) were attempts to avoid postulating non-observable entities as the constituents of culture or as hidden causes of observed behavior. In this, they essentially accepted the positivist critique of theoretical constructs in scientific explanation, a critique that has been shown to be invalid. Although Schneider had emphasized that "the definition of the units and the rules [of a culture] is *not* based on, defined by, drawn from, constructed in accord with or developed in terms of the observation of behavior in any direct, simple sense" (1980:6), and asserted: "I am not a positivist" (1980:128), he continued to hold that the construction of a "cultural account" of a particular domain is a matter of correctly abstracting symbols and meanings from one's observations and interviews (1976: 198, 1980:127-133). He defined an abstraction as "simply an analytically defined operation that is applicable to, and can be drawn from, observations of behavior" and that "exists in the mind of the observer" (1976:198) rather than in some external reality. He argued that "I do not take the position that culture is *sui generis*, a thing in and of itself, or that it has any existence outside the construction of the anthropologist who builds that structure of abstractions" (1980:128).

The methodological implications of the view I have criticized, that culture is an abstraction from behavior, also need to be addressed. For the reasons given above, Schneider held that it constituted "cheating" to present informants' statements as evidence for the validity of a cultural account:

> Since data and analysis are inextricably intertwined, it is a direct corollary that statements by informants, quotations of what the natives actually said, observations about what they actually do can constitute nothing more than examples, or illustrations, and can in no sense be regarded as proving anything. . . . I have frequently been offended by other anthropologists, sociologists and psychologists who play what I think of as the questionable game of suggesting that their generalization is "proven" or "supported" by some appropriately chosen excerpt from the field materials (1980:124).

The realist approach to culture that I present here has quite different methodological implications. Since culture refers to mental and symbolic entities, rather than physical or behavioral ones, its characteristics must be inferred rather than observed or "abstracted" from observations. These inferences must be supported by evidence and defended against various "validity threats" (Cook and Campbell 1979; Maxwell 1992). A cultural analysis should not only meet criteria of simplicity, adequacy, and logical coherence, but should be tested against the full range of relevant data and all plausible alternative analyses (Maxwell 1995). Schneider acknowledged the importance of evidence as well as internal consistency in deciding between alternative theories of society (1984:5), but did not incorporate this concern for evidence into his theory of culture.

Culture Is Not a "Level"

A second implication of Kroeber and Parsons's model is that culture is not a "level" that stands in a hierarchical relationship to the other "levels" of social structure, personality, and biology, although "culture" and "social structure" do refer to a higher level of organization than the individual. This "levels" conception of the relationship among the four concepts, ironically, was later elaborated by Parsons (1966:6-29), who saw these as comprising a hierarchy of control agencies, proceeding from the cultural system (values) downward to the social system (norms and collectivity), personality (the learned behavioral organization of the individual), and the organism (genetic constitution), which is the point of interaction of the system of action with the physical environment. A similar account of the relations among these concepts has been given by Schneider (1976). Parsons apparently shifted from the first to the second view of culture, but never resolved many of the difficulties with the latter conception (Schmid 1992).

This hierarchical formulation is in conflict with the one advanced here. The most serious point of disagreement is that, with the definition of the society-culture distinction as norms vs. values, much of what I have considered culture was assigned by Parsons to the social sphere. One consequence of this is that the development of cultural theory was directed along more limited and less productive lines (Sheldon 1951:40-42). This "stratigraphic" conception of the four concepts was also criticized by Geertz (1965:50-55), who argued that this formulation, and the attempt to tie putative cultural universals to presumed requirements of the lower levels, have in fact hindered the theoretical integration of the four fields and the discovery of genuine functional interrelationships between them.

The more important consequence, however, was that the analysis of normative systems was confounded with that of the interaction of physical individuals and groups, the field to which I have limited the term "society." The alternative position that I take is similar to Parsons's earlier views, cited above, and to the work of Witherspoon (1975:3-9, 67) and Yanagisako (1975). It is also similar to the distinction made by Toulmin (1972:142) between two perspectives on scientific endeavors, seen as human action: as traditions of procedures, techniques, and concepts, to be studied as the history of ideas, and as professions consisting of organizations, roles, and individuals, to be understood in terms of the activities of individual scientists and scientific groups. The problem of the relationship of norms to values is an important and difficult one, but I do not think that a separation of the two into different levels or hierarchically related systems is the best approach to it.

The stratigraphic view of the relationship between symbolic, normative, and behavioral "systems" was also criticized by Yanagisako (1975, 1978) as empirically inadequate for the understanding of Japanese-American kinship. Yanagisako faults this approach, as employed by Schneider and Parsons, both for assuming one-dimensional causation in the system (i.e., that change is determined by exogenous factors rather than by interaction between endogenous structures of the system), and for assuming that norms are more closely tied to particular contexts than are symbols.

The view that culture, society, personality, and organism are linked in a linear sequence of control implies that a society's adaptation to its environment is initially mediated by the "lower" levels in the hierarchy, such as subsistence activities, and that the "higher" levels, especially ideational systems, have a less direct role in the adaptation process. This approach has been challenged by, among others, Keesing (1974:76-77) and Rappaport (1967, 1971). In contrast, Kroeber and Parsons's model, as I employ it, does not entail any particular theory of sociocultural change, and is compatible with the work of Rappaport and others (e.g. Maxwell 1978) who see culture as having a direct role in environmental adaptation.

Culture Is Not Necessarily Shared

From the realist position that I have taken here, the assumption that culture is shared should be a matter for empirical research, not definitional fiat. Berkhofer, a historian, argues that the "consensus" definition of culture:

incorporated a complete theory of culture without a valid foundation in research. By assuming the components of culture in the definition, anthropologists presumed the results of their analyses of various cultures. . . . Moreover, they hypothesized the articulation of these components according to the definition, so their research more frequently proved how things related according to the mind of the anthropologist than according to the minds of the people said to bear the culture (1973:91).

The view that culture is by definition shared has been subjected to repeated challenges in anthropology. These attacks have been both theoretical (Aberle 1960; Hannerz 1992; Linton 1936; Pelto and Pelto 1975; Rosaldo 1989; Wallace 1970) and empirical (D'Andrade 1984; Gardner 1976; E. Heider 1972; K. Heider 1978; Pollnac 1975; Sanjek 1977; Sankoff 1972; Swartz 1982). Further, the idea that what is shared by individuals is most central to the functioning of a socio-cultural system has also been questioned; diversity may be of equal or greater significance (Roberts 1961, 1964; Wallace 1970). Even when diversity is acknowledged it has generally been treated as abnormal, and rarely incorporated into theoretical explanation (Pelto and Pelto 1975).

From these perspectives, the concept of culture cannot be restricted to a set of *shared* concepts, symbols, and beliefs. A culture is a *system* of individuals' conceptual/meaningful structures (minds) found in a given social system, and is not intrinsically shared, but participated in (Aberle 1960); although sharing is one *possible* form of participation, it is not the only one. Culture cannot be represented by a model on the same scale as the individual, i.e., as a "shared" set of meanings or beliefs, but requires a model at a higher level of complexity.

The most systematic alternative conception of culture is that of Wallace (1970), who pointed out the lack of evidence for the functional necessity of shared goals, motives, or beliefs, and the increasing empirical evidence for cognitive diversity. Wallace drew a distinction between what he called the "replication of uniformity" and "organization of diversity" approaches to culture, and argued that ordered, stable societies depend not on a uniformity of beliefs and motives, but on a systematic relationship between diverse cognitive systems that permits prediction of behavior.

Hannerz has taken Wallace's concept of "the organization of diversity" and used it to develop a general approach to cultural complexity, focusing on what he calls the distributive dimension of culture. He argues that "The premise of cultural sharing, continuously reproduced in textbook definitions as well as in advanced theoretical treatises, is obviously deeply entrenched in anthropological thought, an intellectual default position to which one falls back whenever there is no insistent reason for thinking otherwise" (1992:11). His own approach abandons this premise:

> Rather than trying to find, somewhere in the structure of social relationships, a common denominator for the widest possible range of cultural phenomena—an enterprise which even in its more successful versions tends to be quite incomplete in its coverage—I am interested here in the sources of diversity, and in its consequences. This is a matter of confronting a customary commitment, in anthropology and elsewhere, to one particular understanding of culture as collective, socially organized meaning—the idea of culture as something shared, in the sense of homogeneously distributed in society (Hannerz 1992:11).

A similar point is made by Hutchins, who claims that:

> the ideational definition of culture prevents us from seeing that systems of socially distributed cognition may have interesting cognitive properties of their own. In the history of anthropology, there is scarcely a more important concept than the division of labor. . . . The emphasis on finding and describing "knowledge structures" that are somewhere "inside" the individual encourages us to overlook the fact that human cognition is always situated in a complex sociocultural world and cannot be unaffected by it (1995:xiii).

The idea that culture is intrinsically shared is an example of what the evolutionary biologist Mayr (1982:45-47) has called "essentialism": the view that the norm or the "typical" individual is the important characteristic of a species. However, the essence of the Darwinian revolution is that it replaced a Platonic view of variation among organisms (that variations were simply imperfect approximations to an "ideal" or "type") with a realist view that saw actual variation as the fundamental fact of biology and the cornerstone of evolutionary theory (Gould 1996:41-42; Lewontin 1973; also, cf. Pelto and Pelto 1975:14-15). Mayr states that "the most interesting parameter in the statistics of natural populations is the actual variation, its amount, and its nature" (1982:47).

This critique can be applied to the majority of anthropological work on culture. Cultural phenomena are normally presented in terms of an "ideal" individual to which actual individuals more or less correspond, a bias that Pelto and Pelto (1975:1-2) call "uniformism." Furbee and Benfer (1983:307) note that quantitative ethnographic studies of semantics generally use pooled data from a number of individuals, and warn that "pooling may produce a weighted composite which no individual possesses." They argue that "there is value in retaining the individual as the unit of analysis, because differences among informants can help to evaluate the stability and generality of an ethnosemantic model" (1983:308).

In anthropology, the most common approach to intracultural diversity has been to see surface variation as based on an "underlying" or a "higher-level" uniformity (e.g. Schneider 1980:122-123; Moffatt 1979). This explanation of diversity has been criticized by Yanagisako, who states that the premise that "higher" levels are less variable than "lower" ones "has nowhere been adequately supported by cultural data" (1978:26), and argues that the assumption is not true for Japanese-American kinship.

These arguments for the importance of diversity are strikingly similar to Durkheim's distinction between mechanical and organic solidarity. For Durkheim, "mechanical solidarity, or solidarity by similarities" derives from those beliefs and sentiments that the members of a society hold in common—what he called the "*conscience collective*," generally translated "collective consciousness." Organic solidarity, in contrast, is based on individual differences. Durkheim argued that:

> Whereas the other [mechanical] solidarity implies that individuals resemble one another, the latter assumes that they are different from one another. . . . This solidarity resembles that observed in the higher animals. In fact each organ has its own special characteristics and autonomy, yet the greater the unity of the organism, the more marked the individualisation of the parts. Using this analogy, we propose to call "organic" the solidarity that is due to the division of labor (1984[1893]:85).

However, Durkheim later shifted his position to argue that organic solidarity had to be based on a continuation of mechanical solidarity (the *conscience collective*), and his abandonment of the concept of organic solidarity is probably responsible in part for the lack of impact that "organization of diversity" approaches have had on the concept of culture. Parsons, for example, incorporated in his influential theories of society Durkheim's later assumption that shared values were the source of social order. Challenges to this position came almost exclusively from theorists holding a conflict model of society that denied the very existence of the sort of integration that Parsons's concept of culture was intended to explain, so that the possibility that solidarity could be based on complementarity was never systematically developed in sociology. Schmid argues that: "Parsons seems unable to imagine the empirical possibility of conflict-free social relations where actors are orienting themselves, not to a common culture, but to quite different, and possibly contradictory, parts of it" (1992:99).

Methodologically, the view of culture presented here implies that uniformity or sharing must be demonstrated rather than assumed; statements about a particular culture must be based on more than a few "key" informants. Not only must systematic sampling be done in order to insure the validity of such statements (E. Heider 1972; Sankoff 1971), but there is evidence that key informants themselves assume greater uniformity than actually exists (Pelto and Pelto 1975:7; Poggie 1972). Shweder and Bourne argue that:

> Confronted with the apparent diversity of human understandings, there are two powerful ways to discover universals in one's data: (a) emphasize general likenesses and overlook specific differences ("the higher-order generality rule"); and/or (b) examine only a subset of the evidence ("the data attenuation rule") (1984:159).

While Shweder and Bourne are referring here to cross-cultural diversity, the strategies can be (and often have been) used to find or emphasize intracultural similarities and ignore differences. A valid cultural analysis must incorporate procedures designed to counteract these biases (Maxwell 1996).

A concept of culture that explicitly incorporates individual diversity is strikingly similar to the domain of phenomena in psychology known as "socially situated cognition" (Hutchins 1995) and to what Perkins (1992) calls "distributed intelligence," although it is not necessarily limited to cognition but can include affect as well. However, many of those writing about situated cognition use this phrase interchangeably with "socially shared cognition," obscuring precisely what I see as most important about the concept. Cole (1991) argues that the term "shared" is ambiguous, since it has two distinct meanings: "held in common" or similar, and "divided up" or distributed. He elaborates on the latter meaning as "the division of cognitive labor."

Postmodernism

This emphasis on the diversity that is inherent in culture is where the realist perspective I present connects most directly with post-modernism. Rosenau identifies as key characteristics of post-modernism its search for "diversity rather than unity, difference rather than synthesis, complexity rather than simplification" (1992:8) and the possibility of a plurality of interpretations of any text, rather than a single message (1992:35). Wolf likewise sees diversity as central: "The postmodernist goal is, I take it, to encourage the author to present a less tidy picture with more contradictory voices" (1992:53). The additional contribution of my realist conception of culture is that it applies the concept of polyvocality and the rejection of "totalizing metanarratives" not just to the texts that anthropologists create in describing other cultures, but to the phenomena of culture itself.

Hannerz takes a similar position. He states that "Postmodernism comes close enough to the view of culture as an organization of diversity which I take here" (1992:35). However, he also warns that: "It is a problem of postmodernist thought that as it has emphasized diversity and been assertively doubtful toward master narratives, it has frequently been on the verge of becoming another all-encompassing formula for a macroanthropology of the replication of uniformity" (1992:35).

I am well aware that, as Rosenau (1992:14) warns, the absence of unity in postmodernism itself allows anyone to find points of agreement with it. However, I think that the mutual emphasis on diversity in critical realist and postmodern views of culture is not a superficial or chance similarity, but is indicative of a wider and more important connection between the two (Maxwell 1996). For example, another connection between critical realism and postmodernism includes their rejection of a unitary, objectivist concept of truth, and their affirmation of the grounding of accounts in perspectives that are inevitably local rather than universal. (Clearly, the major affinity here is with what Rosenau calls "affirmative" rather than "skeptical" postmodernism.)

Richard Bernstein (1992:8-10) likewise sees the abandonment of a belief in the possibility of an ultimate reconciliation of all differences as the key feature of what he calls the "modern/postmodern condition." He turns to Adorno's concepts of "constellation" and "force-field" as a way of connecting these differences without imposing uniformity. Adorno saw modern thought as characterized by the "logic of identity," a metaphysics that denies difference. He rejected the Hegelian ideal of dialectic as "the ultimate totalizer, bringing the oppositions generated by metaphysical logic into ultimate unity within a totality" (Young 1990:304). In opposition to this, Adorno developed what he called "negative dialectic" and the concepts of "force-field" and "constellation." Jay, commenting on Adorno's work, defines "force-field" as: "a relational interplay of attractions and adversions that constitute the dynamic, transmutational structure of a complex phenomenon" (1984: 14), and "constellation" as: "a juxtaposed rather than integrated cluster of changing elements that resist reduction to a common denominator, essential core, or generative first principle" (Jay 1984:15).

The concepts of force-field and constellation can be seen as ways of recognizing coherence that does not depend on similarity or require reconciliation of difference. In doing this, they implicitly involve the concept of contiguity, derived from linguistics (Jakobson 1956; Saussure 1986 [1916]), as an alternative to similarity. I have argued elsewhere (Maxwell n.d.) that contiguity is an alternative to similarity as a source of social solidarity, and provides the missing component in Durkheim's concept of organic solidarity.

The concept of contiguity-based coherence thus constitutes a third possibility, as an alternative to the two prevalent views of cultural integration: the view that cultural integration is inherently a matter of sharing, and the view that culture is characterized by conflict rather than integration. Smelser (1992:5) distinguishes two aspects of cultural integration: "coherence" (how unified the elements of a culture are) and "consensus" (the degree to which the elements are shared). Unfortunately, he tends to see both of these forms of integration as mainly a matter of similarity. "Consensus" is similarity-based by definition, while Smelser treats "coherence" as largely a matter of the existence of an overarching principle or principles from which the specific elements are derived (a view he attributes to Sorokin). In this, he treats contradictions or a lack of reflection of basic principles in specific elements of culture as incoherence by definition, ignoring the ways in which contradictions may be integral to the functioning of a sociocultural system (see Maxwell 1978). I am arguing that contiguity can be a principle of integration for both of these aspects of culture: that cultures can be "coherent" in other ways than hierarchical consistency, and integrated in other ways than by sharing.

This argument parallels Lakoff's realist account of categorization

(1987:153-154), in which he argues that the members of a category do not necessarily have any property in common, nor are they necessarily united by a general principle for determining membership. Instead, they can be organized metonymically (by contiguity) as well as metaphorically (by similarity). In the same way, cultures are not necessarily integrated by similarity or by overarching principles, but can exhibit a diverse set of links among the elements and the individuals who possess these.

Contiguity as a source of coherence does not fit well with many postmodern views, which reject both contiguity-based and similarity-based integration (e.g. Young 1990). However, contiguity-based integration is compatible with postmodernism's emphasis on local rather than general narratives, since contiguity is inherently a local connection. What I take as most valid from postmodernism is not the rejection of coherence per se, but the rejection of similarity as the fundamental source of coherence. I am arguing for a recognition of contiguity as a real phenomenon that provides an alternative to similarity, an alternative that avoids many of the "totalizing" features that postmodernism has attacked. A realist approach to culture can reveal diversity that the traditional concept has ignored, and can suggest forms of cultural integration that are compatible with diversity. This perspective can provide one way out of the "hegemony of mimesis" that postmodernism has identified.

References

Aberle, David F.
   1960   "The Influence of Linguistics on Early Culture and Personality Theory." In Gertrude Dole and Robert Carneiro, eds., *Essays in the Science of Culture in Honor of Leslie A. White*. New York: Thomas Y. Crowell.
Bateson, Gregory
   1971   "The Cybernetics of 'Self': A Theory of Alcoholism." *Psychiatry* 34(1): 1-18.
Berkhofer, Robert
   1973   "Clio and the Culture Concept: Some Impressions of a Changing Relationship in American Historiography." In Louis Schneider and Charles M. Bonjean, eds., *The Idea of Culture in the Social Sciences*. Cambridge: Cambridge University Press.

Bernstein, Richard
    1992   *The New Constellation: The Ethical-Political Horizons of Modernity-Postmodernity.* Cambridge, MA: MIT Press.
Bhaskar, Roy
    1989   *Reclaiming Reality: A Critical Introduction to Contemporary Philosophy.* London: Verso.
Boulding, Kenneth
    1956   *The Image: Knowledge in Life and Society.* Ann Arbor: University of Michigan Press.
Bruner, Jerome S., Jacqueline J. Goodnow, and George A. Austin
    1956   *A Study of Thinking.* New York: John Wiley and Sons.
Campbell, D. T.
    1988   *Methodology and Epistemology for Social Science: Selected Papers.* Chicago, IL: University of Chicago Press.
Carnap, Rudolph
    1956   *The Methodological Character of Theoretical Concepts.* Minneapolis: University of Minnesota Press.
Cole, Michael
    1991   "Conclusion." In Lauren B. Resnick, John M. Levine, and Stephanie D. Teasley, eds., *Perspectives on Socially Shared Cognition.* Washington, DC: American Psychological Association.
Conant, James
    1990   "Introduction." In Hilary Putnam, *Realism with a Human Face.* Cambridge, MA: Harvard University Press.
Cook, Thomas D., and Donald T. Campbell
    1979   *Quasi-Experimentation: Design and Analysis Issues for Field Settings.* Boston, MA: Houghton-Mifflin.
D'Andrade, Roy G.
    1984   "Cultural Meaning Systems." In Richard A. Shweder and Robert A. LeVine, eds., *Culture Theory: Essays on Mind, Self, and Emotion.* Cambridge: Cambridge University Press.
Dobzhansky, Theodosius
    1962   *Mankind Evolving.* New Haven, CT: Yale University Press.
Durkheim, Emile
    1984   *The Division of Labor in Society*, W. D. Halls, trans. 1893. Reprint, New York: Free Press.
Feyerabend, Paul K.
    1981   *Realism, Rationalism, and Scientific Method: Philosophical*

Papers. Vol. 1. Cambridge: Cambridge University Press.

Fodor, Jerry A.
  1980   *The Language of Thought.* Cambridge, MA: Harvard University Press.
  1981   "The Mind-Body Problem." *Scientific American* (January):114-123.

Frazer, Elizabeth, and Nicola Lacey
  1993   *The Politics of Community: A Feminist Critique of the Liberal-Communitarian Debate.* New York: Harvester Wheatsheaf.

Furbee, Louanna, and Robert A. Benfer
  1983   "Cognitive and Geographic Maps: Study of Individual Variation Among Tojolabal Mayans." *American Anthropologist* 85:305-334.

Gardner, Peter M.
  1976   "Birds, Words, and a Requiem for the Omniscient Informant." *American Ethnologist* 3:446-468.

Geertz, Clifford
  1962   "The Growth of Culture and the Evolution of Mind." In J. Scher, ed., *Theories of the Mind.* Glencoe, IL: Free Press.
  1965   "The Impact of the Concept of Culture on the Concept of Man." In John R. Platt, ed., *New Views of Man.* Chicago, IL: University of Chicago Press.
  1973   "Thick Description." In Geertz, *The Interpretation of Cultures.* New York: Basic Books.

Gould, Stephen Jay
  1996   *Full House: The Spread of Excellence from Plato to Darwin.* New York: Crown Publishers.

Hammersley, Martyn
  1992   *What's Wrong with Ethnography? Methodological Explorations.* London: Routledge.

Hannerz, Ulf
  1992   *Cultural Complexity: Studies in the Social Organization of Meaning.* New York: Columbia University Press.

Harris, Marvin
  1964   *The Nature of Cultural Things.* New York: Random House.
  1979   *Cultural Materialism: The Struggle for a Science of Culture.* New York: Random House.

Hawthorn, Geoffrey
  1987   *Enlightenment and Despair: A History of Social Theory.* 2nd edition. Cambridge: Cambridge University Press.

Heider, Eleanor Rosch
  1972   "Probability, Sampling, and Ethnographic Method: The Case of Dani Colour Names." *Man* 7:448-466.
Heider, Karl
  1978   "Accounting for Variation: A Nonformal Analysis of Grand Valley Dani Kinship Terms." *Journal of Anthropological Research* 34:219-261.
Heinrich, Albert W.
  1972   "A Non-European System of Color Classification." *Anthropological Linguistics* 14:220-227.
Hempel, Carl
  1952   "Methods of Concept Formation in Science." *International Encyclopedia of Unified Science* 2, 7. Chicago, IL: University of Chicago Press.
  1956   "A Logical Appraisal of Operationalism." In P. Frank, ed., *The Validation of Scientific Theories*. Boston: Beacon Press.
House, Ernest
  1991   "Realism in Research." *Educational Researcher* 20(6):2-9.
Howard, George S.
  1991   "Culture Tales: A Narrative Approach to Thinking, Cross-Cultural Psychology, and Psychotherapy." *American Psychologist* 46(3):187-197.
Huberman, A. Michael, and Matthew B. Miles
  1985   "Assessing Local Causality in Qualitative Research." In D. N. Berg and K. K. Smith, eds., *Exploring Clinical Methods for Social Research*. Beverly Hills, CA: SAGE Publications.
Hutchins, Edwin
  1995   *Cognition in the Wild*. Cambridge, MA: MIT Press.
Jakobson, Roman
  1956   "Two Aspects of Language and Two Types of Aphasic Disturbance." In Roman Jakobson and Morris Halle, *Fundamentals of Language*. The Hague, Netherlands: Mouton.
Jay, Martin
  1984   *Adorno*. Cambridge, MA: Harvard University Press.
Keesing, Roger
  1974   "Theories of Culture." *Annual Review of Anthropology* 3: 73-97.
Keller, Evelyn Fox
  1983   *A Feeling For the Organism: The Life and Work of Barbara*

McClintock. New York: W. H. Freeman.

Kleinman, Arthur
1986 *Social Origins of Distress and Disease.* New Haven, CT: Yale University Press.

Kroeber, A. L.
1949 "The Concept of Culture in Science." *Journal of General Education* 3:182-196.

Kroeber, A. L., and Talcott Parsons
1958 "The Concepts of Culture and of Social System." *American Sociological Review* 23:582-583.

Lakoff, George
1987 *Women, Fire, and Dangerous Things: What Categories Reveal about the Mind.* Chicago, IL: University of Chicago Press.

Leplin, Jarrett, ed.
1984 *Scientific Realism.* Berkeley: University of California Press.

Levine, George, ed.
1993 *Realism and Representation: Essays on the Problem of Realism in Relation to Science, Literature, and Culture.* Madison: University of Wisconsin Press.

Lewontin, Richard C.
1973 "Darwin and Mendel—The Materialist Revolution." In J. Neyman, ed., *The Heritage of Copernicus: Theories "More Pleasing to the Mind."* Cambridge, MA: MIT Press.
1974 *The Genetic Basis of Evolutionary Change.* New York: Columbia University Press.

Linton, Ralph
1936 *The Study of Man.* New York: Appleton-Century-Crofts.

Manicas, P. T.
1987 *A History and Philosophy of the Social Sciences.* Oxford: Basil Blackwell.

Maxwell, Joseph A.
1978 "The Evolution of Plains Indian Kin Terminologies: A Non-Reflectionist Account." *Plains Anthropologist* 23:13-29.
1992 "Understanding and Validity in Qualitative Research." *Harvard Educational Review* 62:279-300.
1995 "Biology and Social Organization in the Kin Terminology of an Inuit Community." In R. J. DeMallie and A Ortiz, eds., *North American Indian Anthropology: Essays on Culture and Society.* Norman: University of Oklahoma Press.

1996 "Diversity and Methodology in a Changing World." *Pedagogía* 30:32-40.

n.d. "Diversity, Solidarity, and Community" (forthcoming in *Educational Theory*).

Mayr, Ernst
1982 *The Growth of Biological Thought: Diversity, Evolution, and Inheritance.* Cambridge, MA: Harvard University Press.

Moffatt, Michael
1979 "Harijan Religion: Consensus at the Bottom of Caste." *American Ethnologist* 6(1):244-260.

Norris, Stephen P.
1983 "The Inconsistencies at the Foundation of Construct Validation Theory." In Ernest R. House, ed., *Philosophy of Evaluation.* San Francisco: Jossey-Bass.

Parsons, Talcott
1961 "Introduction." In Talcott Parsons et al. *Theories of Society.* New York: Free Press of Glencoe.

1966 *Societies: Evolutionary and Comparative Perspectives.* Englewood Cliffs, NJ: Prentice-Hall.

Pateman, Trevor
1987 *Language in Mind and Language in Society: Studies in Linguistic Reproduction.* Oxford: Clarendon Press.

Pattee, Howard H., ed.
1973 *Hierarchy Theory: The Challenge of Complex Systems.* New York: George Braziller.

Pelto, Pertti, and Gretel Pelto
1975 "Intra-Cultural Diversity: Some Theoretical Issues." *American Ethnologist* 2:1-18.

Perkins, David
1992 *Smart Schools: From Training Memories to Educating Minds.* New York: Free Press.

Phillips, D. C.
1987 *Philosophy, Science, and Social Inquiry: Contemporary Methodological Controversies in Social Science and Related Applied Fields of Research.* Oxford: Pergamon Press.

Poggie, John J., Jr.
1972 "Toward Control in Key Informant Data." *Human Organization* 31:23-30.

Pollnac, Richard B.
1975 "Intra-Cultural Variability in the Structure of the Subjective

Color Lexicon in Buganda." *American Ethnologist* 2:89-109.

Portmann, Adolf
1961   *Animals as Social Beings.* New York: Harper and Row.

Pratt, Mary Louise
1987   "Linguistic Utopias." In Nigel Fabb et al., eds., *The Linguistics of Writing.* Manchester: Manchester University Press.

Putnam, Hilary
1975   "The Meaning of 'Meaning.'" In K. Gunderson, ed., *Language, Mind, and Logic.* Minneapolis: University of Minnesota Press.

1981   *Reason, Truth, and History.* Cambridge: Cambridge University Press.

1987   *The Many Faces of Realism.* La Salle, IL: Open Court Press.

1990   *Realism with a Human Face*, J. Conant, ed. Cambridge, MA: Harvard University Press.

Rappaport, Roy
1967   *Pigs for the Ancestors: Ritual in the Ecology of a New Guinea People.* New Haven, CT: Yale University Press.

1971   "The Sacred in Human Evolution." *Annual Review of Ecology and Systematics* 2:22-44.

Roberts, John M.
1961   "The Zuni." In Florence Kluckhohn and Fred L. Strodtbeck, eds., *Variations in Value Orientations.* Evanston, IL: Row, Peterson.

1964   "The Self-Management of Cultures." In Ward Goodenough, ed., *Explorations in Cultural Anthropology.* New York: McGraw-Hill.

Rorty, Richard
1979   *Philosophy and the Mirror of Nature.* Princeton, NJ: Princeton University Press.

Rosaldo, Renato
1989   *Culture and Truth: The Remaking of Social Analysis.* Boston, MA: Beacon Press.

Rosenau, Pauline Marie
1992   *Post-Modernism and the Social Sciences.* Princeton, NJ: Princeton University Press.

Ryle, Gilbert
1949   *The Concept of Mind.* London: Hutchinson and Co.

Salmon, Wesley C.
  1984 *Scientific Explanation and the Causal Structure of the World*. Princeton, NJ: Princeton University Press.
  1989 "Four Decades of Scientific Explanation." In Philip Kitcher and Wesley C. Salmon, eds., *Scientific Explanation*. Minneapolis: University of Minnesota Press.

Sanjek, Roger
  1977 "Cognitive Maps of the Ethnic Domain in Urban Ghana: Reflections on Variability and Change." *American Ethnologist* 4:603-622.

Sankoff, Gillian
  1971 "Quantitative Aspects of Sharing and Variability in a Cognitive Model." *Ethnology* 10:389-408.
  1972 "Cognitive Variability and New Guinea Social Organization: The Buang Dgwa." *American Anthropologist* 74:555-566.

Saussure, Ferdinand de
  1986 *Course in General Linguistics*. 1916. Reprint, La Salle, IL: Open Court Press.

Sayer, Andrew
  1992 *Method in Social Science: A Realist Approach*. 2nd edition. London: Routledge.

Schmid, Michael
  1992 "The Concept of Culture and Its Place within a Theory of Social Action: A Critique of Talcott Parsons's Theory of Culture." In Richard Münch and Neil J. Smelser, eds., *Theory of Culture*. Berkeley: University of California Press.

Schneider, David M.
  1976 "Notes Toward a Theory of Culture." In Keith H. Basso and Henry A. Selby, eds., *Meaning in Anthropology*. Albuquerque: University of New Mexico Press.
  1980 *American Kinship: A Cultural Account*. 2nd edition. Englewood Cliffs, NJ: Prentice-Hall.
  1984 *A Critique of the Study of Kinship*. Ann Arbor: University of Michigan Press.

Secord, Paul
  1986 "Explanation in the Social Sciences and in Life Situations." In Donald W. Fiske and Richard A. Shweder, eds., *Metatheory in Social Science: Pluralisms and Subjectivities*. Chicago, IL: University of Chicago Press.

Sheldon, Richard C.
   1951   "Some Observations on Theory and Social Science." In Tal-
          cott Parsons and Edward Shils, eds., *Toward a General
          Theory of Action*. New York: Harper and Row.
Shweder, Richard A.
   1991   *Thinking Through Cultures: Expeditions in Cultural Psy-
          chology*. Cambridge, MA: Harvard University Press.
Shweder, Richard A., and Edmund J. Bourne
   1984   "Does the Concept of the Person Vary Cross-Culturally?"
          In Richard A. Shweder and Robert A. LeVine, eds., *Cul-
          ture Theory: Essays on Mind, Self, and Emotion*. Cam-
          bridge: Cambridge University Press.
Simon, Herbert A.
   1969   *The Sciences of the Artificial*. Cambridge, MA: MIT Press.
Slotkin, J. S.
   1952   "Menomini Peyotism: A Study of Individual Variation in a
          Primary Group with a Homogeneous Culture." *Transactions
          of the American Philosophical Society* 42(4).
Smelser, Neil J.
   1992   "Culture: Coherent or Incoherent." In Richard Münch and
          Neil J. Smelser, eds., *Theory of Culture*. Berkeley: Univer-
          sity of California Press.
Strawson, Galen
   1989   *The Secret Connexion: Causation, Realism, and David
          Hume*. Oxford: Oxford University Press.
Suppe, Frederick
   1977   "Afterword." In Frederick Suppe, ed., *The Structure of
          Scientific Theories*. 2nd edition. Urbana: University of
          Illinois Press.
Swartz, Marc J.
   1982   "Cultural Sharing and Cultural Theory: Some Findings of a
          Five-Society Study." *American Anthropologist* 84:314-338.
Tinbergen, Niko
   1961   *The Herring Gull's World*. New York: Basic Books.
Toulmin, Stephen
   1972   *Human Understanding: The Collective Use and Evolution of
          Concepts*. Princeton, NJ: Princeton University Press.
von Bertalanffy, Ludwig
   1968   *General System Theory*. New York: George Braziller.
Wallace, Anthony F. C.
   1970   *Culture and Personality*. New York: Random House.

Werner, Oswald, and G. Mark Schoepfle
  1987   *Systematic Fieldwork: Foundations of Ethnography and Interviewing*. Vol. 1. Newbury Park, CA: SAGE Publications.
Witherspoon, Gary
  1975   *Navajo Kinship and Marriage*. Chicago, IL: University of Chicago Press.
Wolf, Margery
  1992   *A Thrice-Told Tale: Feminism, Postmodernism, and Ethnographic Responsibility*. Stanford, CA: Stanford University Press.
Yanagisako, Sylvia
  1975   "Two Processes of Change in Japanese-American Kinship." *Journal of Anthropological Research* 31:196-223.
  1978   "Introduction to Special Section: 'American Kinship.'" *American Ethnologist* 5:1-29.
Young, Iris Marion
  1990   "The Ideal of Community and the Politics of Difference." In Linda J. Nicholson, ed., *Feminism/Postmodernism*. New York: Routledge.

IMMANENT HOLISM:
ON TRANSFER OF KNOWLEDGE
FROM GLOBAL TO LOCAL

Peter Harries-Jones

In a long disciplinary tradition espousing both the holism of cultures and the unities of historical experience, many anthropologists, quite surprisingly, have taken an ideological stance against notions of totality and unity in ecology. Since the 1960s, Friedman and others writing in the Marxist tradition have rejected the holism of an ecosystem approach. Gregory Bateson, of whom I will speak further below, and Roy Rappaport were particular targets. Both were criticized for their uses of cybernetic models for what Friedman regarded as Bateson's fanciful "pan-Hegelian" spiritualism (Friedman 1974, 1979). Non-Marxists, such as Roy Ellen, agreed that the ecosystem approach was well meaning but was tied to a salvationary epistemology that found support and moral legitimation in the spread of political ecological movements. This combination of anthropology, ecology and politics was full of polemic and pretension, he stated. Anthropologists espousing it gave the impression that holistic understanding would lead to epistemological nirvana; but careful reading reveals that their rhetoric soon dissolves into a messy functionalism (Ellen 1982:92-93).[1]

Thinking about the unity and totality of ecosystems, especially how totality sustains its own organization, is a difficult task. Until the 1950s, ecological anthropology was dominated by the view that environmental factors determine cultural characteristics. An unrefined Darwinism was the inspiration for this approach. In the early 1960s, Julian Steward focused on the process of resource utilization, how this process depicted material features of given environments and how processes of interaction between culture and environment were cognized by a cultural group. The cultural generalities that Steward depicted drew criticism from those in touch with the environmentalism of that era (Vayda and Rappaport 1968). Both authors pushed the study of cultural ecology towards the analysis of units more definite than the somewhat arbitrary boundaries of "culture" that Steward had used. They began to integrate political economy and demography into this frame of reference and from there moved towards a systematic understanding of interaction between humans and environment. Rappaport, in particular, utilized a cybernetic model, demonstrating how feedback loops linked population to biological units within ecosystems. He argued that cultural institutions act as control mechanisms regulating the intake of nutrients and maintaining overall "self-regulation" between human units and natural resources (Rappaport 1990).

This initial brush of anthropology with an epistemology of cybernetic holism in the late 1960s had reverse effects. Instead of promoting anthropological case-studies informed by an ecosystemic and cybernetic epistemology, the discipline generally accepted the view of the critics of the ecosystem approach. The subject matter of the interrelation between culture and ecology became invaded in the 1970s by economic formalism and methodological individualism. The approach stressed how individuals within small-scale cultures transacted with each other for natural resources, the aggregate of individual transactions supposedly constituting a set of cultural strategies for resource utilization. Postmodernist ideas followed on this trail of transactionalism, and as postmodernism emerged in the 1980s, so the whole notion of "environment" as an important aspect of cultural strategies began to recede. The anthropological task of relating social relations to their ecological surround, an interactional framework of inquiry, became replaced by studies of the cultural constructions of individuals in a variety of small-scale environments.

According to the constructivists, all reality is learned through meanings derived from participation in human society. Descriptions of culture based on a constructivist model make little or no reference to anything outside themselves and their processes of cultural construction. Constructivists, like the Marxists before them, ignore the possible existence of a biological world devoid of cultural construction. Thus they deny any role for the environment itself, and are unsympathetic to any ecocentric perspective (Milton 1996:52). Postmodern constructivists reduce an understanding of how we, as both biological and social beings, produce and reproduce ourselves, or how we are transformed by use of natural resources into the kinds of social beings who seek to maintain access to our own habitats, that is, to familiar types of resources in a particular ecological setting. In its most extreme form, postmodernists negate the possibility of any study of how people relate to their physical and social surroundings (Moran 1990, 1996:532-533). In the face of such extreme examples of constructivism, the prospects for ecological anthropology collapse.

With hindsight it is evident that the initial thrust of the cybernetic paradigm as an explanatory principle for understanding ecosystems was inadequate because its interpretative melange of ideas centered on the small-scale and the local. Nevertheless, issues of scale were ignored by the discipline in favor of leaving the cybernetic paradigm alone, regarding it as fascinating, but largely unusable. So it is no wonder that anthropology gave a very cool reception to a major totalizing ecological hypothesis, the Gaia hypothesis, put forward by James Lovelock in the late seventies (Lovelock 1979). The Gaia hypothesis states that living organisms, including human beings, maintain the biosphere in a condition able to sustain life; thus the biosphere, both in its biotic and abiotic elements, is an integrated whole, a complex living system. In the late 1970s caution was advisable, since Gaia was, in Lovelock's original formula, presented as a "superorganism" that can look after its own interests with or without humanity. This notion was considerably revised in *The Ages of Gaia* (Lovelock 1988). By 1993, it could be said that Gaia in its revised form—stating that the planet behaves like an integrated living system—had reached the status of a working proposition throughout the whole environmental field, and was supported by major agencies in the scientific world and in the United Nations' Environmental Program. Yet even the more sympathetic anthropologists, like Milton, still argue that the implications of Gaia for anthropology are not clear. Milton cites a mixed response to Lovelock's propositions among both environmentalists and natural scientists as a reason for caution in accepting them, and contends that since the hypothesis does not develop a discourse on where power is located in human-environment relations, therefore Gaia does not suggest what humanity can do (Milton 1996:132, 133).[2] However, I shall argue below that an overall understanding of the biosphere as cybernetic system, and the consequences of its "immanent holism," is Bateson's legacy to anthropology.

The Importance of the Kyoto Conference

The 1997 global conference on climate change in Kyoto, Japan, is a marker for our discipline in relation to the Gaia hypothesis. Though many political and economic issues brought to the conference table remained unresolved, considered as an exercise in ecological epistemology, Kyoto was a far greater success. For the first time ecology, as epistemology, emerged on the international scene. Ecological epistemology had convinced world leaders that human activity is a major factor in transforming nature and that natural resources are indeed finite.

Kyoto could not be said to have provided a clear break with the economics of growth, or with neo-liberal politics that have supported growth, or with a socio-political philosophy of developmentalism that has dominated the thinking in social science for the last century. Yet some of the prevailing assumptions of neo-liberal economists, especially that natural resources are a given and can be made subject to infinite transformation through technology, no longer hold as well as before the conference began. Kyoto established that global pollution, waste, and the degradation of water, forests and maritime resources, are no longer figments of an environmental ideology, but are a compelling part of international economics and politics. They have real costs, not only registered in global market values but to human life (*Guardian Weekly* 1997b:13).

The Kyoto conference also established the ecological proposition that human life depends upon a life-support system drawn from nature and that this life-support system, "nature" to use a substantive term, is best represented as a set of dynamic processes in a type of homeostasis. Such processes embrace both biotic and non-biotic elements in interaction with one another. They are self-regulating or self-maintaining. In other words, the Gaia hypothesis—perhaps not in the same terms as James Lovelock originally proposed it—has entered into global politics: the biosphere approximates a natural homeostatic or cybernetic system which is affected by human activity.

The Kyoto conference was replete with its own metaphors of immanent holism, one of which was the evident presence during the pre-conference events of the most severe El Niño effect on record. The phenomenon of El Niño, though primarily driven by the physical factors of the interaction between ocean current and weather pattern—abiotic factors—also responds to human activity, namely anthropogenic warming of ocean-atmosphere interaction. El Niño is a good metaphor for depicting a change of setting in a global cybernetic thermostat in Gaia-like manner. Another metaphor was the smog drifting backwards and forwards across six southeast Asian countries just prior to the Kyoto meetings. The smog arose from forest fires burning in Indonesia. The smog affected more than 70 million people and some 100,000 people across Southeast Asia sought medical help for respir-atory problems. Vast portions of Indonesia literally went up in smoke, perhaps as much as 1.7 million hectares of forests and other land were affected by the fires.

The natural circumstances contributing to the severity of the fires was a drought in the first quarter of 1997 propelled forward by a monsoon that would not come. The fires were started deliberately as part of the current Indonesian practice of clearing land to prepare a multitude of plantations. The major reason for the fires spiralling out of control was a weakened ecology. Having cut down almost 50 million hectares of forest in the past twenty-five years to sell timber cheaply to Japan, Indonesia is now "industrializing" the degraded clear-cut land as rapidly as possible.[3] When land cleared of forest is laid bare for conversion into large plantations for pulp and paper, or palm oil and rice, this weakens the natural ability of the forests to rebound. The World Wildlife Fund (WWF) noted that the 1997 fires occurred on top of the chronic deterioration of the forest ecosystems which has been going on year after year in Indonesia. The fires started in palm-oil or timber plantations, spread into peatlands, where the fires could not be contained, and from peatlands into primary forest. WWF called the fires a "global catastrophe" whose longer term effects are unknown. If there is another drought in the next years, a distinct possibility according to WWF, the fires will be far worse (*Guardian Weekly* 1997a:30-31).

After three hundred years of successful industrial strategies through which human activity was to a large extent uncoupled from the physical constraints of its production—at least in the Western world—humanity now has to confront all possibilities of constraints on its own activity in a total or global context. I would describe the Southeast Asian smog as a metaphor for "Nature's Veto" (Harries-Jones, Rotstein, and Timmerman 1992; Timmerman 1996:222-223). To my own way of thinking, Nature's Veto evokes a "real" global holism, a holism which is "meta-" to local environments, yet, at the same time, requires detailed analysis in local cultural contexts in order to understand the complexities of interaction. One of the original slogans of the environmental movement was "Think globally, act locally," but a revised slogan, especially in the light of events in and around the time of Kyoto, would stress that it is necessary to *think and act* both at the global level and at the local level at the same time.

In effect, issues of scale, time, space and ideas, are crucial both to ecological understanding and political resistance to environmental degradation. As Moran (1990) so cogently argues, the human dilemma requires a careful study of both cultural constructions and physically observable realities if we are to understand if our own cultural knowledge is out-of-phase with current physical environmental conditions. To which I would add that the implications of out-of-phase knowledge between culture and environment is magnified in situations where the interaction of the biological and the social, the genetic and the cultural attitudes towards natural resources are treated as separate sub-disciplines as it often is the case in anthropology. Ingold is also adamant in this respect: "Far from reproducing, in our writing, the ossified separation of humanity and nature, we should thus be leading the way in showing how it is possible, in thought and practice, to move beyond it" (Ingold 1992:693-698). A manifestation like the loss of biodiversity is consequential for global ecology. It is at once genetic and ecosystemic and combines with normative issues of human rights and conflict resolution at local levels. However paradoxical the notion of thinking and acting at both local and global levels may seem at first sight, the paradox is an essential challenge for the twenty-first century (Karliner 1997:199).

The Transfer of Knowledge and "Affirmative Theory"

The postmodern penchant for radical relativism has encouraged progressive diminution of the normative and the social and has increased the distance of anthropologists of the developing world from the inner circle of practicing social scientists in western Europe and the United States. Karim, for example, argues that while the field of theoretical anthropology in the West may be enriched by every new discourse it adopts, the people of the world from which anthropologists have traditionally drawn their theoretical understanding have gained little from such new theoretical discourse. Western theory is failing to take up themes that most concern anthropologists of the South, the "real" in which the South lives. In Karim's view that reality is a powerful combination of Western economics plus military strategy, which creates a constellation of events in time and space perpetuating violence, greed and transnational tragedy (Karim 1996, see also Harries-Jones 1996a). Anthropology not only seems unwilling to undertake a critique of this set of conditions, but most Western anthropologists seem totally unconcerned with the shape that dominant forms of Western knowledge take in an international context.

Karim argues that the general dynamics of global power criss-crosses the lines of least resistance and are selective. One can easily predict who its victims are—indigenous minorities rather than majority populations, women and children rather than men, the elderly rather than youth, workers rather than producers, destitute states rather than the wealthy. Thus anthropology ought to be aligned with some form of "affirmative theory," which recognizes these global conditions and is responsive to them. Affirmative theory, as its name suggests, is oriented towards action and its very orientation makes the transfer of social knowledge from the West to the South much more significant and palatable for the "locals" in the South.

In a minimal sense, an affirmative stance confirms and assents to a set of propositions—about social equity or social equality—and refuses to support and/or implement an alternative or contrary set. The concept, with its implication for action, implies rejection of inaction. Anthro-pology has to learn to back away from serving the elite communities that it currently socializes with its knowledge. It must learn to demystify itself theoretically, Karim says. In addition, anthropology must refute the argument of those popular actors who continue to make use of the combination of ethnocentrism and materialism in order to create their own versions of racism. And it must consider why some forms of ethnocentric violence are condoned by the West while other forms are marginalized as "evil." The next step is more complicated. The secular language of affirmation and confirmation of human rights and other similar issues is commonplace in social movements operating in nations of the South but is entirely absent from anthropology, she observes. In order to change its focus, anthropological research must be undertaken in the light of a close relation between that which the discipline takes as the subject matter for research and the forms of activity typical of social movements.

As a "local," Karim is not entirely opposed to the whole of post-modern discourse. Her third point concords to some extent with the emergence of anthropology as "cultural critique" (Marcus and Fisher 1986). Typically, postmodernist discourse takes the cultural production of sign systems as the central, if not the exclusive, arena of its struggle. For postmodernists, both writer and reader live face-to-face with a sign producing system and its technical amplification, and, postmodernists argue, the operations of this sign producing system must be confronted—especially wherever and whenever the significant text promotes itself as an "objective" account or production. So Karim agrees that anthropology should not continue as a social science whose primary aim is to give an objective account of the ethnographic other. Rather Karim spells out the limitations of opportunistic choice of research questions in anthropology tailored to the production of texts for self-serving academic ends, which a postmodernist perspective so readily promotes. Above all, Karim states, the discipline should give some relief to the native world from which it draws—if only by lessening the shame of poverty, extinction and genocide which are the recurrent features of the societies of the South. Social movements are collectivist in orientation. By contrast, postmodern "hyperreality" enjoins us henceforth to abandon any thought of solidarity based on communal perceptions and interests.[4]

Karim makes her plea for an affirmative theory in terms of human rights and peace, but the same pattern holds with cases of ecological destruction, as holds for any other human rights and/or peace issue. A recent collection of case studies points out that large development projects in the South transfer the loci of power over resource value, access, use and control from resident peoples to external power structures (Johnston 1997). There are few or no opportunities for resident peoples to assess or, more importantly, decide whether the development of resources is, in itself, an appropriate path to take. Once the transfer of power and authority takes place, redirecting the products from household subsistence and regional markets to national and transnational global markets, the meaning and value of resources critical to a traditional way of life become re-defined. This brings in its train a marginalization of various groups attached to a more traditional lifestyle. Human rights and environmental crisis thus become "inextricably linked" (Johnston 1997:19).

The Place of Gregory Bateson in Ecological Science

Wherever issues of ecology are present it is difficult to discuss ecological issues without invoking scientific criteria. For much of the world, especially the South, the notion of environment is defined, assessed and articulated by a Western-dominated science in its most positivistic mode. Western science defines a vision of nature through which natural resources are re-configured as human property, and then are "developed" as human property. The Western scientific vision is rigorously applied in the major developmental projects, down to its deeply functionalist rationale. Thus, biologists might report upon the dangers of pollution, environmental engineers might report upon prudent technological restrictions in the development project, and economists might warn about the need for assessing short-term benefits against longer term management strategies. But their briefs and their regulatory powers are almost always limited and few of them are in a position to undertake a proper holistic examination of habitat integrity (Johnston 1997:17-18).

The first step for anthropology is to be "affirmative" against such functionalism in environmental appraisal as it has so often been in relation to functionalism in sociocultural studies. This brings me back to the issues of ecological holism and the place of Gregory Bateson in linking anthropology to something like a Gaian model of the biosphere. For Bateson the ideas that humans have about ecological systems are such a part of those systems that good thinking about ecology must itself be ecologically sound. The models for such thinking lie in cybernetics. The period immediately after World War II brought the inauguration of a new science, that of cybernetics. Steven Heims, a science historian, identifies Bateson as one of the four synthesizers of cybernetic thinking (the others being Norbert Weiner, Filmer Northrop and John Stroud). According to Heims, Bateson's contribution was to take "the concepts of cybernetics and make them serviceable, first for the social sciences, and later as part of a practical epistemology useful outside of social science" (Heims 1991:249-250). Specifically, Bateson proposed that since cybernetics had brought reticulate causal systems and their properties of self-correction and oscillation to full scientific attention for the first time, then it is legitimate to construct hypotheses around the notion that social and biological systems are in fact circular or reticulate.

To Bateson, cybernetics offered the fundamentals to replace outmoded concepts both of human purpose and of evolution. It also offered a whole new approach to and understanding of coding, particularly in assessing the probable interrelationship of codes of communication in both human and animal populations and in developing alternative approaches to the predominant conceptualization of biological order. At first, Bateson reformulated the cybernetics of the late 1940s in order to make them available to social scientists in general and to psychiatrists and family therapists in particular.

Within anthropology, Bateson is readily recognized as part of that brilliant generation of fieldworkers who followed in the immediate footsteps of Malinowski, Boas and Radcliffe-Brown. Outside anthropolology, Bateson is best known for his twenty years in the field of clinical psychology, most of them in the Veteran's Administration hospital in Palo Alto. Bateson and his research team took the lead in transforming the predominant conceptualization of the therapeutic encounter. They re-defined the task of therapists from dealing with individual clients on a one-to-one basis to dealing with clients within the surround of the family as a whole. In addition, therapists were to include themselves as active participants of the therapeutic process. Within this larger system of client, family, and therapist lay a complex array of interpersonal communications and feedback.

The Palo Alto group recognized that presence of feedback loops was by no means random in communicative order; indeed the structure of feedback could be used by the therapist to present to family members as a map of their patterns of interaction and could be used to break or to alter pathologies in communication. During this time Bateson and his team evolved the well-known hypothesis of the "double bind," and in so doing gave currency to a new phrase in the English language. Subsequently, the Palo Alto approach to treating the family rather than the individual as the unit to which therapy should apply has proved extraordinarily popular.

But Bateson did not stop at this major theoretical advance in social constructivist thinking. From the mid-1960s, he turned his attention back to the subject matter of "ecology"—specifically developing how his themes of an "ecology of mind" might be linked, on the one hand, with evolutionary theory and, on the other, with an emerging debate about the degradation of the environment. Thus, in his major work, *Mind and Nature* (Bateson 1979), published a year before his death, he built upon an analogy between cultural aspects of learning and evolutionary adaptation. His book is a *tour de force* in that he finds a holistic framework within which the features of human understanding can be satisfactorily compared with intelligence in nature. The analogies he draws between learning and evolution, elaborate a common ground, especially in pointing out that mind (observation) and evolution (adaptation) can be considered in a recursive framework of inquiry as two sides of the same coin. In *Angels Fear* (Bateson and Bateson 1987), published posthumously, he once more goes over the validation for his approach, beyond the dualism prevalent in Western scientific thinking, and towards a monism. His "ecology of mind" proposes that there is a necessary unity of organism in environment, an "immanent holism." He argues that faulty epistemological premises tear the representation of systemic unity apart, and so mask our understanding of it.

Immanent Holism

Specifically, Bateson denies that biomass and bioenergy should be the fundamental focus of ecological investigation. This focus on bioenergy in mainstream ecology was, in his view, a remnant of nineteenth-century materialist and industrial thinking. To most ecologists, nature is all about biomass, primary production, current of energy, nutrient cycles and biotopes. As a science, ecology remains true to its dualist tradition, separating mind and meaning from material substance—giving predominant attention to the latter; ecologists remain preoccupied with the purely physicochemical interplay of animals and plants and with the impact of human activity upon these.

Bateson's position is that while living organisms require positive energy budgets to survive, the primary issues of ecological degradation are those of breakdown in ecological organization, and ecological organization is not well represented in terms of energy physics. All living systems generate their own internal energy and living organisms go to great length to ensure that their metabolism does not respond in billiard ball fashion to direct increases or decreases of energy. Bateson proposes that ecological organization corresponds more to the characteristics of a communicative order rather than to the quantum bits or waves of energy physics. Here the feedback characteristics of ecological order become the structure upon which an investigation of ecological degradation can be mapped.

Bateson evokes recursiveness between organism and environment, a process in which each in some way mutually specifies the other. Instead of dealing with the statistical relations which occur between gene and environment, Bateson examines how an organism is coupled with environment, as a unity. Recursion is associated with feedback loops. Feedback is normally associated with a system that can be decomposed into inputs and outputs. The feedback is a "feeding back," a transform of output into the input. Under appropriate conditions the recursion settles down into a steady but oscillating form of interaction.

The concept of recursion stresses all aspects of non-linear organizational coupling of humanity with environment. Because of this, Bateson shares some of the same assumptions as chaos theorists. Bateson died in 1980. Gleick's book on chaos appeared in 1987, so any remarks relating Bateson to chaos theory will necessarily be incomplete. Nevertheless, Bateson commented on chaos theory, and Gleick's book (1987) has one reference to Bateson. Bateson's brief comment was that if fractal geometry were to become the standard reference in chaos theory, then the interest in chaotic patterning might well give rise to a new determinism which had little reliability for social or biological systems. Interpreting his remarks, we may note that all evolution eventually overcomes the habituation of recursive self-similarity. Fractal geometry, on the other hand, presents its models of recursion without an underlying theory of how its change occurs through such self-similarity in patterning. Recursion is often interpreted as a form reentering itself; this is true of fractal geometry, where a recursive iteration as a complex plane in a crystal is mapped onto itself across a hierarchy of scales. Here recursion is treated as a quality of self-similarity, and self-similarity is conceived in turn as a sort of generalized symmetry. But all non-linear patterns in the biological world change, Bateson said, and they evolve from the ways in which form continually re-enters itself. The iterated re-entry of a complex plane of a crystal, as in fractal geometry, was, therefore, a bad metaphor for recursion of biological forms.

There are clear normative themes in Bateson's writing. For Gregory Bateson, as for his father, the issues of evolution and of Darwinism were normative issues. Gregory Bateson regarded Darwinism as a philosophy of fear wedded to mistaken notions of materialism in biological science. The metaphors in Darwinism to which Bateson objected are those of competition and struggle, "progress" (though Darwin himself was ambiguous in attaching this particular metaphor to his own discussion of evolution), and "doing better" through adaptation. Bateson also objected to the preeminence given to a "genocentric landscape" in neo-Darwinism because such a view promoted an instrumental view of the living world, a view which believed that the gene could be mastered by science as if the gene were a "bag of tricks" whose applications could be discovered and controlled. Bateson wished to replace the epistemology on which Darwinism had been constructed by one of "immanent holism."

From this standpoint Bateson attacks the whole culture of control in Western science and presses for its transformation. The object of method in industrial science seemed always to be connected with external control of the territory it surveyed. In social and biological situations this was an impossibility, Bateson believed. Not only was a mental mapping (observation) always more abstract than the features of the territory that it maps, but the product of any mapping always rebounds on the map maker. Science's obsession with quantitative measurement of its objects occluded understanding of the recursive nature of that which it did observe. Quantitative measurement tended to gnore corresponding ambiguities, dilemmas and paradoxes such recursions bring about. Human beings, like other living forms, must content themselves with ambiguity and paradox in the situations in which they find themselves, whether social or ecological, even though perversities inevitably arise. Instead of trying to ban dilemmas and paradox, science should evolve ways of handling the inevitabilities of its occurrence (Harries-Jones 1995:248-249).

A New Semiosis: Biosemiotics

Today Bateson does not find himself alone as he once did on the issues of "immanent holism," nor on its relevance to the micro-world of biology as well as to the macro-world of Gaia. Bateson's epistemological holism embraced both micro and macro dimensions as a monistic "ecology of mind." Within theoretical biology there are some who would now provide a supportive view. They, too, believe that the major problem haunting theoretical biology continues to be the extraordinary influence of the laws of physics on biological explanation. They believe these laws are too limiting to encompass the investigation of the phenomena of life, and they are beginning to sketch a holistic science, a science quite different from that to which eco-feminists have such strong objections (Merchant 1992).[5]

For these theoretical biologists, the study of living systems can no longer be reduced to single-level numerical calculations, nor can biological interaction be explained solely in terms which derive from the "objectivity" of experimentally controlled conditions. This includes experimental controls on DNA within molecules. They note that the context-dependency of living systems, and their multi-level expression, require alternative descriptions. Human beings, in particular, are necessary participants in description of biological order. Given this condition: "there are many ways of describing the same thing (i.e. art, poetry, music) and each description presupposes a set of rules or constraints. Reality has innumerable descriptions" (Pattee 1995:149).

It is among such theoretical biologists that, more recently, the notion of biosemiotics has emerged. Hoffmeyer, drawing on Bateson, argues that every life-form exists both as itself, i.e. an organism of "flesh and blood," and a coded description of itself, the latter being lodged in DNA within molecules, of which the genetic material is composed. Yet what is alive, the organism, is different from what survives, the genetic material. The genetic material, that which is passed on to the next generation, is in fact a code for something else, an image of the subject, and not the subject itself. It is the coded version that survives. From this perspective, "life is survival in coded form" rather than life being the aggregated existence of multiple organisms of flesh and blood and proteins (Hoffmeyer 1996:16).

Hoffmeyer, without arguing against the evident, that DNA is a source of genetic instructions, shows that organic coding is decentralized throughout any organism, and that organic coding is present not only at the molecular level but also at both tissue and cell levels, where tissues and cells interpret their own environment and act accordingly (Hoffmeyer, 1996:94). Because of the ubiquity of organic coding throughout any organism, Hoffmeyer concludes that "bodily life" is, in addition to the ongoing molecular processes of protein formation, a network of coding processes—in effect, a network of sign processes bound into each other and into their environments. Beyond this, Hoffmeyer argues that the sign, not the molecule, is the crucial underlying factor in life. More radically, he proposes that biology be considered primarily in semiotic terms rather than primarily as a manifestation of biochemical reactions constituting protein formation. There is, in fact, a semiosphere which like the biosphere incorporates all forms of communication: sound, smell, movement, color, shape, touch, as well as electrical fields, thermal radiation, chemical signals, and waves of all kinds. Every organism is tossed into this semiosphere, to which it must adapt correctly if it is to survive (Hoffmeyer 1996:vii).

Conclusion: Immanent Holism and Affirmative Theory

This chapter has ranged over a number of questions about the transfer of knowledge, on the one hand discussing transfer of anthropological knowledge from the center to the South, and on the other the way in which anthropological issues of culture at the local level have entered into the discussion of ecology. It seeks to conjoin this transfer of knowledge so that we may approach the notion of thinking and acting on issues of ecological degradation at both local and global levels at the same time. The primary call in this chapter is for recognition of a holistic epistemology as the framework for anthropological research on ecological issues, and the resuscitation of an ecosystemic framework, this time on a global scale. The chapter argues that a holistic epistemology should not be passive, introspective and transcendental; rather, it should be enactive. The active nature of the epistemology should recognize an inextricable linkage between ecological issues, economics and local questions of social justice in the South. It should also recognize that the links between environment and social justice are reciprocal and move in both directions. Thus lack of explicit guarantees of human rights in many nation-states, as in the case of Indonesia, accelerates environmental degradation because local populations have no means to resist development programs promoting destruction of their habitat without great risk to their own lives (Aaragon 1997).

This reciprocal linkage is certainly recognized by environmental movements and there is little reason for anthropologists researching these situations to avoid an affirmative stance. Not only does an affirmative stance make scientific sense, but it is in the discipline's own interest to recognize the role of the West in instituting degradation of ecology. While the West is not alone in instituting degradation, an open expression of the concerns of the South makes anthropological knowledge, when transferred from Western centers of knowledge to "locals" of the South, much more palatable.

At a practical level, anthropologists, like environmental NGOs, should undertake a critique of sustainable development whenever and wherever they are convinced that sustainable development is merely a convenient rationale for governments or transnational corporations pursuing a path of ecological destruction. Wolfgang Sachs has argued that far from enshrining an environmental approach to global order, the 1992 Earth Summit in Rio introduced a global technocratic approach to environmental issues that "inaugurated environmentalism as the highest state of developmentalism" (Sachs 1993:3).

As Johnston states, the science that is used in environmental matters is open to variation. And scientific orientations always implicate economic and social justice orientations, whether acknowledged or not. The first consequence of a holistic scientific framework is acceptance of something like a Gaia hypothesis. Anthropologists should press the need for a holistic appraisal of habitat integrity and present the dangers of a refusal to make such a holistic appraisal. The counterpart of an affirmative stance is to give full support in Western academe to a scientific framework of inquiry which once again stresses holism over positivism. We should recall that when Lyotard raised his battlecry of the postmodern, "Let us wage war on totality," he referred to those modernist totalities which—through a culture of excess—have oppressed modern ethics and have demeaned its aesthetics. The notion of eco-systems, of the "totalities" of ecology, was far from his mind.

Finally, this chapter has argued that a holistic epistemology has far-reaching consequences for the discipline's attitude towards the interrelation of culture and nature. Both Bateson and Hoffmeyer propose that all organisms live first and foremost in a world of communication and signification. At the macro level, Bateson argues that communicative organization in the biosphere is primary and of greater importance under conditions of ecological breakdown to the positive energy budgets characteristic of living organisms. Both authors try to remove ecological science from rigid materialism or its opposite, transcendental holism, towards an interpretation of ecological order in another dimension, that of immanent holism. They include genetics in their reinterpretation.

Mainstream biological science argues that the genetic properties of organisms are a sort of material template for life. In contrast, Bateson argues that biology should rid itself of its mechanistic bias and begin to examine the field of relations which the gene proposed. DNA is not in and of itself self-replicating; it is the organism in an environmental field that is self-replicating. As indicated above, Bateson has received strong support for his position in recent years. The DNA of an organism cannot reproduce that organism without that DNA being placed first in an appropriate context or the setting of a dividing cell among dividing cells (Goodwin 1994; Hoffmeyer 1996). Self-description is the fundamental feature of living organisms and description of self-description, together with what rules may be derived from this biological phenomenon of recursiveness, should be the focus of biological and ecological inquiry.

Hoffmeyer's notion of semiosphere removes an irremedial dualism which for too long has separated the materialism of nature from the ideation of culture and made their interrelationship difficult to comprehend except as the dominance of one over the other. The semiosphere provides a conceptual "home" for understanding their interrelationship. At a teaching level, such a recursive framework is rarely, if ever, found in physical anthropology textbooks and is certainly avoided in sociocultural texts. Yet, as one moves towards a wider system of semiosis, a biosemiotics embracing both nature and culture, any semiotics considered from an entirely cultural perspective begins to seem parochial.

An affirmative theory replete with the epistemological approach of "immanent holism" is oriented towards action. It will, in its praxis, refocus runaway cultural relativism, haphazard choice of case studies, and the rampant individualism of postmodernist approaches in anthropology towards a more coherent stream of thinking. An affirmative theory would change a persistent trend which has disembedded the subject matter of anthropology from the interests of the South. The hope for such an affirmative theory would be to move anthropology away from the margins of environmental discourse, where it is currently situated (Milton 1996:24-36).

Notes

1. Neither authors have substantially changed their position. Ellen still criticizes Rappaport for displaying a number of "technical and conceptual shortcomings," among them a "theoretical naivete" in his use of the cybernetic analogue "which underestimated the difficulties of defining [eco]system boundaries" instead of providing "more scientific explanation of their interrelations" (Ellen and Fukui 1996:597). Friedman still objects to any framework of totality on the grounds that ecological paradigms have political relevance (Friedman 1996).

2. Acknowledgment by natural scientists of Lovelock's propositions is carefully documented in Joseph (1990).

3. In many parts of Indonesia, particularly the outlying islands, it pays to burn the land. One view of the Indonesian forest fires, therefore, is that the smog signified prosperity and life. In this view, a "developmental" one, industrializing the land has resulted in average wages rising in Indonesia from less than US$90 in 1970 to US$1,000 today. But as there are significant differences between the central towns of Indonesia and its outer islands in terms of the rewards that development has brought, there are also very different social consequences for the outer islanders who have been marginalized (see Aaragon 1997).

4. Attention to style is important for the effectiveness of resistance to dominant images flowing from the mainstream media. "Environmentalism" has been subjected to a sophisticated public relations exercise by transnational corporations in their effort to change the way that politicians and academics think about environmental issues. Using public relations firms, favored academic think-tanks, marketing campaigns and educational promotion through the mass media, the transnational corporations have attempted to control understanding of environmental concerns and support, instead, untrammeled use of their own products (Karliner 1997:168-196). On the other hand, the sup-

position that style alone, that is fabulation and collage, magically release postmodernists from the entrapments of their own representationalism, is highly questionable (Wasson 1988:93). When the dialectics of resistance privileges sign production of the "virtual" over the "real," this limits the range of its own discourse.

5. I recognize that an appeal to a reformed science may not satisfy the eco-feminists, who have noted quite correctly that science is not only a set of propositions about the world but is also a series of interrelated social networks whose members offer mutual support in their approval of projects and approaches, and that these social networks are mainly male. Nevertheless, theoretical biology's agreement with the elimination of Carolyn Merchant's five assumptions underlying male-dominated science (Merchant 1992:49) must evidently mark the beginnings of a transformed science.

References

Aaragon, Lorraine V.
  1997   "Distant Processes: The Global Economy and Outer Island
          Development in Indonesia." In Barbara R. Johnston, ed.,
          *Life and Death Matters: Human Rights and the Environment
          at the End of the Millennium.* Walnut Creek, CA: Altamira
          Press.
Bateson, Gregory
  1979   *Mind and Nature: A Necessary Unity.* New York: E. P.
          Dutton.
Bateson, Gregory, and Mary Catherine Bateson
  1987   *Angels Fear: Towards an Epistemology of the Sacred.* New
          York: Macmillan.
Ellen, Roy
  1982   *Environment, Subsistence and System: The Ecology of
          Small-Scale Formations.* Cambridge: Cambridge University
          Press.
Ellen, Roy, and Katsuyoshi Fukui, eds.
  1996   *Redefining Nature: Ecology, Culture and Domestication.*
          Oxford: Berg.
Friedman, J.
  1974   "Marxism, Structuralism and Vulgar Materialism." *Man*
          (n.s.) 9(3):444-469.

1979 "Hegelian Ecology: Between Rousseau and the World Spirit" In P. Burnham and R. F. Ellen, eds., *Social and Ecological Systems*. London: Academic Press.

1996 Comments on "Nature/Culture: Gregory Bateson and Modern Environmentalism." Annual Meeting of the American Anthropological Association, San Francisco.

Gleick, James
1987 *Chaos: Making a New Science*. New York: Penguin Books.

Goodwin, Brian
1994 *How the Leopard Changed Its Spots: The Evolution of Complexity*. New York: Simon & Schuster.

Guardian Weekly
1997a "A Smouldering Catastrophe." 157(21) November 23:30-31.

1997b "*Le Monde* Editorial." 157(25) December 21:13.

Harries-Jones, Peter
1995 *A Recursive Vision: Ecological Understanding and Gregory Bateson*. Toronto: University of Toronto Press.

1996a "Affirmative Theory: Voice and Counter-Voice at the Oxford Decennial." In Henrietta Moore, ed., *The Future of Anthropological Knowledge*. London: Routledge.

1996b "Nature/Culture: Gregory Bateson and Modern Environmentalism." Paper presented at the Annual Meeting of the American Anthropological Association, San Francisco.

Harries-Jones, Peter, Abraham Rotstein, and Peter Timmerman
1992 *Nature's Veto: UNCED and the Debate About Earth*. Toronto: Science for Peace (Special Publication).

Heims, Steve J.
1991 *The Cybernetics Group*. Cambridge, MA: MIT Press.

Hoffmeyer, Jesper
1996 *Signs of Meaning in the Universe*, B. J. Haveland, trans. Bloomington: Indiana University Press.

Ingold, Tim
1992 "Editorial." *Man* (n.s.) 27(4):693-698.

Johnston, Barbara R., ed.
1997 *Life and Death Matters: Human Rights and the Environment at the End of the Millennium*. Walnut Creek, CA: Altamira Press.

Joseph, Lawrence, E.
1990 *Gaia: The Growth of an Idea*. New York: St. Martin's Press.

Karim, Wazir Jahan
    1996   "Anthropology Without Tears: How a 'Local' Sees the
            'Local' and the 'Global.'" In Henrietta Moore, ed., *The
            Future of Anthropological Knowledge*. London: Routledge.
Karliner, Joshua
    1997   *The Corporate Planet: Ecology and Politics in an Age of
            Globalization*. San Francisco: Sierra Club Books.
Lovelock, J. E.
    1979   *Gaia: A New Look at Life on Earth*. Oxford: Oxford Uni-
            versity Press.
    1988   *The Ages of Gaia: A Biography of Our Living Earth*. New
            York: W. W. Norton.
Marcus, George, and Michael M. J. Fisher
    1986   *Anthropology as Cultural Critique*. Chicago, IL: Chicago
            University Press.
Merchant, Carolyn
    1992   *Radical Ecology: The Search for a Livable World*. London:
            Routledge.
Milton, Kay
    1996   *Environmentalism and Cultural Theory: Exploring the Role
            of Anthropology in Environmental Discourse*. London:
            Routledge.
Moran, Emilio F.
    1990   "Ecosystem Ecology in Biology and Anthropology: A Criti-
            cal Assessment." In Emilio Moran, ed., *The Ecosystem
            Approach in Anthropology: From Concept to Practice*. Ann
            Arbor: University of Michigan Press.
    1996   "Nurturing the Forest: Strategies of Native Amazonians." In
            Roy Ellen and Katsuyoshi Fukui, eds., *Redefining Nature:
            Ecology, Culture and Domestication*. Oxford: Berg.
Pattee, Howard
    1995   "A Symposium in Theoretical Biology." In Paul Buckley
            and David Peat, eds., *Glimpsing Reality: Ideas in Physics
            and the Link to Biology*. Toronto: University of Toronto
            Press.
Rappaport, Roy
    1990   "Ecosystems, Population and People." In Emilio Moran,
            ed., *The Ecosystem Approach in Anthropology: From Con-
            cept to Practice*. Ann Arbor: The University of Michigan
            Press.

Sachs, Wolfgang
  1993   *Global Ecology: A New Arena of Political Conflict.*
          London: Zed Books.
Timmerman, Peter
  1996   "Breathing Room: Negotiations on Climate Change." In Fen
          Osler Hampson and Judith Reppy, eds., *Earthly Goods:
          Environmental Change and Social Justice.* Ithaca, NY:
          Cornell University Press.
Vayda, A. P., and Roy Rappaport
  1968   "Ecology, Cultural and Non-Cultural." In J. Clifton, ed.,
          Introduction to Cultural Anthropology. Boston, MA:
          Houghton Mifflin.
Wasson, Richard
  1988   "The Contrary Politics of Postmodernism: Woody Allen's
          Zelig and Italo Calvino's *Marcovaldo.*" In Robert Merrill,
          ed., *Ethics/Aesthetics: Post-Modern Positions.* Washington,
          DC: Maisonneuve Press.

TOWARD AN ANTHROPOLOGICAL THEORY
OF NATURAL RESOURCE MANAGEMENT
IN INDIGENOUS COMMUNITIES

Daniel M. Cartledge

Throughout the world today there exist numerous indigenous agricultural communities many of whom have a long history of residence in a particular region, in a particular place. They often possess cultural traditions, local economies, and agricultural practices that are uniquely their own. Concurrently, concerns are being voiced by the scientific community regarding increasing rural populations, environmental degradation, and the need to identify and develop sustainable systems of agriculture and natural resource management. Frequently, debate ensues regarding the extent to which indigenous peoples possess their own conservation or environmental ethics and sociocultural means of actually controlling local resource exploitation. This chapter examines the relationship between conservation ethics and actual resource use and management and hypothesizes likely characteristics of this relationship in indigenous communities such as are found in many parts of the nonindustrialized world.

Indigenous Land Wisdom

The existence of conservation or environmental ethics among indigenous peoples has been most studied in regard to Native North Americans. J. B. Callicott distinguishes four types of American Indian "land wisdom": utilitarian conservation, religious reverence, ecological awareness, and environmental ethics (1990:257). W. C. McCleod (1936) and Frank Speck (1938) both argued that the peoples they studied (Algonkian groups) practiced a utilitarian sort of conservation not unlike that espoused by Pinchot (1909) in his principle of multiple sustained use. This is still the guiding principle of the U.S. Forest Service. This principle entails a conscious and rational use of resources. There is some evidence, however, that indicates that this rational approach to resource management is a product of post-contact interactions with Europeans, especially following the advent of the North American fur trade. Leacock (1954) and Bishop (1970) support this view.

Ironically, both McCleod and Speck also observed a religious reverence for various natural entities, including plants and animals, among these indigenous groups. The nonhuman world was seen to be filled with various natural and supernatural entities that needed to be placated. Such animistic beliefs, may, more than rational decision processes, account for behavior that serves to conserve natural resources.

According to Callicott, accompanying this religious reverence was often a sort of environmental golden rule in which animals and plants were treated in a social, ethical, anthropomorphic manner. They were often regarded as social equals. The social world of these peoples could be regarded as transcending the boundaries of strictly human relations to incorporate other animate beings.

Many, if not all, indigenous groups that have maintained close ties to the land have individuals who possess high degrees of ecological awareness. They have an intimate knowledge of local ecosystems. Various ethnolinguistic studies have made it evident that indigenous peoples often have a large and detailed knowledge of their local ecosystems (see Altieri et al. 1987, or Prance et al. 1987).

Knowledge per se, however, does not directly relate to moral or ethical behavior. A people may know much about local flora and fauna, and still nonconservingly exploit these natural resources. Callicott argues that ethical attitudes toward other living beings derive from social interaction with other humans. In a similar vein, G. H. Mead (1939) believed that a person's self-concept, one's definition of self, could be developed only in the context of social interaction. The case of feral children and their inability to communicate or otherwise appropriately interact with other humans is an example of what happens to the self when social interaction does not occur. Insufficient and/or dysfunctional social interaction in early childhood, or even later in the context of the family, will frequently lead to distorted self-definitions and accompanying social maladjustments (Watzlawick et al. 1967). Through processes of projection and identification, individuals in societies with close ties to local ecosystems might well come to incorporate various flora and fauna into their social sphere of significant others. This is particularly likely if parents, and other figures with whom children strongly identify, hold such beliefs and attitudes (Whiting and Whiting 1975). Other cultural elements, particularly rituals and myths, likely serve to reinforce these beliefs and attitudes (Hill 1989).

The four categories of land wisdom listed above are actually not at all mutually exclusive, as Callicott initially presents them. Rather, in various degrees, they may all occur within a particular culture group, and they may complement rather than contradict one another. For purposes of discussion and analysis, I would propose renaming these as follows:

utilitarian conservation = *rationalism*
religious reverence = *supernaturalism*
ecological awareness = *empiricism*
environmental ethics = (secular) *moralism*

In attempting to determine the role of an ideological cultural component—conservation ethics—in natural resource management, I have placed myself square in the middle of two major theoretical schisms: idealism vs. materialism, and rationalism vs. moralism. The relationship between these and the four titles that I have proposed above is not coincidental. I would argue that the four land wisdom categories are really genres of rhetoric, as are the four theoretical "isms." Each may be seen as a basis for, and concurrently an explanation of, human behavior. Here I am using "rhetoric" in its more general sense, i.e., behavioral influence predicated upon communicative transactions. Following G. H. Mead, and other symbolic interactionists, cognitive decision-making regarding envisioned behavior, including natural resource exploitation, is largely an internalized process of communicating with an other. In this instance, decision-making about anticipated action is a process of communicating with one's self, the self being a cognitive construct developed via the process of socialization.

Each of these genres of rhetoric assumes various antecedents:

rationalism =
logic and the maximization principle as antecedent to behavior
supernaturalism =
religious ideology as antecedent to behavior

empiricism =
sense perception of material world as antecedent to behavior
(predicated upon sociocultural value/belief system)
moralism =
social norms and affective ties as antecedent to behavior
(predicated upon sociocultural value/belief system)
idealism =
ideological aspects of society most influence behavior
materialism =
material aspects of society most influence behavior

Empiricism, as previously discussed, does not in a direct manner relate to actual resource management behavior but rather provides information upon which cognitive processes act, though it must be noted that the perceptual process itself is influenced by antecedent logical and normative elements. Supernaturalism and moralism, as they relate to actual behavior, may both be seen as normative societal elements as they guide behavior and as they are derived via social interaction. These normative processes are in contrast to rationalism, or so it would seem.

Rationality and Irrationality

I would argue that rationality is a characteristic of human decision-making and that all conscious decisions can be seen to involve varying amounts or degrees of rationality. Some may seem to involve almost no rational component, others may clearly adhere to the rational ideal. Schneider makes a corollary statement that somewhat acknowledges this and that considers the place of social norms *vis-à-vis* rational behavior. He says that "norms are always intrusive on rationality to some degree, and those who accuse science in general and anthropologists in particular of being biased are to some extent and perhaps entirely correct. And, by its very nature, the output of a rational system is capable of being used for any normative end" (1974:203).

Rationality focuses attention upon means, not ends. Affective and normative factors, on the other hand, focus attention upon ends, not means (Etzioni 1989). The crux of the substantivist/formalist debate is a conflict between the preeminence of rationality vs. the preeminence of nonrational factors in determining behavior. This ongoing dialectic, however, misses the point that these motive forces may actually be complementary; they are not in necessary opposition.

It has yet to be shown that anyone can consistently perform as a fully rational actor in real-life situations. Barnard (1968) believed that a condition of "decision paralysis" would ensue should a decision-maker attempt to make a fully rational decision. This would entail considering all possible alternatives before making a decision and possessing all relevant information, and this would effectively paralyze the decision-maker due to limits of time, energy, and short-term memory capabilities. Also, in actual decision-making situations, rarely if ever does an individual have access to all possible pertinent information.

For these reasons, both Barnard and Simon (1957) felt that normative factors help make individuals in a sense more rational by limiting alternatives and providing the goals, the ends, toward which people should direct their activities. With these provided, decision-makers can then focus their energies and efforts upon the most rational means of accomplishing the normatively determined ends.

Simon considered both internal and external normative influences as acting upon rational decision-making. External influences include such things as imposed rules or laws and accompanying sanctions including physical force or other coercive measures of enforcement. Internal influences, which Simon believed to be most instrumental in determining the ends of society and thus most affecting rational decision-making, include the internalization of values, beliefs, and norms via socialization and identification with socially significant individuals and groups.

Viewed from this perspective, supernaturalism and moralism act upon behavioral decision premises, the ends of behavior, whereas rational processes function to guide the means of behavior, the strategies that are adopted for anticipated behavior. It may, therefore, be appropriate to consider religious reverence (supernaturalism) and environmental ethics (moralism) as acting in combination with utilitarian conservation (rationalism) to determine indigenous resource management as they act upon data derived via ecological awareness (empiricism).

Culture and Environment

A culture group or population should not be viewed merely as an isolated object of study but rather as being enmeshed within a larger framework, and it is in interacting with, accommodating to, and exerting influence upon this larger framework that a group comes to develop, at least in part, its unique identity. The extent to which this occurs is of course dependent upon the degree of uniqueness found in the group's cultural-historical and environmental milieu. The environment includes not only physical factors but also social components, i.e., other human groups. The culture-nature boundary is an analytic concept derived via dichotomous thinking, not a necessary existential reality.

Adopting a genuinely ecological perspective may provide considerable synthesis of the apparently opposed positions of idealist and materialist thinking, and such an approach is useful when one is attempting to understand the relationship between ethics and behavior in regard to indigenous resource management. A brief analysis of some of the major characteristics of ecological studies will demonstrate this. By examining prominent tenets of ecological anthropology, a clearer view of the legacies of the past may be discerned. The following will be discussed as they help to provide a basis for understanding the relationship between conservation ethics and natural resource management: the use of systems concepts, holism, the concern with biocultural needs, and the evolutionary perspective.

Perhaps the most pervasive characteristic found in ecological studies, either implicitly or explicitly, is that of an underlying systems metaphor or premise. For example, Clifford Geertz's *Agricultural Involution* (1963) is based upon the concept of an ecosystem. Other systems concepts such as feedback, system structure, reciprocal causality, and equilibrium repeatedly occur in ecological anthropology literature. While this may to some extent reflect the influence of general systems theory and work in cybernetics, a systems metaphor or archetype may also be traced more directly back to patriarchal figures in anthropology.

Radcliffe-Brown, in developing his structuralist approach to understanding social relations, made use of this metaphor (1952). Likewise, in the works of R. Benedict and A. Kroeber we can see evidence of systemic thought. Benedict (1934) saw cultures as composed of integrated systems of traits and Kroeber, in his consideration of the superorganic (1948), viewed cultures as configurations of integrated traits. A systems perspective, however, may be traced even further back. E. B. Tylor (1871), in his oft-quoted definition of culture, describes it as "that complex whole." This at the least implies a possible systems orientation particularly when one considers that Tylor adhered in large part to the ideas of H. Spencer. And we find that Spencer, in his theory of social evolution (1876), quite clearly discusses such concepts as system, differentiation, and integration. Thus, a long tributary stream of systems thinking has been incorporated into the ecological perspective.

A second important characteristic of ecological anthropology is its generally holistic approach. While some have argued that ecological anthropologists are guilty of a sort of simple environmental determinism (Johnson 1982), a survey of the broad range of sociocultural phenomena and the multidimensional analyses which are a part of ecological research should suffice to prove otherwise. The complex and multifaceted analyses of Barth (1956), Rappaport (1967), and Harris (1979) are certainly not guilty of simple reductionism. Generally, in ecological research, a wide range of interconnected elements are considered. An emphasis upon holism may also be seen in earlier anthropological endeavors, as, for instance, in the works of Franz Boas and his students.

A strong biocultural orientation exists in many ecological studies as well. This may be at least partially due to the influence of Malinowski's consideration of both biological and cultural needs. These really form the basis for the theoretical framework that Malinowski used to analyze culture groups. And, while he primarily used this biocultural approach in a case study manner, it also might well be used in designing comparative analyses.

Closely allied with a biocultural orientation is the common acceptance of evolutionary concepts by ecological researchers. Julian Steward (1949) is well remembered for his evolutionary view of cultural development. His notion of multilinear evolution infers development based upon differential environmental factors. Leslie White (1943), while disavowing simple biological determinism, clearly embraced evolutionary principles in his consideration of efficiency in the cultural capture of energy. More recently, Marvin Harris (1979) also incorporates evolutionary thinking in his theory of cultural materialism. And this evolutionary thread running through the fabric of ecological studies may be traced back to the nineteenth-century theorists: Tylor, Morgan, and Spencer.

An ecological perspective stresses the interdependence of sociocultural and environmental systems. Emphasis is upon networks of reciprocal relationships. This concern with integrated systems is an obvious legacy of structural-functionalist thought. Dynamism exists in ecological models through the inclusion of an evolutionary underpinning. The structural-functional components of an ecological perspective help explain equilibrium or homeostatic attributes of a population or culture group while the evolutionary principles provide a means for analyzing and understanding change in such systems. This incorporation of otherwise disparate theoretical components adds rigor and increased explanatory potential to this research perspective. It incorporates both synchronic and diachronic elements. From this perspective, culture-environment interactions may be seen as a cyclical concatenation of causal factors.

Cognition influences actual behavior, which has environmental consequences. An individual monitors the environment. This allows for assessment of past behavior and provides information that influences future behavioral acts. Cognition, however, is continuously influenced by ideological and cultural factors. This cycle occurs in a social context. Individual behavioral acts have social consequences, they affect others. Concurrently, individual and group actions influence ideological and societal factors which influence individual cognition.

Some researchers, Weick (1979) for example, argue that a good deal of decision-making is actually retrospective. An individual acts, perceives behavioral consequences, and then makes sense of the act. This would reverse the causal influences linking those elements of the individual cycle. Most likely, such reversals are indeed fairly common, in part due to the bounded or limited nature of human rationality. Ideological factors (norms, beliefs, values, etc.) influence behavior which influences the environment. Concurrently, perceived environmental factors influence individual cognition and, via social processes, the ideologic components of a society. Ideology and material conditions of existence possess a transactional rather than a contradictory or oppositional relationship.

Thought and Action

This theoretical conceptualization assumes that ideological factors come into being via human interaction; they are in some measure socially constructed. These factors consequently influence individual perception, cognition, and behavior. As such, individuals unavoidably act upon a social construction of the environment. Thus, actual behavior may prove to be more or less adaptive *vis-à-vis* the actual environment (which must be assumed as we can never directly perceive it), and the aggregate behavioral adaptiveness of individuals in large measure determines the degree to which groups or societies successfully adapt to changes in the environment.

To better understand the relationship between a sociocultural system of conservation ethics and actual individual behavior, it is necessary to further examine individual cognitive processes. Kenneth Burke (1973) emphasizes the importance of processes of identification in determining individual behavior. According to him, accompanying an awareness of self is a sense of difference from others, a sense of estrangement. It is this inherent estrangement that leads to the process of identification by which an individual comes to experience a psychological union or communion with others. The human condition is seen as one of contradiction, the dialectic occurring between psychological states of congregation and segregation.

Burke considers four elements as central to understanding the place of individuals in social collectivities: hierarchy, order, mystery, and identification. Specialization and division of labor result in the creation of some sort of hierarchical relations within social groups. This also entails order in the sense of authority as it is maintained via various means including rhetoric (persuasive communication) and identification. Hierarchy and order give rise to a sense of mystery or estrangement in individuals at one level in the social collectivity from individuals at other levels. This sense of estrangement gives rise to various forms of identification.

Identification, as a form of unobtrusive control, may operate in a largely covert manner within a social group. As such, identificational processes may help to explain the relationship between ethical systems and individual behavior in a social/cultural group. Burke defines identification in this manner: "A person may think himself as 'belonging' to some special body more or less clearly defined . . . he may identify himself with such bodies or movements, largely through sympathetic attitudes of his own" (1973:263). Herbert Simon explains that "a person identifies with a group when, in making a decision, he evaluates the several alternatives of choice in terms of their consequences for a particular group" (1957:205).

Tompkins and Cheney (1982) build upon this conceptualization of identification in considering it to be an important form of unobtrusive control over individual behavior. For them, identification is seen as a process of inculcating major enthymemic premises. It is an inherently rhetorical process and interacts with various sorts of obtrusive rhetoric in a mutually reinforcing manner.

Kaufman (1960), in his landmark field study of the U.S. Forest Service, provides an insightful analysis of social roles and control with an emphasis upon the process of identification. His is a thorough analysis of the organization and those members singled out for focused study, forest rangers. He denotes various tensions or conflicts between forces of fragmentation and techniques of integration and demonstrates the central role of identification in determining actual individual behavior, especially in regard to resource management and conservation activities.

Those who most control scarce and valued resources in a community will exert substantial influence upon ideological processes, particularly the process of identification. They will also be instrumental in the determination and execution of sanctions against those who violate norms regarding the allocation of these resources. The stronger the group orientation in a community, as opposed to a strong sense of individuality, and the higher the level of conformity, the less deviance will be tolerated and the tighter the fit will be between normative expectation, ideal behavior, and actual, exhibited behavior. Strong identification with a particular community, the people and the land, will interact with these normative factors to increase the concordance between culturally preferred and actually exhibited individual behavior.

Ethics and Behavior

As humans possess bounded rationality, and decisions are based upon a self-rhetorical process involving ideological influences, a model of behavior that is fully rational, and amoral, is not valid. Culturally determined ethics tend to set the parameters of rational behavior by providing first premises for decisions and subsequent behavior. Humans are concerned with quality as well as quantity in life. Social relationships are important for human development and survival. Thus, altruistic or other-accounting first premises, in association with the process of identification, have strong persuasive influence over individual decisions and behavior. So, for most individuals, decisions and subsequent behavioral acts involve both moral and rational components.

The extent to which a people are in an interactive relationship only with local ecosystems influences their ethical system and their behavior toward the environment. These will be more social and familial the more that people are dependent upon the local resource base. In an adaptive society, the rules of its conservation ethics will likely be homologous with the exigencies of its local environment. However, culture is inherently conservative, as it is based upon the perception and interpretation of past successful behavior. As such, a lag will tend to exist in a society between actual environmental conditions and culturally determined behavioral responses. Furthermore, the adaptability and sustainability of cultural ecological strategies and behavioral repertoires are, in part, a matter of the time frame involved. As the environment changes, so does the culture, and vice versa, so long as the culture continues to exist as an identifiable entity. Therefore, various societies may be more or less adaptive in the short or long term.

The environment does not strictly determine religious ideology, ethics, or behavior but rather sets parameters or constraints as defined by the articulation of existent technologies and social structure with the environment. Generally, under relatively stable environmental conditions, traditional religio-ethical systems operate as the main influence upon resource use and management. In times of relatively rapid environmental change, traditional systems may break down. Innovations may well be encouraged (in successfully adapting groups), though this would likely occur after a period of closure (Colson and Scudder 1991, personal communication), wherein conservatism and an adherence to traditions help to preserve a sense of stability in the face of rapid change. This is likely when cultural evolution occurs as a relatively rapid but discontinuous process, akin to Kuhn's (1970) paradigmatic revolutions. Successful groups adapt and work on satisfactory new behavioral repertoires, unsuccessful groups may vanish.

Many if not most indigenous agricultural communities have a history of relative autonomy and dependence upon a local resource base. A high degree of conservatism, a strong adherence to traditions, will likely coincide with a more well-developed local religio-ethical system, with clear normative prescriptions and sanctions against deviant behavior in regard to local resource management. Relative isolation from other social groups should help to perpetuate this situation. Additionally, small, relatively closed communities possess more behavioral accountability, and more monitoring of individual behavior due to the prevalence of face-to-face contact. This will likely increase the fit between local environmental ethics and actual resource use and management. However, it should be noted that the pragmatics of survival, preservation of self and family, may well override community ethics and social expectations in extreme cases, such as famine. And, outside sociocultural, political, and economic influences may erode the saliency of traditions, local social structure, accountability, and normative prescriptions in determining the sort of environmental ethics and conservation practices existent in a given community.

A relatively low level of technology limits the ability of individuals to amass or control access to resources. This may frequently act as a limitation on the procurement of political power. In rural communities this may create a more egalitarian ethos similar to that found among hunter-gatherers and result in similar conservation practices. Also, the more that foraging forms a major component of a community's subsistence system, the more its conservation ethics and natural resource practices may approach those of hunter-gatherer groups. So, in agricultural communities where a low level of technology exists and/or where foraging is an important activity, some of the following might be expected:

* A norm of reciprocity in terms of food resources and in giving others access to one's land for foraging.

* Myths and/or rituals in regard to valued resources similar to those among hunter-gatherers.

* Animal and/or plants conceptualized as social beings.

* Norms regarding the sustained yield of valued resources.

* A norm against the waste of valued resources.

(This is a representative, not exhaustive, list following Martin 1974, and Nelson 1983.)

In general, conservation ethics may be viewed as largely determined by the interaction of limited human rationality, identification processes, social structure, and the perceived environmental consequences of past behavior. There is a need, however, to assess the extent to which the actual conservation of resources is conscious and intentional rather than latent and unintentional. There is also a need to understand more clearly how marketed and/or exchanged resources are conceptualized and managed in indigenous communities. Are these treated in a manner similar to those consumed locally? In what ways do macrosocial influences change the cognitive evaluation of local resources resulting in changes in management activities?

Questions such as these are difficult to answer. However, given the environmental issues facing many developing regions of the world today, it is imperative that they be tackled. More and more, state conservation authorities, as well as numerous academic researchers, are in agreement that, for conservation programs to work in rural communities, the active involvement of the local population is needed.

Consequently, research designed to better understand indigenous systems of conservation management is needed to provide a baseline for such programs and to better allow for the incorporation of indigenous ethics and practices.

References

Altieri, M. A. et al.
  1987 "Peasant Agriculture and the Conservation of Crop and Wild Plant Resources." *Conservation Biology* 1(1):49-58.
Barnard, C. I.
  1968 *The Functions of the Executive.* Cambridge, MA: Harvard University Press.
Barth, F.
  1956 "Ecologic Relationships of Ethnic Groups in Swat, North Pakistan." *American Anthropologist* 58:1079-1089.
Benedict, R.
  1934 *Patterns of Culture.* Boston, MA: Houghton Mifflin.
Bishop, C. A.
  1970 "The Emergence of Hunting Territories Among the Northern Ojibway." *Ethnology* 9:1-15.
Burke, K.
  1973 "The Rhetorical Situation." In L. Thayer, ed., *Communication: Ethical and Moral Issues.* London: Gordon & Breach.
Callicott, J. B.
  1990 "American Indian Land Wisdom." In P. A. Olson, ed., *The Struggle for the Land: Indigenous Insight and Industrial Empire in the Semiarid World.* Lincoln: University of Nebraska Press.
Etzioni, A.
  1989 *The Moral Dimension.* New York: Free Press.
Geertz, C.
  1963 *Agricultural Involution: The Process of Ecological Change in Indonesia.* Berkeley: University of California Press.
Harris, M.
  1979 *Cultural Materialism.* New York: Random House.
Hill, J.
  1989 "Ritual Production of Environmental History Among the Arawakan Wakuenai of Venezuela." *Human Ecology* 17(1): 1-25.

Johnson, A.
  1982   "Reductionism in Cultural Ecology: The Amazon Case."
          Current Anthropology 23(4):413-418.
Kaufman, H.
  1960   *The Forest Ranger: A Study in Administrative Behavior.*
          Baltimore, MD: Johns Hopkins University Press.
Kroeber, A. L.
  1948   *Anthropology: Culture Patterns and Processes.* New York:
          Harcourt, Brace, & World.
Kuhn, T. S.
  1970   *The Structure of Scientific Revolutions.* 2nd edition. Chi-
          cago, IL: University of Chicago Press.
Leacock, E.
  1954   *The Montagnais "Hunting Territory" and the Fur Trade.*
          Washington, DC: American Anthropological Association.
Malinowski, B.
  1944   *A Scientific Theory of Culture.* Chapel Hill: University of
          North Carolina Press.
Martin, C.
  1974   *Keepers of the Game: Indian-Animal Relationships and the
          Fur Trade.* Berkeley: University of California Press.
McCleod, W. C.
  1936   "Conservation Among Primitive Hunting Peoples." *Scientif-
          ic Monthly* 43:562-566.
Mead, G. H.
  1939   *Mind, Self, and Society.* Chicago, IL: University of Chi-
          cago Press.
Morgan, L. H.
  1878   *Ancient Society.* New York: Henry Holt and Co.
Nelson, R. K.
  1983   *Make Prayers to the Raven: A Koyukon View of the North-
          ern Forest.* Chicago, IL: University of Chicago Press.
Pinchot, C.
  1909   "The Fight for Conservation." *Farmers Bulletin 327.* Wash-
          ington, DC: U.S. Department of Agriculture.
Prance, G. T. et al.
  1987   "Quantitative Ethnobotany and the Case for Conservation in
          Amazonia." *Conservation Biology* 1(4):296-310.
Radcliffe-Brown, A. R.
  1952   *Structure and Function in Primitive Society.* New York:
          Free Press.

Rappaport, R. A.
   1967   *Pigs for the Ancestors*. New Haven, CT: Yale University Press.
Schneider, H. K.
   1974   *Economic Man: The Anthropology of Economics*. Salem, WI: Sheffield Publishing Company.
Simon, H. A.
   1957   *Administrative Behavior*. New York: Free Press.
Speck, F. G.
   1938   "Aboriginal Conservators." *Bird-Lore* 4:258-261.
Spencer, Herbert
   1876   *The Principles of Sociology*. New York: Appleton.
Steward, J. H.
   1949   "Cultural Causality and Law: A Trial Formulation of the Development of Early Civilizations." *American Anthropologist* 51:1-27.
Tompkins, P. K., and G. Cheney
   1982   "Toward a Theory of Unobtrusive Control in Contemporary Organizations." Paper presented at the Speech Communication Association Annual Meeting, Lexington, KY.
Tylor, E. B.
   1871   *Primitive Culture*. London: John Murray.
Watzlawick, P. et al.
   1967   *Pragmatics of Human Communication*. New York: W. W. Norton & Company.
Weick, K. E.
   1979   *The Social Psychology of Organizing*. 2nd edition. Reading, MA: Addison-Wesley.
White, L.
   1943   "Energy and the Evolution of Culture." *American Anthropologist* 45:335-356.
Whiting, B. B., and J. W. M. Whiting
   1975   *Children of Six Cultures: A Psychological Analysis*. Cambridge, MA: Harvard University Press.

RECAPTURING ANTHROPOLOGY
IN MARGINAL COMMUNITIES

Parin A. Dossa

Reflecting on my childhood experiences in the plural society of East Africa, with its numerous indigenous groups and heterogeneous Asian population, I find it odd that we drew predominantly upon the British tradition, represented first by the colonial administrative power and later by its institutional infrastructure, which became a permanent fixture of the East African landscape. During the independence period of the early 1960s, East Africa was artificially divided into the three countries of Kenya, Uganda and Tanzania, and the neocolonial West continued to exercise its hegemony. Mapped as the epicenter of the world, the latter was presented as an imaginary space where things were happening. By contrast, the perception advanced was that East Africa had a long way to go before it could resemble even the shadow of the West. The power of this imaginary construct can be gleaned from the fact that alternative ways of being have been submerged under the catch phrase of "catching up to the West." My "field trips" to the Muslim coastal town of Lamu (Kenya) have been motivated by the need to understand alternative and gendered constructions of modernity that articulate with Western hegemony in their own terms, while at the same time they engage in the reconfiguration of alterity.

Territorial colonization reached its peak in the first half of this century; in the second half, we are part of an emerging global landscape where movement of people, goods, media-generated images, and capital have become the order of the day, leaving little room for anthropology to document its "people-and-culture" centered ethnography (Gupta and Ferguson 1997). An earlier and much cited work of Edward Said (1978) focuses on the way in which the West has established for itself a Subject status through a process of Othering of the "Orient" to such an extent that large numbers of writers have accepted the basic distinction between East and West (them and us) as the starting point for elaboration of theories, epics, novels, and also policies. A critical issue foregrounded here is that a created body of theory and practice gains in durability and strength through techniques of representation. Thus for the West, "the Orient [is] visible, clear, 'there,'" and "these representations rely upon institutions, traditions, conventions, agreed-upon codes of understanding for their effects" (Said 1978:22). This critique has given rise to an intensive debate within the discipline of anthropology. As a Western theory of knowledge about culture and gender (Ong 1996:61), it is imperative for the discipline to engage in a relational account where the existence of other forms of practice and knowledge are valorized. This chapter considers how anthropology can make itself more responsive to identifying originating points of other modernities and gendered forms of cultural knowledge.

Reflexive Turn in Anthropology

Over the last two decades, the discipline of anthropology has been subject to an intensive critique challenging its foundation paradigm of "culture" as bounded and homogenized, and of "identity" as unchanging and confined within parameters of space (Abu-Lughod 1986; Calgar 1997). Conventional notions of nativeness and native places make little sense in a world where people identify themselves in relation to deterritorialized "homelands," "cultures," and "origins," and feel at ease with multiple cultural identities. This shift has problematized the way in which we research and write about cultural others, a theme taken up by Clifford and Marcus (1986), and Gupta and Ferguson (1997) among others. Theoretical projects directed towards salvaging anthropology from remaining parochial (e.g. Bhabha 1994; Cerroni-Long 1995; Clifford 1988; Fabian 1983; Fox 1991), focus on a critique of the way in which anthropologists have constructed the native as abiding in another time and place, and incarcerated in his/her setting so that the anthropologist can emerge as the quintessence of mobility (Appadurai 1992). However, by focusing on the discursive aspects of Western epistemology, this body of work has not been able to advance substantive and systematic suggestions as to how anthropological knowledge may tap into local understandings and specifications at a

deeper structure of theory. As Ong has observed: "We remain comfortably lodged in a Eurocentric notion of modernity, regardless of the
rest of the world's views and plans for the future" (1996:61). It is
questionable whether anthropology, with its vantage point in the West,
has substantively moved away from essentializing notions of culture,
now transplanted into ethnic and gendered identities.

In reformulating its project, anthropology has shifted gears and
found anchorage in the examination of transcultural and hyphenated
identities. These constructs aim to capture the complex cultural configurations of translocal subjectivities. The fluid identities implied by
the concepts of hyphenation and hybridity are understood as products
of multiple social and cultural influences arising from the crossing of
social and symbolic borders. In multicultural Canada, for example,
non-Western immigrants are hyphenated: Chinese-Canadians, Japanese-
Canadians and so on. These identities form part of the popular and
scholarly discourses as much as they are entrenched in state documentation and census data. The informing principle is that of conflation of
culture and place. At this critical juncture, the question for consideration is whether hybridization or hyphenation can break with the ontological premises underlying essentialist notions of culture. Calgar
(1997), for instance, advances the argument that concepts like
hybridization may easily embrace and accommodate the very reification
they seek to overcome.

Citing Abu-Lughod's work (1986, 1993), Calgar observes the
dicrepancy between theoretical attempts to write against culture, and
the practice of remaining confined to "a single Bedouin family, and
particularly of the women's world which she herself perforce
inhabited. The growing impact of external economic and media forces
which she describes makes little advance beyond the usual acknowledgment of 'external' influences characteristic of most 'village
studies'" (1997:170). The terms that have replaced the master concept
of "culture"—"hyphenated," "hybrid," "diasporic"—have been problematized as they continue to remain part of an essentializing
epistemology. "Although hybridity ascribes cultures and identities
with 'fluidity,' they remain anchored in territorial ideas, whether
national or transnational. . . . The sources of identity are pre-given
rather than being practice-bound" (Calgar 1997:172).

Conceptualized as an antidote to the bounded phenomenon of culture, hybrid and/or hyphenated identities continue to be associated with
the existence of *a priori* spatialized communities. The association
between culture and spatiality has ontological status in anthropology.

Popular discourses of nationality and ethnicity evoke ideas of "roots," of attachment to the soil, and of a homeland. This form of landscape generates topographies of what is home and foreign, "us" and "them." Isomorphism of culture, place and people is also entrenched in images of community which underpin our research designs on immigrants. On the basis of such an ontology, a continuity is posited between for example, the Chinese and Chinese culture in China, and the Chinese community in Canada. Moreover, it is not clear how hyphenated identities destabilize existing hierarchies, since they do not strike against the minority-majority dualism based on unequal power relations. These theoretical weaknesses make it difficult to celebrate hybridity as a real break from essentializing notions of culture.

Another dimension that comes to light is the tendency to "ethnicize" cultural differences and spaces as marking the boundaries between people of common stock or origin, as is evident in the literature on immigrants where case studies of groups (Japanese, Chinese, Jews) are profiled for discussion. This line of reasoning extends to the more general "multicultural discourse" which sees cultures as "the reified possession of ethnic groups or communities." The impact of such an imaginary construct is that immigrants, although having full citizenship status, are defined as fundamentally alien, as their roots are deemed to lie elsewhere (cf. Fernando 1979). To freeze cultural difference between groups along ethnic lines is to assume that each culture is homogeneous and that multiple loyalties imply potentially conflictual ethnic/national loyalties. Ethnic identity is only one kind of order of cultural or social difference. In Calgar's words: "Our ethnographic practices must correspondingly abandon implicit ethnicisations and spatializations of cultural differences, or assumptions that such differences are automatically reproduced between generations" (1997: 175). Ethnicity has thus become a naturalized marker of an immutable cultural difference. The emphasis is invariably on the hyphenation of ethnic identities to the exclusion of other forms of identification. What is overlooked here is the fact that the latter may potentially cut across ethnic attachments and generate quite different forms of sociality and alliance, an aspect that we are ill equipped to document.

The assumption underlying hyphenated identities is that of a priori spatialization of cultures making them no different from the cultural concept that anthropology claims to have reworked. The vantage point of anthropology continues to be limited by its own history and geopolitics. Ong (1996), for example, suggests that the current focus on the transnationalism of late capitalism may actually represent anthropological recodification of Western knowledge about those cultures. A viable vantage point would be to engage with other forms of cultural knowledge that are anchored in other historical situations. Such a shift would be significant as it recognizes non-Western cultures as producers of knowledge that are not invariably informed by Western concerns or perpetually engaged with the Western discourse. Our key assumptions about history, capitalism, and modernity have remained largely unchanged by the ways social knowledge elsewhere remakes other worlds. There has been no systematic attempt to consider how non-Western societies themselves make modernities after their own fashion. By reducing crisis of representation to questions of definitions and literary techniques, we continue to skirt the issue of how anthropological knowledge can accommodate alterity.

As a modest attempt to engage with other forms of cultural and gendered knowledge arising out of other historical and social situations, I explore spatial de-framing of a performance that encapsulates global/local interface as these are revealed in narrative scripts and bodily images. The performance to be discussed is that of the celebration of Independence Day in Kenya. Data are drawn from ethnographic research on women and "development" conducted during three field trips, between 1990 and 1997.

De-Framing the Celebration of Independence Day

Since 1970 the coastal town of Lamu (and its archipelago by the same name) has been incorporated into capitalistic development projects framed by the state and international agencies. At one level, it would appear that Lamu's thousand year old history and Islamic heritage are being eroded at the roots owing to the physical deterioration of the town together with staggering poverty. A closer look at the narrative fragments of women and the quotidian world of body postures, however, suggests that there are distinctive cultural and socioeconomic forms of modernity in the making. Some background information is in order.

Lamu is the oldest Muslim town in Kenya and the only Swahili settlement which has retained a thousand year old tradition while sustaining a growing urban community. Its highly stratified Muslim population of Arabs, Bajuni (mainland), Hydramont (Omani ancestry), Bohra (Indian ancestry) and of late Somalis and Orma (displaced groups from the border) is unique as it forms a complex plural society. Lamu's compact townscape of narrow alleys, its distinct architecture of stone built houses, mosques and tombs, with a burgeoning population of 15,000 people, are the features that have made it a target for a complex configuration of development and conservation (Ghaidan 1975; Nagari 1986; Siravo and Pulver 1981). The Kenyan state has embarked upon a narration of modernity of what is perceived to be a "backward" pre-industrial culture. This form of discursive displacement paves the way for foreign intervention. How is the town's conversion to global capitalistic market economy imagined and what insights can we derive from alternative constructs? I suggest that alternative constructs are formulated on the margins and in-between spaces of everyday life.

To begin with, we need to acknowledge that in modernizing societies, issues of economic development are forged in relation to discourses and appropriation of family and gender. It is in this context that we can explain the state's discourse of oppression of Muslim women: "Muslim women are veiled and kept in the house. Muslim women do not work." I want to suggest the dramaturgical metaphor as a point of entry into the margins as it "encourages us to pay analytic attention to audiences as well as actors, to silences between dialogues, to nakedness as well as costume" (Hirsch and Lazarus-Black 1994:14). Using an illustrative example of the Independence Day celebration, I will suggest that alternative constructs of identities, rights, entitlements and relations—forms of modernity—are reconfigured and partially framed through reappropriation of the celebration. Alterity does not lie outside hegemonic domains; it is within the latter that terms of engagement between groups not yet reified under specific categories may be foregrounded. Ironically, it is the state orchestrated ceremony that provides the space for the expression of alterity. Vincent notes that "power and authority are dramatized in big ceremonial occasions" (1994:124). This is only half of the script. I argue that highly structured hierarchical frameworks evoke configurations that form part of the creative response of excluded groups and individuals.

Lamu's centralized marketplace and narrow vehicle-free streets foster face-to-face interaction. Information on celebration of events and festivals, occurrences of births, deaths and illnesses spread like wildfire. There exists an implicit code as to what items deserve attention and need to be collectively shared. Local men's and women's differentiated roles in the construction of knowledge, however, has been partially appropriated by official discourse. The latter is promulgated through news media, radio and official visits of politicians from Nairobi and the metropolitan coastal town of Mombasa. Official discourse exhorts men and women to act as citizens of Kenya and work in the spirit of *harambee* (self help) to build the nation through hard work and dedication. The official narrative of modernization, also referred to as "good life," where people are healthy, well educated, and enjoy the benefits of a comfortable life (*mysha mazuri*), links the achievement of the latter to a united and strong nation-state. This narrative is at loggerhead with on-the-ground reality.

Over the last two decades, the local people of Lamu have observed the appropriation of their land and resources by the state. For example, Lamu's century-old practice of exporting mangrove poles to the Middle East and inland to other parts of Africa has been banned by the government on the grounds that it is leading to deforestation of land. The local people's argument that "mangrove trees can only continue to thrive and grow if they are cut," is not given much weight. Mangrove poles can only be used for local purposes with a government license. In other words, people now have to pay to use what has been in their possession for centuries. On another front, the revenue generating tourist industry is largely operated by upcountry (mainly Christian) Kenyans and some foreign-based Europeans. The unofficial discourse is then directed at subverting what the local people perceive to be alien interventions that have left them with few resources. Local men and women are beginning to formulate their own plans and discourses that form part of the narrative fragments of a different modernity that valorize an indigenous vision of life in active engagement with the global cultural economy.

Although Kenya obtained its independence in 1963, it is only recently that an Independence Day celebration was introduced in Lamu by the government. This is because Lamu was not of much interest to either the colonial power, which bypassed it during the construction of the Ugandan railway in 1920s, or the state, for whom Lamu is an out-of-the-way place. In the 1970s, the town caught the attention of the tourists for whom vehicle-free streets, a thousand year old heritage with a unique architecture, and pollution-free beaches constitute a heavenly resort. An added appeal was its inexpensive lifestyle. The town's capacity to generate revenue from tourism and the fact that there is room for "development" projects has attracted the attention of the government and international agencies. These interventions do not benefit the local people at large; hence, when the government decided to include Lamu in the celebration of Independence Day, the response has been passive, verging on resistance as can be gleaned from the following conversation, one among numerous others, between myself and a female informant (translated from Swahili):

A   I understand that there is Independence celebration this
     Sunday. Could you tell me what time it begins?
B   I don't know (*mimi apana juva*).
A   Do you know where it will be held?
B   Somewhere on the school grounds. It will be held some-
     where there.
A   Do you have any details on the program?
B   See those police men? They have come to town for the occa-
     sion. They will have some information. Once I come to
     know (*na juva*) or come to hear (*na sikiya*) about it, I will let
     you know.

Terms like *sikiya* (heard) and *juva* (know), together with *famu*
(understand) and *hona* (see) form part of the daily discourse in Lamu.
It is only when one has internalized an event or occurrence in the context of this configuration (embodied knowledge) that one is fully convinced of the need to act. Resisting internalization of the event in the
form of not grounding it in bodily spaces (heard, know, etc.) amounts
to discursive displacement, an aspect understood more fully through
comparison with the indigenous festival of Idd. Prior to its celebration, the festival is talked about (*juva*) and heard about (*sikiya*) for
months, and preparations are made for stitching new clothes, planning
food menus, extending invitations, and other related activities. Also,
people have an understanding (*famu*) of what needs to be done in terms
of collective projects, such as distribution of food and clothes to poor
families. Success of a celebration depends on its imaginary construct,
whereby individuals establish their vantage points for participation and
reconfiguration of subjectivities.

Discursive displacement of Independence Day meant that people in
Lamu did not talk about (*juva*) or hear about (*sikiya*) the celebration,
which in local terms did not become spatially integrated into the town's
landscape. The presence of armed policemen and a Kenya flag in the
center of the main street were the only visible signs of the event. Dis-
advantaged groups are well aware of the fact that a non-participatory
stance makes a powerful statement and goes a long way towards subverting hegemonic forms of power. Although the people of Lamu had
deframed the state's plan of a "celebration," it did not preclude inclusion of other scripts.

My premise is that the dynamics of state performance may serve to create spaces which articulate with but resist total incorporation into state practices. In the following section, I offer a gendered reading of women's scripts and bodily images, inscribed on the borders and in-between spaces where alternative configurations may be identified.

Independence Day: Gendered Script

When I arrived on the grounds of the secondary school at the set time of 9:00 a.m., a military band and armed police officers with long pistols were practicing marching past. The military display at the center of the ground was not mere pageantry, as the presence of an army invokes a statement of authority and control. The irony was that this dramaturgical expression of power was lost as there were only a few spectators. Around 10:30, twenty government representatives arrived on the scene and took their positions on the stage set up for the occasion. The "ceremony" commenced at 11:30 with political speeches and the paraphernalia of performance: raising of the national flag, singing of the national anthem, military marching past, secondary school girls parading in uniforms. This "performance" was accompanied by a side show staged by Muslim women in three different spaces. The first group comprised Bajuni and Orma food vendors. Seated on the grass on one side of the field, they had come to the "ceremony" to sell finger foods: fried cassava, fried spiced potatoes, home made popsicles, coconut candies and locally grown seasonal fruits: mangoes and bananas. The second part of the field was occupied by a group of Somali women who were scheduled to perform a traditional dance. Their brightly colored traditional attire and handcrafted jewelry added color to the ceremony and contrasted with the black *bui bui* of other Muslim women. Secondary school girls in uniforms stood on the third side of the field. A noticeable feature of this group was the absence of Muslim girls who, unlike their Christian counterparts, wear loose-fitting tops with head scarves. Muslim girls, according to one informant, were busy attending Madrasa schools.

The stage and the center space in the field did not draw much attention as there was not much happening at these two sites, except for some political speeches and military displays. Activities in fact centered on the borders of the field, where women were engaged in performing their own scripts. This suggests possibilities for exploring issues of knowledge production on the margins, an "excentric perspective" (Moore 1996:9), that displaces fixed locales of the center. The question as to how one writes about scriptural enactments at the border posits a framework of analysis that is elusive at best. What is enacted cannot be captured; what exists at the border defies containment. These themes are poignantly suggested in the work of Visweswaran, who draws attention to the narrative character of cultural presentations, and the stories built into the representation process. At best, narrative enactments allow us to say that "this is the story about that" (Visweswaran 1994:41). In this text, my concern is to present the significance of women's enactments as these are transferred from oral stories to broader concerns of life. My first aim is to explore women's manipulation of production that is both grounded in survival strategies but goes beyond to encapsulate larger issues of life. My second purpose is to demonstrate how narrators appropriate ambiguous and in-between spaces to reconstruct lives and recapture meaning.

From Narrative Scripts to Enactment of Lived Situations

Before telling their survival stories, the narrators tend self-consciously to proclaim their way of life as it was in the olden days. In the following script, Fawziya, who had sent her niece to sell frozen popsicles and coconut candy, relates and enacts her achievements over a life span of sixty years. Part of her story dramatizes her movements and grounding in situations where, in her words, "we women work with our hands." While Fawziya wants to highlight achievements of women, she is preoccupied with her role as a leader of *mandeleyo ya wanawake* (women and development) project. Her concern is to show that "selling food" is not engaging into petty trade. In her words: "It is the means whereby many women feed their families; it is the means whereby women ensure that their families remain healthy on a day to day basis." When she gets the opportunity to tell her story, she first focuses on the image of herself traveling:

> When Kenya got independence I was appointed as the first woman to lead women's development projects. The government gave us no money. I thought of a plan. I formed women's groups around the town and I asked women to get together and make things. Some women would stitch children's clothes, other women would make baskets and mats. Other women made *Kofia* (embroidered cap worn by men during prayers) and prepared henna. I would collect all the things that women had made and sell them to shopkeepers in Nairobi. With the money I got, I bought stuff that other women had asked me to get for them. Some women would order shoes,

other women would ask for jewelry. These women would then sell
to other women. I opened a shop in my house. I used to carry
Khanga (two piece loose garment worn by women in the house),
shoes, mats, baskets and ready-made clothes.

Fawziya then proceeded to relate how she and other women's lives had
fallen into disarray because of outside interventions. She attributed the
negative change to *Sarkari*'s (the government's) unwillingness to give
any money.

The government wants to take the money from us (people of Lamu).
It has taken and taken and left us with nothing. The big people in
the government want to eat and drink. (At this point Fawziya sat
forward in her seat, put her hands in the mouth and enacted the act
of drinking.) We have to eat and drink too. How do we do this?

When I tried to pursue this question further, Fawziya did not reply. It
was later on, through more intensive reflection on my field experiences, that I began to realize that Fawziya wanted me to learn through
women's bodily engagements in the world and experiential understanding of life. Many times, when I visited Fawziya at her shop/house, I
observed her making candies. Fawziya would first purchase a sack
(*guni*) of unrefined sugar. Every few days, she filled a large bucket of
sugar and asked her niece to take the bucket to her next-door neighbor
who had purchased a grinding machine. The preparation activity
reveals how women deploy their bodies in ways that bespeak a mode of
communication. Balancing a sack or buckets of water on the shoulder
or the back symbolizes women's use of bodies in everyday life situations. When the sack is brought back to the shop, Fawziya would
divide the mixture into equal portions with swift usage of hands. The
portions served two purposes: they helped her have an exact measurement for a batch of candies and they could be easily packaged for
resell. Fawziya did not have a fixed price for the packaged sugar or
the candies. This in no way reflects "inefficiency" or "indeterminacy."
Fawziya's price was contingent upon the financial status of the purchaser. When a woman came into the store with three children, she
bought two candies for two shillings. As the woman was leaving,
Fawziya gave a third candy saying: "three for two," knowing that the
woman could not afford to buy more. Likewise, when another woman
came into her store to buy one bunch of spinach, Fawziya took a second bundle and put it in her basket. She explained to me afterwards

that the purchaser has a lot of mouths to feed. In turn, Fawziya charges more to wealthy families and twice or three times to tourists. Of interest is the fact that goods are not given in the form of charity. Putting an item in a basket is indicative of giving more gently through expressive usage of the body. No words were exchanged during the time of giving. Gestures and an implicit code of recognition seemed to suffice. The redistribution of goods at this micro level was reflected during the Independence Day celebration, when female vendors shared food, assisted each other in child care, and exchanged information. Conversation in a group context included such examples as:

A   My child has a bad cough. It is not going away.
B   Did you go to the hospital?
A   They do not do much at the hospital. They give medicine; it is expensive and I am not sure it would work.
C   My father-in-law has made a mixture from herbs (Swahili medicine). If you come by this evening, I will give it to you. My son also had a cough. It worked on him.

*****

D   My daughter is getting married in a few months.
E   That is good news. Whom is she marrying?
D   My uncle's relative. He lives in Mombasa. I will visit her there. She had another proposal from someone in Dubai. I did not want her to go far from me. Mombasa is not too far.
F   Where are you having the wedding?
D   It will take place near the medical clinic. There is open space there. My uncle's sons will help prepare the wedding.
G   If you need mats (for women to sit on), I know someone who can rent them to you at a good price.
E   I know one woman. She keeps henna and good perfume. Her brother brought a lot of perfume from Saudi Arabia. I will get it for you at a good price. She also has beautiful head scarves and shoes from Saudi Arabia. If you are interested, I will take you to her house.

Exchange of information constitutes an important forum for women to address the tension created by the market economy in the form of keeping up with the demands of consumerism while leaving few resources in the hands of consumers. Imports from Saudi Arabia are valued. While they enable women to keep up with "modern fashions," they do so in terms that include an Islamic orientation to life. Lamu's engulfment into capitalistic oriented projects has impacted women's lives as the latter are undertaking trade as well as engaging in waged work. Occupying a space in the market economy has meant modification of attire. More and more women are adopting modern fashions from Saudi Arabia which comprise a loose black or colored buttoned gown and a colored and designed head scarf. This attire contrasts with traditional all black loose *bui bui*. A major problem facing women is that of finding the resources to purchase these new and relatively expensive products. A strategy resorted to by women is to continue exchange of services and products at a level that includes market economic ventures as well as non-capitalistic modes of interaction. It is at this wider level that one can appreciate women's scriptural and bodily communications during the Independence Day celebration. Local understandings and knowledge required to deal with market economic pressures are juxtaposed and intertwined in the context of everyday life situations. In this respect, the Independence Day celebration was an "ordinary" day which food vendors identified as one of the occasions when they can engage in trade in their own terms. An appealing aspect was the presence of other women. As one vendor explained:

> When I heard about Independence Day, I thought, well, let me make the *bhajiyas* and see if I can make some money. I am collecting money for my daughter's uniform. Then I said, well, even if I don't sell what I make, at least I will meet other women. You know what happened? I met another woman there who said if I cut the cloth, she would stitch the uniform for me. She has a sewing machine at home.

Through the process of combining cash economic concerns with the noncapitalistic pool of resources, women appropriate and cope with the pressures of consumerist gaze in a market economy. Resource sharing strategies deployed for new purposes indicate that women are not passive onlookers on change, but astute negotiators of what appears to be small, micro-level happenings. As one woman stated it: "It is little things that add up and it is little things that make a difference in a crisis situation." It is in marginal spaces that Lamu women engage with terms of market economy trade. The fact that these negotiations take place at any appropriate available site indicates the fluidity of women's social relationships. The above scripts reveal that women have access to information that makes a difference to their daily lives.

Recognition of the way in which women's scripts are juxtaposed with that of the political agenda of the celebration should facilitate a fruitful examination of the process through which women engage in transforming meanings through re-telling narratives of their lives. While women represent the past through elements of the traditional scripts, they simultaneously interrogate the ideals of the nation-state. Aisha's narrative script is telling.

> I am an Orma. Our cows were taken away from us. Then came the *shifta* problems. Times were very uncertain. My father got me married at a young age. I was very unhappy. I ran away. I joined other families who were on their way to Lamu. I did not know that I would have to live on a coconut farm. I almost starved. I looked for work in the town. Here I met a Christian boy. He is a *Giryama* (tribe). I am going to marry him. He will have to become a Muslim. This is the only way. His family was also displaced by *sarkari* (government). His family lost everything when the government people moved into their land. The two of us will build our lives together. We want to live in the town and have a house of our own. This is the story I have to tell.

The script first talks about the displacement of a woman (Aysha), brought about by a political situation through which pastoral tribes experienced depletion of their resources: "There was no further land to move to, we had nowhere to go. We were trapped." In telling her story of struggle, Aysha simultaneously affirms her status as a protagonist. It was her courage in crossing boundaries, running away from an unhappy marriage, establishing a "home" in the coconut farm, and her bold step in marrying a Christian man that she foregrounds in the context of a broader story of displacement as indicated in the opening words: "I am an Orma. Our cows were taken away from us." These sentences convey the message of displacement. The end of the script asserts rebuilding of lives through innovation. To marry outside the tribe for a Muslim woman is a rare occurrence. In the process of telling her story, seated on a stool in contrast to other vendors sitting on the grass, Aysha draws the attention of other women from the town who have overlooked the plight of women and men on the coconut farms. It is not surprising then that the narrator ends her script with a direct plea to women: "This is the story I have to tell." This estab-

lishes the idea of multiple audiences as the listeners belong to interlocking female-centered networks. Her marriage to a potential Muslim
convert is a news item that would be of interest to other women whose
daughters and sons go to mixed schools. The dual audience of the
physically present and absent women constitutes an important
indigenous avenue for sharing information. Aysha's telling of her
story to the assembled group of women is accompanied by bodily gestures and postures integral to traditional storytelling. One story leads
to another. Rashida's rejoinder to the script is illustrative of the way
in which women in their talk reinforce breaking of gendered norms and
behavior patterns.

> I lost my mother when I was very small. We were raised by my
> father and grandmother. When my grandmother was sick, a medi-
> cal aide used to visit us. He was not from our community. I fell in
> love with him. I eloped. I wore the Arab *bui bui* when I ran away
> so that no one could recognize me. My father could not believe
> what I did. He did not think that I had the courage to run away.
> He was so ashamed of what I did that he left town. I don't see
> much of him but I have support from some women in Lamu.

Telling and re-telling of scripts creates an ambiance of sharing that
includes a broader audience of other women who are not present. It is
in the context of co-performers that women relate to each other, and it
in this form of shared understanding that accepted definitions of
womanhood are reworked or subverted in relation to circumstances, as
I documented through life narratives (Dossa 1994, 1997, and n.d.; see
also Mirza and Strobel 1989; Mugambi 1997).

As women talk and converse about their life situations in scriptural
forms, the specific event in question—food vending on Independence
Day—becomes embedded within a wider context. It is this context that
allows women to have a space where they tell their stories and
determine acceptable and unacceptable forms of change. For instance,
when one woman got up and mimicked what it would be like not to
cover their heads, other women took strong objection in gestures but
also verbally.

> If we do away with the veil, men would not talk to us. Besides,
> how will we be able to move around without a veil? This way it is
> better. We have freedom to move. So far as we are covered no
> one asks us where we are going. Besides we do not want to be like

Wazungus (Europeans).

The parameters of women's movements and actions are not solely determined by neo/post colonial patriarchal discourse. In their own circles and within their own spaces, women also make "collective" decisions on issues that come up when women get together. In this respect the marginal space that female vendors occupied on Independence Day constituted one site among many where women get together to work and talk about whatever they regard as important.

Female vendors then did not come to celebrate Independence Day. Rather, they came to occupy a particular space among other spaces that form part of their everyday work/talk. What was unusual about Independence Day is that female vendors from different areas of town were getting together and sharing a space, an opportunity that does not arise on everyday occasions when women interact within familiar interlocking networks. It is through small acts and scriptural performances that women engage in self-definition, identifying several vantage points to facilitate their own and their families' well-being. Another food vendor (Khadija) related her script:

> My daughter has asthma. We took her to the hospital. The medication that the doctor has asked us to get is very expensive (*kali shana*, phrase accompanied by gesture of spreading out of hands). My mother has come up with a plan. She makes good popsicles. When someone was going to Mombasa, she ordered a roll of tiny bags of plastic wrap. She makes a batch every night and puts the mixture into these bags which are easy to tear off from the roll. Everyday, my mother sells thirty popsicles at one shilling each to school children (accompanied by hand gestures to indicate the act of accumulation). She puts aside thirty shillings each day. Today is Sunday. My mother said there will not be any school children who will come around. Why don't you go on this Independence Day and see if you can sell thirty popsicles?

Khadija's story, though unique to her own situation, is not peculiar. Other women have resorted to collecting money along similar lines knowing that Lamu's poverty level does not offer jobs for them or their husbands to cope with the pressures of change. In the words of one woman:

> We have to send our children to school for education. We have to

buy books, uniform, pencils and lunch boxes. Our children have to be healthy. When we go to the hospital, they ask us to get medicine that Lamu cannot afford. So we think of getting money in other ways.

The strategies adopted by three women included the following:

* Amina saved money and purchased a freezer. Every night she freezes water to make ten bags of ice. The ice is sold to fishermen at ten shillings a bag.

* Mehrun has made arrangements with a boat man to deliver two bags of charcoal from Makowe to her house each week. She divides the charcoal into ten sections and sells each section for ten shillings. Her profit is 50 percent.

* Razia gets tea in bulk from Mombasa. She puts the tea in small bags and sells them for one shilling each. Her profit margin is 60 percent.

Given the above scenario, it would be inappropriate to consider food vendors as petty traders. Women selling food were engaged in "projects" that they had initiated both for purposes of survival as well as participation in the market economy that has come to stay. In the words of one woman: "There is no going back. The old way of living has gone. We have to learn to move forward." In their own ways, the food vendors with performative scripts were engaged in creating a space to inscribe stories of their lives.

Women are cognizant of the fact that their survival in the market economy is determined by their ability to pool together resources from the multiplicity of groups that are found in Lamu. Diverging from a homogeneous audience, narrators use scripts as a means of reflecting new ties in the making. Fatima related how her daughter was looked after by her Christian neighbor when she had to travel to Mombasa to see her sick mother. She in turn had offered to assist her neighbor in collecting donations for a blood transfusion. She had come to the ground of the celebration as she was looking for an assembled crowd anywhere in town. This was the quickest way to obtain support.

I have focused largely on narrative scripts and bodily images because they represent indigenous forms deployed to re-create and reconstruct situations of life (cf. Csordas 1994). It is through these forms that we can become more cognizant about "epistemic agency" (Mugambi 1997:213) and women's intervention into the market economy. De-framing and re-appropriation of a state-planned celebration on the margins is one way in which women create a space to address their concerns.

Conclusion

My presentation of the above scripts and images are meant to be investigations in search of a path. Following the footsteps of African women writers, I seek to answer two questions: How can marginal voices be heard? And, in what interest are these voices heard? The answer to these questions requires dealing with the paradox of the feminist project within anthropology, a profile of which would be along the lines of recognizing the dynamics of dialog and polyphony. The feminist critique has focused on the eventual retention of control by the ethnographer who selects and edits the words of the informants (Enslin 1994; Stacey 1988; Strathern 1987). The process of selection invariably leads to representation of some individuals as typical of the culture in question. A more pressing issue is the tension between "theorizing women and presenting women" (Abwunza 1995:250).

At one level, women's intervention reaffirms Abwunza's observation that African women are portrayed as struggling beings who are forever working (1995). Articulation of this activity in economic language trivializes non-capitalistic modes of transaction. To appreciate alternative modes of communication, we need to listen to women's voices and read through women's bodies. Women's enactment of lived situations reveals that the demarcation between waged and non-waged work is not rigid. Women in Lamu do not have access to waged work at all times.

The language of women's bodies at work, in repose, in performance, in interaction, as well as in absent selves, does not suggest that women are continually strategizing to fight capitalist patriarchal order. Women's marginal and differentiated locations in the field show that women continually find means to fulfill their goals. As each voice is heard, as each body engages in communication, as each task is accomplished, women's message is clear: There is need for material about women, collected and explained by African and other Third World women themselves, from which adequate and suitable theories and methodology can be worked out (cf. Abwunza 1995:254).

Analysts of storytellers and performers have observed how women use ambiguity to communicate their revisions of women's conventional roles. In a similar vein, narrators use their own traditional strategies to demonstrate their multiple activities. The message conveyed by the scripts I presented is to the effect that not all Muslim women are "kept within the confines of a home. Women have the capacity to build the nation and work toward its progress!"

Female script narrators' active—albeit unnoticed—use of marginal spaces articulate with the larger and more alien discourse of Independence Day. The shift from home and neighborhood space to that of "ceremonial" space represents a transformative process reflecting changing everyday life situations. In suggesting that women are producers of cultural knowledge in spaces and places that they regard as amenable to their activities, we can begin to identify alterity, the originating point of which is the margins which may appropriate, rework, or subvert occurrences at the center.

References

Abu-Lughod, Lila
    1986   *Veiled Sentiments: Honor and Poetry in a Bedouin Society.*
            Berkeley: University of California Press.
    1993   *Writing Women's Worlds: Bedouin Stories.* Berkeley: University of California Press.
Abwunza, Judith
    1995   "Conversation Between Cultures." In S. Cole and L. Phillips, eds., *Ethnographic Feminisms: Essays in Anthropology.* Ottawa: Carleton University Press.
Appadurai, Arjun
    1992   "Putting Hierarchy in its Place." In G. Marcus, ed., *Rereading Cultural Anthropology.* Durham, NC: Duke University Press.
Bhabha, Homi
    1994   *The Location of Culture.* London: Routledge.
Calgar, Ayse
    1997   "Hyphenated Identities and the Limits of Culture." In T. Modood and P. Werbner, eds., *The Politics of Multiculturalism in the New Europe: Racism, Identity and Community.* London: Zed Books.

Cerroni-Long, E. L., ed.
  1995   *Insider Anthropology.* Arlington, VA: American Anthropological Association.
Clifford, James
  1988   *The Predicament of Culture.* Cambridge, MA: Harvard University Press.
Clifford, J., and G. Marcus, eds.
  1986   *Writing Culture: The Poetics and Politics of Ethnography.* Berkeley: University of California Press.
Csordas, Thomas, ed.
  1994   *Embodiment and Experience: The Existential Ground of Culture and Self.* Cambridge: Cambridge University Press.
Dossa, Parin
  1994   "Critical Anthropology and Life Stories: Case Study of Elderly Ismaili Canadians." *Journal of Cross-Cultural Gerontology* 9:335-354.
  1997   "Reconstruction of the Ethnographic Field Site: Mediating Identities—Case Study of a Bohra Muslim Woman in Lamu (Kenya)." *Women's Studies International Forum* 20(4):505-515.
  n.d.   "On Law and Hegemonic Moments: Looking Beyond the Law Towards Subjectivities of Subaltern Women." In D. Lacombe and D. Chunn, eds., *Law as Gendering Practice: Canadian Perspectives.* Cambridge: Cambridge University Press (forthcoming).
Enslin, Elizabeth
  1994   "Beyond Writing: Feminist Practice and the Limitations of Ethnography." *Cultural Anthropology* 9(4):537-568.
Fabian, Johannes
  1983   *Time and the Other: How Anthropology Makes Its Object.* New York: Columbia University Press.
Fernando, Tisa
  1979   "East African Asians in Western Canada: The Ismaili Community." *New Community* 7(3):361-368.
Fox, Richard G., ed.
  1991   *Recapturing Anthropology: Working in the Present.* Santa Fe, NM: School of American Research Press.
Ghaidan, Usam
  1975   *Lamu: A Study of the Swahili Town.* Nairobi: Kenya Literature Bureau.

Gupta, A., and J. Ferguson, eds.
1997   *Culture, Power, Place: Explorations in Critical Anthropology.* Durham, NC: Duke University Press.

Hirsch, Susan F., and M. Lazarus-Black
1994   "Introduction." In M. Lazarus-Black and S. F. Hirsch, eds., *Contested States: Law, Hegemony and Resistence.* New York: Routledge.

Lazarus-Black, Mindie, and S. F. Hirsch, eds.
1994   *Contested States: Law, Hegemony and Resistence.* New York: Routledge.

Mirza, Sarah, and Margaret Strobel
1989   *Three Swahili Women: Life Histories from Mombasa, Kenya.* Bloomington: Indiana University Press.

Moore, Henrietta L.
1996   *The Future of Anthropological Knowledge.* New York: Routledge.

Mugambi, Helen
1997   "From Story to Song: Gender, Nationhood, and the Migratory Text." In M. Grosz-Ngate and O. Kokole, eds., *Gendered Encounters: Challenging Cultural Boundaries and Social Hierarchies in Africa.* New York: Routledge.

Nagari, John
1986   *Conservation, Regional Planning and Development.* Nairobi: Physical Planning Development.

Ong, Aihwa
1996   "Anthropology, China and Modernities: The Geopolitics of Knowledge." In Henrietta L. Moore, ed., *The Future of Anthropological Knowledge.* New York: Routledge.

Said, Edward W.
1978   *Orientalism.* New York: Random House.

Siravo, F., and A. Pulver
1981   *Planning Lamu: Conservation of an East African Seaport.* Nairobi: National Museums of Kenya.

Stacey, Judith
1988   "Can there be a Feminist Ethnography?" *Women's Studies International Forum* 11(1):21-27.

Strathern, Marilyn
1987   "An Awkward Relationship: The Case of Feminism and Anthropology." *Signs* 12(2):276-292.

Vincent, J.
1994   "On Law and Hegemonic Moments." In Mindie Lazarus-

Black and S. F. Hirsch, eds., *Contested States: Law,
Hegemony and Resistence*. New York: Routledge.
Visweswaran, Kamala
1994   *Fictions of Feminist Ethnography*. Minneapolis: University
of Minnesota Press.

HUMAN MATERIALISM:
A PARADIGM
FOR ANALYZING SOCIOCULTURAL SYSTEMS
AND UNDERSTANDING HUMAN BEHAVIOR

Paul J. Magnarella

Introduction

Human materialism is a systematic paradigm designed to bridge the gap between scientific and humanistic approaches to understanding human behavior, culture, and society. It conceptualizes humans as rational, cost-benefit calculating, scheming, emotional, loving and hating, social creatures who are indoctrinated to some degree in ideological, ritual and symbolic systems that influence their thought, behavior and perceptions of their natural and sociocultural environments. Even though human materialism eschews the simplistic, reductionist characteristics of human nature, it still manages to offer a framework or research strategy for investigating human sociocultural systems and generating hypotheses and theories that facilitate understanding, explanation, and prediction.

Some of the ideas that contributed to this paradigm and to my book expounding it (Magnarella 1994) had been developed by many people over many centuries. Among those who stimulated my thinking are Durkheim, Weber, Marx, Freud, Lévi-Strauss, Harris, as well as Adler and other humanistic psychologists. Unlike many Marxists or Freudians, however, I feel no compelling need to determine exactly what the master meant by each word or set of ideas. Instead of pursuing the truths of the prophets, I employed the ideas of their traditions, as I interpreted them, along with my thoughts as well as ideas from other scholars, and mixed them with designs I cannot trace easily to any particular source. Over the past twenty years, as I studied, applied and taught anthropological, political and economic theory, I have tried to weed out sterile ideas from the fecund and integrate the latter into a logical, empirically relevant formulation. In this way, I moved progressively closer to the human materialist paradigm.

My interest in paradigm building has been stimulated by my colleague Marvin Harris (1979) and his insistence that anthropologists compare currently competing anthropological research strategies and opt for the most explanatory one. In so doing, anthropology can exit the Kuhnian pre-paradigmatic morass and progress as other disciplines have.

I, too, believe we need more direction in anthropology. Currently anthropology consists of a series of theories, some competitive, others complementary, and still others mutually exclusive. We have many localized, effectively uncorrelated or insular and context-dependent ethnographic studies, largely unresponsive to any particular theoretical envelope. At this point in the history of our discipline, achieving needed direction requires a research strategy that can logically integrate the most promising existing theories into a forceful, unified approach to the field of inquiry. With human materialism, I offer an integrative research strategy that accommodates the confluence of a variety of existing sociocultural theories, without being hopelessly eclectic or random.

Science, like art, is a human endeavor. Analysis proceeds at two levels: that of *phenomenology*, involving direct experience, encompassing perceptions, feelings, thinking, will, etc.; and that of *conceptual constructs*, reconstructing direct experience into systems of symbols, culminating in science. No absolute gap between precept and concept exists; the two levels intergrade and interact (von Bertalanffy 1967:94).

A social scientific paradigm or research strategy must serve a number of functions. *Selectivity*: The paradigm must tell the researcher where to focus attention and what to select for description. Explanation requires a description of the conditions under which designated phenomena vary. *Organization*: The theoretical structure superimposes on the data an organizational structure designed to enhance the explanation of relevant relationships according to an assumed set of relevant criteria. *Integration*: The research strategy must be capable of bringing together theoretical constructs and propositions into a unified whole. *Generation*: It must be productive, capable of providing the insights for a steady stream of testable hypotheses. In addition, a comprehensive anthropological research strategy must be able to address three central problems: (1) how ongoing sociocultural systems function; (2) why they function as they do, and (3) how they change through time. Because of cultural anthropology's broad scope, a comprehensive, integrative research strategy must be sufficiently abstract to adequately deal with pre-industrial/non-centralized societies as well as with industrial/centralized societies.

A social scientific paradigm or research strategy, being an abstract model of sociocultural systems without empirical content, is not directly testable. What is testable are the empirically related hypotheses that can be generated from it. A paradigm that can be used as the basis for generating more useful and numerous empirically supported hypotheses than alternative paradigms is a superior way of understanding sociocultural systems.

Although the theoretical construct presented here attempts to serve the functions of selectivity, organization, integration, and generation, it has certain shortcomings. Like any paradigm, it is an incomplete product. It does not deal with everything anthropologists find interesting, nor does it explain everything anthropologists feel needs explaining. It contains many open categories, such as the psychobiological characteristics of humans, which can be progressively filled as more knowledge becomes available. The model's openness makes it amenable to new information and complementary theories. Future discoveries in anthropology and related disciplines concerning the nature of people, society and culture can be easily integrated into the paradigm to enhance its explanatory and productive powers.

A Model of Sociocultural Systems

A nuclear family, a peasant village, a single or a group of hunting and gathering bands, a city, a nation-state, an international alliance, the countries of the earth, or any set of people with some common connection that a researcher chooses as a unit of analysis can be effectively conceptualized as a sociocultural system. Culture is conceptualized as what people think, say, do, and create to the extent that these processes or elements are either created or learned and not wholly biologically determined. Specific sociocultural systems interface with a natural context and a larger sociocultural environment; they have spatial and temporal dimensions.

The human materialist conception of sociocultural systems consists of an asymmetric structure comprised of infrastructural, social structural, and superstructural components. While the last three rubrics resemble those employed in Marvin Harris's cultural materialist model, here they stand for different sets of contents and relationships. The characteristics of a human materialist system include:

1. Etiologic and systemic sets of relationships within and among infrastructure, social structure, and superstructure, with each major component exerting positive (system altering) and negative (system maintaining) forces on the other two.

2. Asymmetry: the forces of infrastructure are more determinative than those of social structure and superstructure. In turn, social structural forces outweigh superstructural ones.

3. Internal contradictions or conflict exist, but not necessarily class dialectics.

4. Process of tension management with strains towards integration.

5. Hierarchical levels of control.

6. Openness: System viability depends on a continuous interchange with successively more encompassing systems. Each sociocultural system interfaces with a natural and a larger sociocultural environment (see Lewin 1951:151).

Infrastructure

The infrastructure consists of three sub-structures: material, human, and social infrastructures. The material infrastructure includes technology, tools, machinery, productive capital equipment, modes of production, the productively relevant parts of science, as well as the environmental resources and factors (e.g., land size and character, minerals, climate, soil types, water, etc.) that have been harnessed or that impinge on the system.

The human infrastructure includes demographic factors, such as population size, growth rates, sex ratio, age profile, life expectancy, immigration-emigration rates, etc., as well as the psychobiological characteristics of people (both actual and potential).

Human psychobiological characteristics represent one of the model's important open categories, to be enriched by future psychobiological research. The psychobiological characteristics of humans include such universals as the drives to satisfy hunger, thirst, and sexual gratification; the need to maintain body temperature within a survival range; mother-child bonding; a need for social affiliation; the natural propensity to learn and communicate through language; feelings of love, happiness, hostility, pride, shame, and sorrow; the human propensity to plan, design strategies, and estimate the costs and benefits of potential courses of action; as well as humankind's susceptibility to indoctrination by ideologies that present faith-worlds and faith-facts (such as the existence of heaven and hell) that cannot be empirically validated (see Brown 1991 for a discussion of human universals).

Because of natural selection pressures and exposure to different ideologies, the biological or psychological nature of people may vary somewhat from society to society (see Geertz 1966). Examples are the abilities of high altitude dwellers to live comfortably at great heights because of their specially adapted breathing apparatus and elevated metabolism (Molnar 1983:152-155), or those Iranian Shiites who, in the 1980s, were true believers in the Hidden Imam, the divine mission of Ayatollah Khomeini and the inevitable injustice of secular government (Magnarella 1981).

Social infrastructure includes the effective ownership and control of the forces of production. It consists of the persons in positions of economic and political power, as well as the positions they hold. Such persons are somewhat like orchestra leaders directing available musical resources. By including the persons in positions of power and the structural positions they occupy, human materialism assumes that the personality characteristics of powerful individuals must be taken into account. Decisions by elites are not the exclusive result of their structural positions and environmental pressures. Personality characteristics also come into play. Hence, human materialism looks to psychology, especially to personality theory, to amplify the analysis of elite behavior.

This category becomes especially important when we consider the roles of charismatic leaders. Working with the concept popularized by Max Weber, Willner (1984:8) defines charismatic leadership as a relationship between a leader and followers that exists when the followers regard the leader as somewhat superhuman and accept his statements without question. They comply unconditionally with their leader's directives for action and give the leader unqualified emotional commitment. Actual persons who have achieved the rank of charismatic leader (e.g. Castro, Gandhi, Hitler, Mussolini, F. D. Roosevelt, Sukarno, Khomeini, Mao, Joan of Arc and Mohammad, the prophet of Islam), generally had spellbinding oratory powers, unusual strength of personality and presence, as well as the ability to instill confidence and win commitment. On the strength of their personalities, intellects, and discourse skills, they were able to command people and resources to an extraordinary degree. Many of them created and occupied unique, one-person statuses to which there could be no immediate successor.

The cultural and behavioral aspects of a charismatic leader vary from society to society. The leader's manner, appearance, actions and discourse style must be appropriate to the superstructural component (see below) of the sociocultural system in which he/she operates. As Willner (1984:63) notes, it is hard to image Gandhi arousing the Germans to mass passive resistance. Gandhi's ascetic practices and sexual celibacy (*brahmachari*) were appropriate and powerful in India's Hindu context. In Latin America, by contrast, *machismo*, and the virility syndrome, are culturally appropriate and necessary character-istics of the *caudillo*, or political leader (Gillen 1955).

Social infrastructure overlaps with social structure (see below), which contains the remainder of the relations of production. By plac-ing persons of economic/political power in the infrastructure, certain theoretical problems raised by structural Marxists are solved. For instance, Marshall Sahlins in his critique of Worsley's view of kinship among the Tale, writes: "Tallensi fathers are not related as father and son by the way they enter into production; they enter thus into produc-tion because they are related as father and son" (1976:9). Note that in Tale society, fathers are the heads of kin groups and they own the land. Thus, in the human materialism conceptualization of Tale families, fathers occupy infrastructural positions of political and economic power *vis-à-vis* sons. In modern industrial societies, these positions are anal-ogous to those of corporation chief executive officers or board chair-persons. In many case studies, researchers must take into account the goals, agendas, and personalities of the systems' politically and/or eco-nomically powerful people in order to understand the systems and to predict their future course (see Magnarella 1994:Chap. 2).

Social Structure

Social structure includes all forms of social organization: family and kinship organization; social organization; political, religious, economic organization, and work relations (see G. A. Cohen 1978:11-12), with the exception that persons with political and economic power are in the social infrastructure. Owing to the psychobiological nature of humans, primary kinship groupings are assumed to be natural. People naturally form such groups to rear children and to cooperate in the achievement of universal natural needs. The forms that such kin groups take are determined by other infrastructural factors; previous, historical social arrangements; and contact with other societies, especially those that have an impact on the infrastructure. An example of this historic process is the Muslim Persian and Arab impact on Turkish social norms. Prior to their migration from Central Asia into the Middle East in about the tenth century A.D., the Turks practiced bilateral kindred exogamy. That is, they observed a prohibition against marrying first and second cousins and anyone within five genealogical degrees of kinship. After converting to Islam as a consequence of their interactions with Persian and Arab Muslims, they adopted Persian and Arab social norms. They altered their traditional exogamous rules and, like Persians and Arabs, permitted marriage with first cousins generally.

Societies become more complex and differentiated as technology develops, partly because the new technologies require societal members to engage in longer training periods to acquire advanced skills. More specialists are needed, and societal integration is based on the interdependence of specialized functions. Simultaneously, more non-kinship statuses and new socioeconomic arrangements are created. Effective kin relations are progressively confined to fewer people as other social ties carry more of the economic, political, educational, and social burden. The universality of sexual prohibitions (incest taboos) between primary kin remains, however, probably because the intensity of emotion associated with such prohibitions has become, through intensive learning in each generation, part of the psychobiological makeup of most societal members. Consequently, this deep-seated emotion may be independent of other infrastructural elements (cf. Y. Cohen 1978).

"Faction" versus Class

The concept of class refers to a horizontal slice of society characterized by group solidarity based on similar socioeconomic status and shared perceptions of self-interest (Collins 1982:32). Most Marxists conceptualize society as being class structured. In many cases, however, this may not be the most useful conceptualization. Human materialism employs the concept of "faction," which can be a class or a vertical section of society comprised of elites and their followers. Factions stand opposed to each other. The subordinate members of each faction see it in their best interest to support a single elite or group of elites rather than band together with other subordinates against the class of elites. For example, in multiparty political systems characterized by coalition governments, the elites of minor parties have loyal, lower economic class supporters who hope to be awarded secure government jobs once their minor party becomes part of a government coalition and takes control of a government ministry.

Superstructure

The superstructure consists of the ideologies, rituals and symbols associated with various organizations in social structure and of rival or alternative ideologies, rituals and symbols espoused by rival, minority or marginal members of the population. The strength of an ideology's influence within the sociocultural system is related to the degree to which it is promoted by those in positions of economic and political power and the extent to which the population has been indoctrinated with it. Persons occupying power positions within the social infrastructure devise ideologies or commission others to do so, or co-opt and/or alter existing ideologies to promote their positions and agendas by legitimizing the real relations of production or by masking them in the minds of the population. "Ruling groups throughout history and prehistory have always promoted the mystification of social life as their first line of defense against actual or potential enemies" (Harris 1979:158).

Well-intentioned intellectuals may inadvertently serve a system they miscomprehend. For instance, Marxists argue that modern liberal intellectuals fail to perceive the underlying forces of capitalist society. They see each new event—a strike, a colonial revolt, a war—as a separate phenomenon arising from a particular evil or injustice. They support justice against injustice so long as justice only makes for a temporary easing of the tensions and does not threaten to end the oppressive system in place. In effect, they counsel the bourgeoisie on the degree of concession needed to survive. When they inadvertently help to release mass forces which acquire their own momentum, they advocate retreat, urging the working mass not to go beyond a reasonable alleviation of their misfortunes. Marxists further maintain that this basic pattern did not arise with capitalism. The role of the intellectual attached to a ruling class has been the same for some three thousand years. It reflects the integration of professionals economically dependent on a property-owning system into the ruling class, where they generally act as a moderating force countering the possibly self-destructive conservatism of the owners of land and capital (Cameron: 1985:139).

Infrastructure and superstructure do not necessarily bear a direct one-to-one relationship. In socially ranked and stratified societies, persons in political/economic power often create or sustain ideologies that mask real relationships. They promote belief systems that indoctrinate the masses into believing things are their opposites: that a military, interventionist foreign policy exists to promote democracy, when it actually protects large overseas investments by powerful owners of capital.

According to Joll, the Italian philosopher Antonio Gramsci believed that "the rule of one class over another does not depend on economic or physical power alone but rather on persuading the ruled to accept the system of beliefs of the ruling class and to share its social, cultural and moral values" (1977:114). Gramsci correctly assessed the power of elite persuasion, but he apparently failed to note that the elites often persuade the masses to believe in social, cultural and moral values that they, themselves, secretly reject.

Such false ideologies may contain the seed of a major contradiction, which in the long run can work to the detriment of those in power. The masses, who have been led by the words of democracy, may begin demanding democracy in fact, by agitating for just legislation and political reforms. Rulers may find it expedient in a cost/benefit sense to accede to some of these demands, rather than risk revealing their true agendas. Through time, however, the political process may become progressively democratic, thus representing a threat to the prerogatives of those in power. In such a situation, rulers may attempt to overpower the democratic masses by military means and then change the process. Or they may redouble efforts to indoctrinate a large part of the masses into seeing what does not exist, or into not seeing at all.

To accomplish this, leaders often magnify internal and external threats to sacred values (e.g. capitalism as a threat to the Soviet way of life, or the evils of communism as a danger to the right of religious worship) and they foster major distractions, such a patriotic celebrations and sports events. They honor the major distracters, such as sports and entertainment heroes, in widely publicized, official ceremonies.

Ideology's Interface with Infrastructure and Structure

Leaders and organizations need a validating ideology. For people with economic and/or political power such an ideology serves to convince subordinates that the powerful few occupy their privileged places legitimately. An ideology begins to die out (i.e., have progressively fewer adherents) if those who promote it fail to gain infrastructural power or lose such power. Hence, the *sine qua non* of the relations of production is a validating ideology, and both depend on the ability of the elite to control the forces of production.

Productive forces, which are infrastructural elements that can be combined in effective ways (e.g. industrialization, mechanization of agriculture), also depend on a validating ideology. However, this ideology is more abstract. It merely justifies technological progress, the practical application of science, the goodness of innovation, the harnessing of nature's power, and the like. Being so abstract, it rarely conflicts with lower-level ideologies that attempt to justify the positions of certain power elites and the relations of production from which they benefit.

Ideology as Infrastructure

Human materialism is not intended to be a static, mechanical model. The shortcomings of such a model have been spelled out by Karl Deutsch, who has argued that the mechanical ideal-type carries with it some logical conclusions that are effectively inapplicable to our current knowledge of social and human phenomena. Among them is the notion of a whole completely equal to the sum of its parts; a model which can run in reverse; which behaves in the same fashion no matter how many times the parts are disassembled and reassembled; a model whose parts are not significantly modified by each other, nor by their own pasts. The mechanical model is based on the assumption that each part once placed in its appropriate position with its appropriate momentum, will stay exactly there and continue to fulfill its completely and uniquely determined function.

The human materialism model is designed to be dynamic. Rather than consisting of stationary, hierarchical categories, the relative positions of the analytic components shift with conditions and time. For example, conceptually, a new ideology is introduced into a system's superstructure and stays there until it has been spread to and inculcated by some segment of the population. Once it becomes a society's dominant ideology, that is, once societal members have become thoroughly indoctrinated by it, the ideology becomes part of their being and conceptually shifts to the human infrastructural component, not merely as a feedback loop, but as a constituent characteristic of population.

In socially ranked and stratified societies, each ideology may have its complement—one held by the ruling elite and another for mass indoctrination. The elite may purposefully promote an ideology they do not believe in, so long as that ideology contributes to the maintenance and/or enhancement of their dominant positions. The elite's own ideology (the complement of the one they promote) will probably be more blatantly self-serving. For example, during European Medieval times, the ideology for the masses was "rule is by divine right," while the elites' ideology involved exploiting religious beliefs to the extent possible to secure and enhance their ruling positions.

Societies whose rulers rely heavily on religious indoctrination and symbolism to secure and legitimize their positions of economic and political power exhibit a different reward system than do secular societies. In "religious" societies, rulers control the population (promote and reinforce their conformity) through a combination of spiritual and material rewards and a variety of spiritual, economic, and physical punishments. A recent example is Iran, where the ruling *mullahs* inspired men and boys to march to the front against Iraq by imbuing them with promises of heaven if "martyred" in battle and of economic security if Allah should permit them to live.

Spiritual Experience and Reinforcement

A spiritual sensation resulting from such activities as deep prayer or meditation, focusing on god or the guru, or chanting into ecstasy makes some people experience psychological and physical elation. Such spiritual euphoria constitutes the reward or reinforcement for the behavior that preceded it. People so rewarded repeat the behavior, seeking further elation or reinforcement. These people develop strong emotional attachments to the institutions that provide the context for the behavior and experience: institutions like churches, mosques, synagogues, ashrams, etc. Consequently, the institutions through their leaders can call on these people for financial, social, and political support. The success of these institutions may be measured in terms of their longevity, membership, and ability to command the support of the faithful. The old, conventional religious institutions that enjoy large, accumulated memberships can rely more on their well-established economic and political ties within their communities to command the faithful than on their ability to provide spiritual euphoria. New religious institutions, however, especially cult movements that lack the benefits of establishment ties, often attempt to win a loyal following by appealing to or creating emotional needs.

In secular societies, leaders must rely heavily on a system of material rewards and punishments to control the masses. But even in societies with secular governments, rulers search out and utilize sacred or near-sacred (e.g. patriotic) ideologies and symbols to persuade the masses to follow their directives. In such societies, tension exists between secular rulers and religious leaders, with the former circumscribing the political power of the latter, but drawing on that political power when it serves their needs.

Interface with Other Systems

A sociocultural system interacts with a variety of other systems. Rather than speak of boundaries, systems theorists employ the concept of "interface." They pay more attention to system-environmental connections and interpenetrations than to separations. At any point in time, an open system is characterized by both initial state conditions and external influences. An open system engages in interchanges with its sociocultural and natural environments, and these interchanges are essential to the system's viability, continuity and change. Open systems may respond to environmental intrusions by elaborating their structures to more complex levels. Human materialism assumes that an environing system's influence on the subject sociocultural system will be greatest when it impacts on the infrastructural component. Human materialism is compatible with world-system theory in that both conceptualize the contemporary world economy as consisting of interacting socioeconomic units tied together by a complex network of global economic exchange (see Wallerstein 1979).

Teleology

Many social scientists hope to make anthropology or sociology a "natural science" paralleling physics, biology, chemistry, etc. This suggests explaining human behavior in precisely the same fashion as the physical sciences have explained the behavior of inanimate, "natural" events, such as the motion of the stars, earthquakes, rain. It denies the usefulness of conceiving of human behavior as in any way mental, self-directed, or organized by the individual. Deterministic theories in the natural sciences explain the present as conditioned by the past. Teleological or final cause explanations may be quite inappropriate for the physical universe, but what about human behavior? If human behavior is nothing more than the result of material causes, then there is no room for self-directed, alternate actions. I argue that social science should readmit individual level teleology.

An approach is teleological when it explains either natural phenomena or human behavior on the basis of its purposive or intelligent striving towards some goal. A teleological explanation places as much emphasis on the future as it does on the past. Teleological theories concerning natural phenomena or systems are sometimes called "vitalistic," in contrast to more "mechanistic" theories, which stress the efficient causes of the past. Teleological theories of human behavior are often called "humanistic." Humanism implies that people differ from natural phenomena or systems in that they actively cognize their environment, and select goals and strategies to achieve them. Humanists argue against relying exclusively on efficient causes to capture the essence of human behavior. Bacon feared that if scientists accepted formal and final causes as explanatory, they would not actively seek empirical knowledge through experimentation. To experiment is to ask "What caused this state of affairs?"—not the teleological question, "What is the purpose of this object?" Bacon helped fix this attitude as the proper one for natural science. He limited explanation to material and efficient causes, and natural scientists have followed this path to the present. Formal and final causal explanations were left to the field of ethics (Rychlak 1968:122-123).

Human Teleology

A satisfactory sociocultural paradigm should take into account the dynamic forces motivating the people being studied, and the proponents of such models should reveal their assumptions about human nature. On the level of the individual actor, human materialism assumes "individual-level teleology." People in political/economic power positions are presumed to act in ways that maintain or enhance their positions. For example, they will promote legislation that favors themselves. The promoted legislation and especially its interpretation and application through time may not simply reflect the existing mode of production or relations of production. Rather, such legislation may reflect the strategies of the politically and economically powerful to maintain or enhance their positions in the face of changing circumstances, such as the shift from feudal to industrial economies.

In general, people are presumed to act to further their own well-being by trying to maximize *perceived* benefits, be they material, affective, or spiritual. For the relatively weak, the maximizing strategies may involve subordinating themselves to the powerful elite, or banding together with others to oppose those in power.

The above may be restated in terms of the following testable propositions. (1) Most persons in positions of economic/political power want to secure and enhance their positions or maximize their perceived benefits/resources, therefore they will promote courses of action they believe will accomplish these aims. (2) Some persons not in positions of economic/political power are dissatisfied with their statuses and will attempt to create strategies to elevate themselves to higher positions. Such strategies might include: (a) allying with elites so as to profit from their superior positions, even though this means remaining in a subordinate role, or (b) trying to displace elites, either with themselves or others who they believe will promote their cause. But, (3) if subordinate persons have been indoctrinated with the ideology for the masses, then they will accept the system in place.

Human materialism maintains that we cannot understand people if we assume that their states of mind are inconsequential. Whether one believes the goal of social science is interpretive understanding or casual explanation influences one's method and theory. Even if one is primarily interested in causal explanation, one cannot escape the question of whether people act because of environmental contingencies or because they have certain needs, desires, and perceptions of environmental contingencies. Rappaport (1967, 1979) has fruitfully distinguished between cognized and operational environments. A people's understanding of an environment constitutes their cognized environment. It may diverge from the operational environment or the actual set of environmental forces impinging upon them. In some societies, where voodoo and witchcraft beliefs are firmly held, the mind appears to dominate over objective environmental conditions, as when one's fear of voodoo death is so intense, that fear actually causes death (Cannon 1942).

In his study of the *Isoma* ritual of the Ndembu, Victor Turner (who wed structural, symbolic, and functional analysis) maintained that the symbols were not merely "a set of cognitive classifications for ordering the Ndembu universe. They are also, and perhaps more importantly, a set of evocative devices for rousing, channeling, and domesticating powerful emotions" (1969:42-43).

The Cyrenaica Bedouins, described by Peters (1967) have, according to their own conceptions, a segmentary system with political ties based on patrilineal descent. They explain that political alliances should be and are based strictly on the degree of relationship through males (agnatic ties). Yet when Peters mapped out the organization of political ties in actual situations, he discovered alliances were influenced heavily by ecological factors and were more often formed with distant lineages rather than with the ideals resulting from the application of agnatic rules. The Bedouin explain away the various exceptions, thereby maintaining the pretense that the ideals do govern behavior. Demographic and ecological factors may largely explain why certain numbers of people ally in a given ecological niche. But such factors do not explain which people will ally and why the Bedouin insist on conceptualizing their politico-economic behavior in terms of the particular legitimizing ideology of patrilineal descent.

Explanation and Testing

The human materialist paradigm assumes that infrastructural arrangements exert limitations on social structural and superstructural possibilities. A particular infrastructural base may be associated with a limited variety of social organizations and dominant ideologies. Given a certain socio-cultural system's infrastructural arrangement, social scientists should be able to predict, with some accuracy, what types of social organizations and ideologies are highly probable or highly improbable for most societal members. For example, given the technological base, mode of production and population density of a modern city like Chicago, a human materialist can predict that the hunting and gathering band type of social organization and nature religion (e.g. "the forest is god") that characterized the Pygmies of the Ituri Forest, are highly improbable for most residents, because they are functionally unsuited to this infrastructural context. Instead, small, sedentary family or household units and ideologies emphasizing individualism and the acquisition of material wealth, such as money and prestige goods, are more probable. However, this does not mean that some Chicago residents cannot choose to organize themselves into Pygmy-like bands and worship nature. Strong ideological commitments may cause some residents to act in unique ways. All of human teleology (goal directed behavior) cannot be accounted for by infrastructural deterministic explanations.

As stated above, a social scientific paradigm or research strategy, being an abstract model of sociocultural systems without empirical content, is not directly testable. Its empirically related hypotheses are testable. Support for a hypothesis comes in two forms: statistical and reasonable. The first is quantitative and refers to the proportion of empirical cases that exhibit the relationship predicted by the hypothesis. The second is the degree of plausibility of the posited deterministic relationship between and among the empirical elements of the hypothesis. For example, suppose the hypothesis is that prolonged infant nursing and a long post-partum sex taboo (2 + years after birth) are more probable than not in societies (1) practicing protein-poor forms of horticulture as the predominant mode of food production, and (2) experiencing a high incidence of kwashiorkor (a protein-deficiency condition). Suppose also that an examination of a large, random sample of societies with characteristics (1) and (2) shows that in a high proportion (say 80%) mothers generally do breast-feed their infants for two or more years and during that time avoid sexual intercourse. Then we can conclude that the hypothesis has statistical support.

An infrastructurally based explanation of the observed relationships could go as follows: societies that experience high rates of kwashiorkor due to insufficient protein in available foods must, in order to enhance the survival of new members, develop means of increasing the protein content of their diets. Because a mother's milk is richer in protein than available alternatives, such societies are likely to develop practices, such as prolonged infant nursing and a long post-partum sex taboo (to prevent the birth of another child during the nursing period), that enable newborns to benefit from mother's milk during the critical early years of life. The causal arrows of the correlated elements go from infrastructure (mode of food production and environment), to social structure (mother-child, father-child, and wife-husband relationships), to superstructure (an ideology proscribing sexual intercourse with women during the prolonged nursing period). The degree to which this explanation is logically and factually constructed and reasonable to knowledgeable persons is the degree to which the hypothesis is plausible.

Although a social scientific paradigm may be used to develop generalizations or nomothetic explanations, as illustrated above, it may also be used to explain the single case, e.g., the meaning of a Koryak incest myth (see Magnarella 1994:Chap. 4). Support for the posited explanation of a single case may rest on logical and factual construction and plausibility only, without resort to statistical proof.

Summary and Conclusion

The human materialist paradigm offers both an abstract model of socio-cultural systems and a research strategy. It combines in a unique and fruitful way a number of established theoretical perspectives. One of its major strengths and innovations is its blending of infrastructural causality with humanistic teleology. That is, it places human behavior within its effective environmental context and also focuses significantly on human thought, especially the plans, strategies, and agendas of societal leaders. The paradigm analytically divides sociocultural systems into three major interfacing components—infrastructural, social structural, and superstructural—and suggests, for the purpose of hypo-thesis formation, a sequence of causal relationships. Although the model assumes mutual causality within, between and among the three major components, it hypothesizes that the direction of the more powerful causal forces goes from infrastructure to social structure to superstructure.

The human materialist paradigm is designed to be dynamic, rather than simply mechanical. It is comprehensive enough to deal with sociocultural systems as small as families or hunting and gathering bands, or as large as modern states and interstate systems. It can address questions in any of the social sciences areas: kinship, society, politics, economics, religion, law, education, etc.

I have applied human materialism to a variety of case studies, derived from tribally to state organized peoples (Magnarella 1994). This is a series of case studies that further develops the human teleological component of the model and applies it to an actual case of peasants undergoing change; deals with an Islamic-political movement in early twentieth-century Arabia and offers an analysis of the causal-teleological interrelationships among environment, technology, elite-and-follower political aspirations and religious indoctrination; offers analyses of the Siberian Koryak's mythology, religion, symbolism and ritual by combining human materialism with French structuralism and various interpretative approaches; applies human materialism to state level politics in Turkey by offering an analysis of elite behavior, especially attempts by political leaders to employ civic and religious ideologies to indoctrinate and control the masses; presents a human materialist theory of civil violence and applies the theory to Turkey. On the basis of an assessment of the current debate in cultural anthropology over proper goals and methods it can be concluded that an integrative paradigm such as human materialism can accommodate those seeking scientific explanations as well as those searching for meaning.

References

Brown, Donald E.
    1991   *Human Universals*. New York: McGraw-Hill.
Cameron, Kenneth Neil
    1985   *Marxism: The Science of Society*. South Hadley, MA: Bergin & Garvey.
Cannon, Walter B.
    1942   "Voodoo Death." *American Anthropologist* 44:169-181.
Cohen, G. A.
    1978   *Karl Marx's Theory of History: A Defence*. Princeton, NJ: Princeton University Press.

Cohen, Yehudi
    1978   "The Disappearance of the Incest Taboo." *Human Nature*
            1 (7):72-78.
Collins, Hugh
    1982   *Marxism and the Law.* Oxford: Clarendon Press.
Geertz, Clifford
    1966   "The Impact of the Concept of Culture on the Concept of
            Man." In J. Pratt, ed., *New Views of the Nature of Man.*
            Chicago, IL: University of Chicago Press.
Gillen, John
    1955   "Ethnos Components in Modern Latin American Culture."
            American Anthropologist 57:488-99.
Harris, Marvin
    1979   *Cultural Materialism: The Struggle for a Science of Culture.*
            New York: Random House.
Joll, James
    1977   *Antonio Gramsci.* London: Penguin Books.
Lewin, Kurt
    1951   *Field Theory in the Social Sciences.* New York: Harper.
Magnarella, Paul J.
    1981   *Iranian Diplomacy in the Khomeini Era.* In M. D. Zamora
            et al., eds., *Culture and Diplomacy in the Third World.*
            Williamsburg, VA: College of William and Mary.
    1994   *Human Materialism: A Model of Sociocultural Systems and
            a Strategy for Analysis.* Gainesville: University Press of
            Florida.
Molnar, Stephen
    1983   *Human Variation.* 2nd edition. Englewood Cliffs, NJ:
            Prentice-Hall.
Peters, Emery
    1967   "Some Structural Aspects of the Feud among the Camel-
            Herding Bedouin of Cyrenaica." *Africa* 37:260-282.
Rappaport, R. A.
    1967   *Pigs for the Ancestors.* New Haven, CT: Yale University
            Press.
    1979   *Ecology, Meaning, and Religion.* Berkeley, CA: North
            Atlantic Books.
Rychlak, Joseph F.
    1968   *A Philosophy of Science for Personality Theory.* Boston,
            MA: Houghton Mifflin.

Sahlins, Marshall
    1976   *Culture and Practical Reason.*   Chicago, IL: University of
            Chicago Press.
Turner, Victor
    1969   *The Ritual Process.* Chicago, IL: Aldine.
von Bertalanffy, Ludwig
    1967   *Robots, Men and Minds.* New York: George Braziller.
Wallerstein, Immanuel
    1979   *The Capitalist World-Economy.*   Cambridge: Cambridge
            University Press.
Willner, Ann Ruth
    1984   *The Spellbinders: Charismatic Political Leadership.* New
            Haven, CT: Yale University Press.

Conclusion

FORECASTING THEORY: PROBLEMS AND EXEMPLARS IN THE TWENTY-FIRST CENTURY

Stanley R. Barrett

Anthropologists justifiably celebrate the ethnographic tradition, the eye-witness documentation of cultural variation around the globe. Yet as we gaze back over the twentieth century, what is equally impressive is the sheer range of theorizing that has been accomplished. It would seem that almost every conceivable theoretical position has been formulated, from the scientific to the humanistic, from the general to the local. In the early days there was Boas's historical particularism competing with Radcliffe-Brown's structural functionalism, and more recently the different camps occupied by Harris and Geertz, plus the thought-provoking approaches of postmodernism and feminist anthropology.

One thing is certain: over and above the discipline's reputation for the close descriptive account of specific cultures, or parts of cultures, based on participant observation, anthropology has harbored huge theoretical ambitions. But it is not simply the amount of theorizing that is noteworthy. Instead, it is the impact of theory. From the advent of professional anthropology, the progress of the discipline (or at least changes in perspective) has been stimulated as much by the key theoretical work as by the impeccable ethnographic monograph. Thus, not only did we have Malinowski's *Argonauts* early on, but also Radcliffe-Brown's *A Natural Science of Society*.

By the time the careers of the first generation of modern fieldworkers were spent, it became even more probable that the publication with the greatest impact on the discipline, promoting a new way of looking at the world and doing research, would be a work of theory.

Consider, for example, the influence of *Theory of Culture Change* (Steward), *The Elementary Structures of Kinship* (Lévi-Strauss), *Purity and Danger* (Douglas), *Political Systems of Highland Burma* (Leach), *Schism and Continuity in an African Society* (Turner), *Models of Social Organization* (Barth), *Custom and Conflict in Africa* (Gluckman), *Stratagems and Spoils* (Bailey), *Time and the Other* (Fabian), *The Revolution in Anthropology* (Jarvie), *Orientalism* (Said), and *Writing Culture* (Clifford and Marcus).

It will be noted that this sample list of key publications does not include textbooks on theory. Textbooks have their place. They clarify what has been going on, synthesize fields of research, identify problems and trends, evaluate perspectives, and give a glimpse of the big picture. At times they may promote a specific research program, such as cultural materialism in Harris's *The Rise of Anthropological Theory* (1968), but for the most part textbooks serve a didactic purpose aimed at the classroom. The key theoretical study is a different animal. Its essence is innovation. Its impact is revolutionary—not just in the classroom, but in the fieldwork setting itself. Such works shift the way practicing ethnographers look at the world, and influence the kinds of data collected and the manner in which data are interpreted.[1]

It will also be noted that the publications identified as pivotal ones are full-length books, not articles. It is understandable why the book is the preferred form of publication for ethnographic reporting: the sheer amount of data—qualitative for the most part—leaves little option. What is curious is that the book has been the main vehicle for the influential theory statement as well. There have been exceptions, such as Radcliffe-Brown's "The Mother's Brother in South Africa," Foster's "Peasant Society and the Image of the Limited Good," Sahlins's "The Original Affluent Society," Nader's "Up the Anthropologist. Perspectives Gained from Studying Up," and Strathern's "An Awkward Relationship: The Case of Feminism and Anthropology." Occasionally anthologies organized around a specific theme such as *African Systems of Kinship and Marriage* (Radcliffe-Brown and Forde) and *African Political Systems* (Fortes and Evans-Pritchard), or a collection of an author's previously published pieces (perhaps with a new introduction such as "Thick Description" in Geertz's *The Interpretation of Cultures*), will have an impact. But these are exceptions. Anthropologists aspiring to become the pied pipers of theory would be wise, at least if the past tells us anything, to record their seductive melodies in the single-authored, full-length monograph.

There is something else characteristic of the key books in theory:

they are ethnographically friendly. Although abstract by definition, they are often constructed from existing ethnography, certainly illustrated by ethnography, and capable of directing future fieldwork. An especially appropriate example is the transactional model advocated by Bailey in *Stratagems and Spoils* (1969). To turn this around, those theory books (and theoretical orientations) that fail to inspire considerable fieldwork activity, that stand splendidly independent of research, perhaps because they constitute meta-theory or are simply too fanciful to have any pragmatic application, rarely endure, even if they stimulate the brain cells. Cases in point may well be Lévi-Strauss's structuralism and the current front-runner, postmodernism. The influential theory books in the twentieth century might be regarded as the discipline's exemplars—works that have not only shaped the discipline, but also reveal its nature.

My assumption is that progress in the future, as in the past, will hinge largely on the key theory books that will eventually be written. My aim in this chapter is to identify some of these potential works. For at least two reasons, this task, while daunting, is not entirely a matter of guesswork. One is that the forces that will generate the next generation's theoretical positions already are in operation. Put otherwise, at any given time the social and cultural (including intellectual) environment is pregnant with theory. A second reason is that the sources of theoretical development are not entirely mysterious. As I shall argue, the books about to be born in the early decades of the twenty-first century will be sired and nurtured partly by the particular nature of social change in society at large, as well as by the internal dynamics of the discipline itself.

A Framework for Forecasting Theory

1. Social Change

Kardiner and Preble (1963:189) have ventured that the history of a field such as anthropology is not so much a history of falsehoods and truths as it is a record of man's attempts to solve the problems that a constantly changing world presents. This alludes to a significant difference between the database of the natural sciences and the social sciences. In the natural sciences a pig does not change into a hippopotamus over the course of a few generations. But in that same time span a socialist society can become a capitalist society, and women can leave the kitchen and join men on the assembly line or in the boardroom. Unlike Kuhn's (1970) version of the hard sciences, where new theoretical perspectives (or paradigms) are generated by anomalies (puzzles which persist), in the social sciences they are generated by changes in the subject matter itself: society.

Just as a particular theoretical orientation is being elaborated and refined, a world war erupts, the Berlin Wall comes down, or a technological revolution ushers in the computer age. The old theories become obsolete, and scholars scramble to erect new ones appropriate to the transformed world. There is nothing controversial in the suggestion that society is constantly in flux, and that our theories must adapt to a mutable database. But there is something special about the kinds, and sheer range, of social change that have materialized in recent decades. Human society is in the process of being transformed to a degree possibly not seen since the Industrial Revolution. This process can be summed up by the term globalization. Multicultural corporations in search of cheap labor and new markets have spread across the globe, challenging the integrity of the nation-state, weakening trade unions and undermining social programs, polarizing wealth and poverty, shifting power from one region to another, prompting massive population movements, and creating simultaneously a trend towards a homogenized world culture and a celebration of a newly conscious local culture.

This massive transformation of society on a world scale has obvious implications for anthropology. Our theories must be rebuilt to cope with the new realities. But there is another implication that is not so obvious, yet enormously significant. As a result of globalization, anthropology may finally be entering an era in which the sense of crisis that has dogged the discipline for decades will wither away.

Let me explain. The big event for early anthropology, spawned in the age of imperialism, was the discovery of "the other" (the primitive, the native). This gave rise to the discipline's central problematic: how to square the immense range of cultural variation with the presumed underlying psychic and biological unity of *Homo sapiens*? This problematic, which endured up to the Second World War, and provided the discipline with at least a loose sense of direction and coherence, was explored in the context of colonialism, resulting in both humanistic and racist responses. Similarly, the big event for sociology was the Industrial Revolution, shaping its central problematic, social class, as feudalism and mercantilism gave way to capitalism. Behind both disciplines were the ideals of the Enlightenment: individual worth, rationality, and progress.

The crisis that emerged in anthropology in the 1960s was a signal that its central problematic had lost much of its relevance. Social change had dealt it a death sentence: the impact of two world wars, the end of colonialism, development in the Third World, and a globe made smaller by population movements, communications, and international politics. This brings us back to my central (perhaps audacious, and at this point certainly speculative) thesis: a new all-embracing problematic may be crystallizing around globalization, articulated with capitalism, and informed by the tenets of postmodernism rather than by the Enlightenment. Should this be the case, it is improbable that a single, dominant theoretical orientation will emerge, or that paradigmatic status will be achieved. That pleasant state of affairs never existed when the influence of the old problematic was at its height. But it may mean that once again there will be a sense of direction to the discipline, and a degree of confidence among practitioners unknown since the days of Radcliffe-Brown, Steward, and Firth.

2. Internal Dialectics

The task of adapting our theories to changes in society is challenging enough, but there are additional complicating factors. Theory is driven in part by an internal dialectic; or, rather, a complex of dialectical forces. One dialectic, deeply embedded in the discipline, consists of conceptual contradictions (or oppositions) such as dynamic vs. static, conflict vs. harmony, individual vs. group, emic vs. etic, unique vs. regular, and unconscious vs. conscious (see Barrett 1984:Chap. 4). A theoretical orientation rarely expresses both sides of the conceptual contradictions, otherwise it would lack coherence. Moreover, there is at least a loose logical fit between combinations of concepts (for example, harmony, group and regular; or dynamic, conflict and unique), which partly explains why new models often resemble long-discarded ones. Because these contradictions have not been resolved (and probably never will be), there is a tendency to build the next generation's theoretical perspective around the concepts that have been suppressed in current orientations.

The embedded conceptual contradictions are not the only ones that stir the anthropological stew. The entire history of theoretical orientations, on that level, contains its own peculiar dynamic. New approaches certainly address changes that have taken place in society, but to some degree they are trapped by the achievements of the past. In other words, the collective body of theory in the discipline constitutes a social fact (to borrow from Durkheim), or a frozen dialectic, as Murphy (1971) has put it, from which new orientations only partially escape. What I am arguing, in a nutshell, is that theoretical orientations bounce off each other. For example, it is improbable that a new version of evolutionism would be crafted without considering early evolutionary theory and neo-evolutionism, plus the principal critiques of this perspective mounted by historical particularism and structural functionalism. The tendency for scholars to engage in a debate with their own history impacts on theory in two related ways. New models usually reverse the direction of those they aspire to displace, and they often resemble those that long ago were discarded. For example, Gluckman's conflict theory supposedly obliterated structural functionalism while at the same time resuscitating Simmel's perspective.

So far, I have suggested that theory is shaped by a triple dialectic: the adaptation of theory to changes in society, the influence of the raw conceptual contradictions, and the reaction of theoretical orientations to each other. It may make sense to talk about a fourth and fifth dialectic. Knowledge of the world modifies the world. Theories of social action do more than explain: they potentially change the nature of social action itself. As Friedrichs (1972a, 1972b) has argued, the social scientist's analysis of behavior and belief feeds back into the social realm, thus altering it.

Finally, just as there is an internal dialectic within the corpus of anthropological theory, there may be one within social action itself. Dahrendorf (1959:viii) has remarked that a unique human phenomenon is that social structures create permanently and systematically some of the determinant forces of their change within themselves. Van den Berghe (1967:295) has pointed out that while tending toward stability, consensus, and equilibrium, societies also generate within themselves the opposite conditions. And let us not forget Murphy's dialectics (1971), in which norm and act clash, transforming each other and culture more generally.

This complex of dialectical forces not only helps to explain an otherwise baffling phenomenon—the repetitive, oscillating, noncumulative character of anthropological theory—but also to anticipate its future direction. The history of the discipline can be crudely divided into the long run of positivism (evolutionism, historical particularism, cultural ecology, structural functionalism, etc.) and the recent era of post-positivism (structuralism, interpretive anthropology, postmodernism, and feminist anthropology). Solely on the basis of dialectics internal to theory (conceptual contradictions, and the impact of theoretical orientations on each other), it would appear that many of the assumptions within and positions taken by post-positivism are about to be reversed. The anti-scientific thrust of postmodernism and feminist anthropology (especially the sub-variant, feminist methodology), and the peculiar version of science within structuralism (non-empirical, and characterized by transformation and inversion rather than cause and effect) and interpretive anthropology (non-generalizable and non-verifiable) may well give way to a revived, if less arrogant, positivism. There already has been a sizable backlash against feminist methodology, especially the distinction between male and female science, and Lévi-Strauss's halo has long since dimmed.

The emphasis on the particular, as in the work of Geertz and Abu-Lughod, may be reversed, rendering generalization across cases legitimate once again. The justification will be readily available despite Abu-Lughod's (1991) persuasive argument that cultural generalizations freeze, homogenize, and distort the individual, and that a focus on the individual does not ignore broader historical and structural forces; indeed, it is at the level of the local and particular that such forces are manifested and thus recognized by the investigator. It will be argued, perhaps especially by British social anthropologists, that if patterns of social action, or properties of the social structure, are not critical, the discipline might as well be abandoned, because it will lack an autonomous conceptual territory. It might also be pointed out that the tendency to eschew social facts provides credibility to right-wing politicians such as Margaret Thatcher who declared that society does not exist, only individuals do. If generalization across cases makes a comeback, we can expect the life history, only recently revived, to sink back into oblivion.

Also on shaky ground will be the privileged position occupied by things said rather than things done, by interpretation, subjectivity and meaning rather than objective data, social structure and behavior. The justification here will be that social structure (or material culture) shapes people's lives at least partly independent of their consciousness, and therefore constitutes a basic dimension of inquiry.

It is always possible that sanity will prevail, so that not every idea and procedure associated with post-positivism will be thrown out. An anthropology that fails to assign a central position to interpretation, à la Geertz, is difficult to imagine. The same is true with regard to the issue of representation explored by postmodernists and feminists: the image respectively of "the other" and of women under patriarchy. Then, too, there is the analysis of ethnographic authority, and the promotion of a dialogic anthropology. Most surprising of all would be the failure to protect a place for gender in our conceptual framework.

My views on the literary analysis of ethnography are quite different. To paraphrase Rabinow (1986:243), the news that ethnography constitutes a text replete with literary devices is interesting, but hardly earth-shattering. The view from the English department certainly adds to our understanding, as does Geertz's reduction of ethnography to an assemblage of texts, a fiction, something made. But that is only one slant on the subject, and in my judgment hardly the most significant one. What is rather astounding is that any of us should have assumed that literary criticism has anything more profound and less jargonistic to offer than our conventional tools of analysis. If ever there was doubt about the crisis in anthropology and the vulnerability of its practitioners, the intellectual *coup d'état* engineered by Clifford and company should have laid it to rest. Besides, the literary theorists have had their fun, and are ready to drop us and move on to fresh pastures.

If sanity does not prevail, we may be in for a sterile stretch. The healthy critical thrust within postmodernism and feminist anthropology may give way to a conservative era, and some of the most value-laden perspectives of the past, such as evolutionism and structural functionalism, or at least heavily disguised aspects of them, may creep back in. If the discipline does swing towards conventional science, there may be some pressure to replace qualitative methods by quantitative ones, but it will be resisted by the effort to keep our distance from sociology. Even if it is the softer versions of scientific anthropology from the past which resurface—Bailey's transactional model and Murphy's dialectical approach—the overall prognosis is hardly inspiring: warmed-up porridge, the old story of repetition and oscillation from which the post-positivists had temporarily escaped.

3. Salvage Theory

While the impact of social change and the internal dialectic constitute the basic sources of theoretical development, they are not the only ones. Some theoretical work will be devoted to propping up orientations that have been discredited, or at least increasingly neglected. This is what I call salvage theory. For example, the old Weberian-influenced modernization theory of the 1960s, with its emphasis on individualism, the Protestant ethic, middle-class values, and culture rather than economics, was shaken to the roots by the emerging Marxian-influenced alternative, with its emphasis on Western (capitalistic) hegemony, core-peripheral relations, and the process by which under-development was developed. Yet few modernization theorists abandoned the ship. Instead, they tinkered with the framework, stressing the psychological basis of development (*n*Ach, or the need to achieve), promoting a top-heavy model orchestrated by the state rather than the uncoordinated efforts of individual entrepreneurs, and even advocating that the military in new nations assume the leading role in the development process.

Just as there still were positivists in the 1980s and 1990s, there also will be post-positivists when the theoretical orientations lumped under this label lose their steam, which almost certainly will be the case. Salvage theory, in other words, will continue to occupy a corner of the discipline in the twenty-first century, and for understandable reasons. It is asking a lot for individual scholars who have devoted their careers to a particular version of anthropology to accept that they have been misguided all along. Moreover, it is highly improbable that the superiority of the sparkling new orientation (or orientations) over previous ones will have been clearly demonstrated. Even in the hard sciences, Kuhn contends, new paradigms are embraced largely on the basis of faith, in a process comparable to religious conversion.

4. Unfinished Business

Some theoretical work in the future will address issues and puzzles that have long existed in the discipline, but have never been adequately resolved. Galton's problem comes to mind, involving the difficulty of identifying discrete units of culture given the potential contamination of diffusionism. Then there is the matter of value-neutrality. Under the current era of post-positivism, the goal of a value free, objective social science has been massively rejected. This is not only because it is assumed that objectivity is unattainable, but also because it obfuscates power and privilege, and thus helps prop up the *status quo*. Yet if the discipline does swing back to a more conventional scientific style, the dream of a value-free anthropology will once again rock us to sleep.

A number of other unresolved issues and problems lurk in the shadows: What is the difference between culture and society? What comes first: thought or action, idea systems or social systems? How to handle the gap between things said and things done? Then there are the perennial dilemmas of deductive versus inductive and macro versus micro, as well as the conventional textbook questions: Does language dictate thought and behavior? Is the family (or religion, or racism or gender inequality) universal?

Not surprisingly, these same issues and puzzles formed the basis for heated debate when we were students. In time, most of us professional anthropologists set these issues aside and got on with our work. But that does not mean we had come up with answers. We simply lost interest, or wrote the whole business off as beyond rational solution.

5. Individual Creativity

Nobody writes in a vacuum. Even the most imaginative scholars have intellectual pedigrees. However, every now and again a man or woman comes along with a message so novel as to stun the rest of us. Since the Second World War, two anthropologists have taken the discipline by storm: Lévi-Strauss and Geertz. Their unique—even idiosyncratic—achievements push the borders of anthropology beyond what most of us thought was possible, and where few of us dare, or have the capacity, to follow. In this context it may be warranted to evoke the notion of innate creative genius. Some theorizing in the generations ahead, if we are lucky, will carve out the equivalent of the structuralist analysis of myth or thick description.

In a sense, of course, innovation is a goal institutionalized into anthropology (and the social sciences in general). Lodged at the pre-paradigmatic stage, the discipline does not engage in the mopping-up operations that Kuhn associates with normal science, where novelty is a nuisance. Instead, we seek out and reward novelty, whether of fact or theory. Anthropologists, in other words, at least when it comes to choosing pet theories, are programmed to be promiscuous.

6. Order as a Constraint

Contradicting, and thus limiting, the emphasis on innovation for its own sake is the desire for order. Festinger (1957:260) has argued that among lay people there is an incessant drive to reduce dissonance, to achieve harmony and order in one's life. Academics are little different. Not only do they attempt to demonstrate that beneath the apparent chaos of life there is order, but the evidence suggests that many of them cannot tolerate disorder. Herbert Spencer, for example (Kardiner and Preble 1961:33), could not accept an inefficient salt cellar any more than he could abide a disorderly universe. His life was obsessed with the need to fit all of nature—the inorganic, the organic, and the superorganic—into a neat, perfectly axiomatized system. Tyler (1969:6) has observed that we classify because life in a world where nothing was the same would be intolerable. Lévi-Strauss (1978:11), who has described his mandate as the search for order behind apparent disorder, declared that it is absolutely impossible to conceive of meaning without order.

The commitment, both intellectual and emotional, of anthropologists to the discovery of order will undoubtedly help shape theory in the next generation. Given the bias towards order, it is all the more surprising that the inconclusive, fragmented ethnographic products advocated by postmodernists and feminist methodologists attracted as large an audience as they did.

Key Books on the Horizon

My purpose now is to speculate about the kinds of studies that will provide the discipline with new vigor. Note that I employ the word vigor rather than progress. It is dubious whether progress is an appropriate term in the context of anthropological knowledge. Rather than being cumulative, with each successive model resting on its predecessors, our theories rise and fall according to the nature of social change. To make matters worse, these theories are sometimes deflected away from the ethnographic target that social change does produce by virtue of the dialectics contained within them.

The conventional way to measure the significance of a book (or article) is to ask whether further research in the same field of inquiry can afford to ignore it. Who would examine suicide or ritual without consulting Durkheim and Turner? This makes a lot of sense to me, but I want to put a different twist on significance. To rip a famous concept out of its usual context, those books that have made, or will make, a critical contribution contain what might be labelled intellectual surplus value. That is, they erect an explanatory system that avoids (at least partially) the internal dialectic that drives theory in a repetitive direction, and surmounts some of the peculiarities of the social structure at the point in time in which they are composed. A theoretical work rich in surplus value, in other words, opens up a new way of looking at the world which remains efficacious even after the changes in society that prompted it have given way to fresh waves of change. It is in this context that progress may be said to be meaningful in anthropology.

All of the books outlined below—my version of the top ten—have one thing in common: the potential to create surplus values of theory.

1. Culture

It would not be difficult to explain to a non-anthropological audience why culture has been our core concept. It is culture that separates *Homo sapiens* from other species. Chimpanzees and dolphins may display signs of behavior that are inexplicable in genetic terms; but to paraphrase Marvin Harris, there would not be enough room in the local library to store a complete record of the cultural acts performed by human beings in a small village on a single day (at least before the era of the computer disc)! It is also culture that separates the behavior of human beings which is learned and created from that which is biologically determined. Culture, as we say, is adopted, shared, and transmitted by socialization from one generation to the next. At the very heart of culture, White (1949) points out, is the capacity to symbolize; human beings, for example, are the only species capable of distinguishing holy water from ordinary water.

Yet if culture has been our most significant concept, it simultaneously has been maddeningly elusive. Half a century ago, Kroeber and Kluckhohn (1952) were able to identify more than one hundred different definitions of culture in the literature. Over the years the explanatory value of the concept has been questioned. Radcliffe-Brown flatly declared that a science of culture was nonsensical (but not a science of society). A generation ago Tyler pointed out that too much has been expected from the concept:

> Culture, conceived as the totality of human behavior, ideas, history, institutions and artifacts has never been particularly useful as a meaningful method of explaining ethnographic facts. Such a conception merely asserts that culture is equivalent to the whole of human knowledge. As a device which purports to explain all of man's learned behavior, motivations, prehistoric record, ecological adaptations, biological limitations, and evolution it attempts too much (Tyler 1969:14).

More recently, Abu-Lughod (1991) has declared that the time has come for anthropologists to write against culture. Her argument is that the concept has begun to resemble race. It promotes a viewpoint in which people around the globe are separated into distinctive blocks, homogenized and stereotyped, and arranged in an implicit hierarchy of superiority and inferiority.

As we enter the twenty-first century, the clarity and utility of the concept of culture appear to be more dubious than ever before. By the grace of globalization, and its engine capitalism, Western ideology has stretched into the furthest reaches of human habitation. At the same time there has been a massive population movement, what Appadurai (1991) labels deterritorialization, of political and economic refugees, and others rich in capital or imagination, into the towns and cities of the West. The impact on culture has been enormous. Former citizens of Calcutta, Fiji and Estonia now reside next to each other in Philadelphia and Toronto. Protestants, Catholics and Jews on the way to worship cross paths with Hindus, Muslims and Buddhists. Restaurants (thank God!) offer a choice between roast beef, curry and couscous. In view of such heterogeneity, the idea of culture as a coherent, unified, distinctive whole no longer is tenable. But this is not reason to jettison the concept. Human beings will continue to distinguish holy water from ordinary water, and the ideas and traditions of one generation, even if they are more diffuse than those of the past, will still be passed on to the next. What is required is a key theoretical work that will salvage the concept of culture in a transformed world. The starting point, I think, will be to revise the concept so that it reflects the heterogeneity and fragmentation generated by globalization, and to cut the concept down in size so that it does not promise more than it can deliver.

2. Class

The old distinction between kinship-organized and class-organized societies conveyed the assumption that class belongs to sociology, not anthropology. The trend towards anthropology at home, by now a well-established tradition, should have undermined that assumption, one would have thought, but no such luck. As Ortner has pointed out, the bulk of ethnographic studies in America cavalierly ignore social class. Rather than focusing on the core of capitalist society, they search out marginal groups such as retirement communities, street gangs and religious sects. Moreover, these studies have tended "to 'ethnicize' the groups under study, to treat them as so many isolated and exotic tribes" (Ortner 1991: 166). The significance of social class for anthropology does not rest solely on the trend for ethnographers to work in their own class-based societies. Globalization has also transformed kinship-organized societies at least partly into class-organized ones; the implication is that social class now has analytic pertinence regardless of geographic setting.

There is an urgent need, thus, to pull class into the center of the discipline's conceptual territory. Attempts to do so will not be starting from scratch. There is Warner's (1949) well-known, albeit strongly criticized, Yankee City series, and more recently Bourdieu's influential *Distinction* (1984); for decades scholars favoring a political economy perspective have grappled with class in their research in developing nations, and here at home an occasional ethnography comes on the market, such as Dunk's (1991) elegant analysis of working-class culture in a northern Canadian city; class and status, I might add, were critical variables in one of my own recent projects (Barrett 1994).

If logic does prevail, and class is adopted as a basic concept in anthropology, there will be some unsurprising consequences. Kinship studies may slip even further from the center, and ethnographers will have to return to Weber and Marx as much as to Boas and Malinowski. There may also be a rather fascinating unanticipated consequence. My impression is that students in sociology have begun to lose sight of social class. This may be because class has been pushed aside by other variables, notably gender and to a lesser degree ethnicity, deflating the attraction of the classics. The irony would be delicious if it took the example of anthropology to instruct sociology about the fundamental importance of class.

3. Gender

There is an enormous, important, and stimulating literature on feminist anthropology, and on feminist scholarship more generally. But in my judgment, if I might be so bold, some sizable gaps remain. For example, while writers such as Whittaker (1994) and Strathern (1987) have articulated the principles of a unique feminist perspective in anthropology, their works might be described as preliminary. What is missing is the authoritative book on the feminist paradigm that the majority of anthropologists (male or female) cannot afford to ignore, and which will have an enduring influence on ethnographic research over the next several decades.

It is well known that anthropology as a profession has proved attractive to women. There exist specific studies devoted to women who have had outstanding careers, and to the impact of gender on the research setting (Golde 1970; Warren 1988), as well as bibliographical sketches of women in the discipline (Gacs et al. 1988). Yet to my knowledge there is nothing in anthropology comparable to McDonald's studies (1993 and 1994) on the critical contribution of women to early sociology. What is surprising is that there has been little written, and certainly no book-length treatment, on a figure as prominent as Audrey Richards, an early British social anthropologist whose work can still be read with profit today.

While there is nothing very provocative about calling for a key book on feminist anthropology, or for studies that document the contributions of women founders, some eyebrows might be raised if I suggest there is a place for texts on theory and methods that draw primarily from female sources. I do so with Eichler in mind. Her position (1986) is that while non-sexist research is the ultimate goal, in order to get there it is necessary to first pass through the stage of women-centered research. Similarly, women-saturated textbooks may be an unavoidable prelude to gender-blind ones, if only for their political clout. Such texts, of course, will be hardly more gender-biased than those in print at present.

4. Power

Power, Edmund Leach once observed (1954) is the most basic dimension in human interaction. It follows logically that anthropologists, even if they wished, could not avoid dealing with power at least implicitly, for it is an analytic aspect of all social behavior, embedded by definition in ethnography. In the sub-field of political anthropology, the analysis of power occasionally has been explicit. Bailey (1980), for example, has advocated that power (and authority) be replaced by influence. Influence here connotes force at one end of a scale and rational argument at the other, with manipulation somewhere in between.

Bailey's contribution notwithstanding, what has been missing in the discipline has been the path-breaking work on the theory of power. Anthropologists looking for direction about the meaning and operation of power have to return to Marx and Weber, or raid more contemporary ideas and concepts from neighboring disciplines. There is, for example, the top-down and bottom-up view of power (Hunter 1953; Dahl 1961), intentional (subjective) versus unintentional (structural) power (Baldus 1975; Giddens 1979), decisions versus non-decisions (Bachrach and Baratz 1962, 1963), and Gramsci's distinction between force and consent (Merrington 1968).

Postmodernists and feminist anthropologists, notably in relation to the analysis of representation and the once unproblematic authority of the researcher/writer, have helped to show how power operates. Until, however, a key theoretical work bounces off the press, reflecting the discipline's special perspective and taking into account recent global changes, perhaps even rendering obsolete Lukes's thin volume on power (1974), anthropologists will be derelict in their duty.

5. Racism

Some of the most prominent anthropologists in the world, such as Boas and Montagu in America and Banton and Little in Britain, have focused their minds on the analysis of racism. This makes it all the more difficult to understand why the subject of racism does not occupy a more central position in the discipline. My impression is that while the majority of anthropologists are disturbed about racism when it crosses paths with their personal lives, they generally ignore it or are at a loss about how to deal with it in their professional lives. Part of the explanation concerns the influence of the great European theoreticians, Marx, Weber and Durkheim, whose great achievement was to carve out social structure as a distinctive disciplinary territory. Yet Marx did write about racism, referring to the Irish as Britain's niggers, and explaining racism as one of the ideological props of capitalism; Weber, for his part, was sensitized to the issue of racism by his visit to America, and theorized about ethnic-based social action. The tendency to ignore racism also can be traced back to the battle between race and culture in early American anthropology. Victory went to culture, but it apparently left anthropologists partly blind about a non-biological phenomenon: racism.

One of the most contentious issues in the literature has been the status of racism as an independent entity. The conventional Marxist perspective (Cox 1948) is that racism is an epiphenomenon of class, a mechanism that divides the workers along color lines for the benefit of the owners. The conventional liberal perspective (Rex 1970) accepts all this, but insists that racism is also to some degree a thing in itself; that is, it contains an autonomous zone irreducible to the division of labor. Equally provocative has been the argument that only white people can be and are racists. The explanation for this argument is that racism is above all else an issue about power; because people of color as a whole do not have power in society, they cannot be racists.

Marxists are inclined to dismiss the liberal notion of racism as a thing in itself as so much mystical nonsense, something that can't be articulated. However, what might be meant by the autonomous zone are the various pan-human psychological propensities such as xenophobia, scapegoating, ethnocentrism, insecurity in the face of disorder and complexity, plus the sheer classificatory function of the human mind. These same propensities might help to remove some of the controversy from the claim that only white people can be racists. That is, racism revolves primarily around power, which for the past few centuries has been lodged in Western society, but complementing the power element are things like ethnocentrism and scapegoating, and they can invade the minds and actions of *Homo sapiens* everywhere.

In the decades that lie ahead, Rex has predicted, racism will increase rather than decrease. There is nothing about globalization to make me disagree, especially as regards the power dimension of the phenomenon. The time has certainly come, therefore, for racism as a social fact to be inserted firmly into our core conceptual territory. In view of the loss of nerve among anthropologists to which Geertz has alluded, it may be that European-origin anthropologists will turn their backs to the challenge, and even feel that they have no business in getting involved with it—that is the special mandate of the victims of racism. Yet Harding's (1992) argument about the obligation of men to produce feminist scholarship applies equally to racism. Only people of color can write *as* people of color. But white scholars can meaningfully write *about* people of color; and in some areas of research they may even have an advantage: studying victimizers rather than victims, especially those located in the corridors of power.

6. Anthropology at Home

As recently as the 1960s it was rare for ethnographers to ply their craft at home; the exceptions were Third World students who were expected to do fieldwork in their own societies. Yet by the 1980s Messerschmidt was able to state: "Anthropology at home is not a fad; neither is it a stopgap for unemployed Ph.D.s. It is, instead, a wellestablished branch of anthropology that . . . is here to stay" (1981: 1).

Anthropology at home was born from the same conditions that saw the classical problematic, what to make of "the other," give way to problems connected to deterritorialization and similar early signs of the globalization to come. Frank (1975), for example, pushed for fieldwork at home in order to sever the discipline from the era of colonial exploitation. Nader (1972), too, advocated that Western scholars focus on their own societies, countering the criticism that to do so would be the end of the cross-cultural perspective by pointing out that these societies were by then inhabited by people from all points of the globe. Among students today, armed with Said's *Orientalism* and the postmodernist deconstruction of the ethnographic enterprise, there almost seems to be an attitude that research abroad is unethical.

As Geertz has observed in passing, the turn to anthropology at home not only is profoundly important, but also brings into play "a few tricky and rather special second order problems" (1973:14). What happens, for example, to the notion that objectivity is enhanced by studying in other cultures? Or the claim that if one does not do research abroad one takes for granted and is blind to the most basic facts in everyday life? What about stranger value and the cross-cultural perspective? Certainly Nader is correct that fieldwork on an enormous range of cultural groups is possible within the United States, but this is comparative research with a difference, its units of analysis jumbled together, criss-crossed by the force of diffusion. Then there are the political and ethical aspects of fieldwork. Are they reconfigured when ethnographers stay at home? And if so, how?

Messerschmidt's edited volume throws some light on these questions. He breaks down anthropology at home into three categories: insider anthropology, the term applied to anthropologists from dominant groups who do research at home; native anthropology: the term for anthropologists from ethnic minority groups who study their own people; and indigenous anthropology: Third World anthropologists who do fieldwork in their own societies. My guess is that anthropology at home will increasingly define the discipline regardless of the fieldworker's nationality. Should that turn out to be the case, the importance of a definitive work on the topic will be reinforced.

7. Halfie Anthropology

As Abu-Lughod points out, *Writing Culture* ignored not only feminists but also halfies. Halfies (Abu-Lughod 1991:137) are "people whose national or cultural identity is mixed by virtue of migration, overseas education, or parentage." Anthropologists, asserts Abu-Lughod, always argue from a position that reflects their sense of self. The self, in turn, is defined in relation to the other—the subject of research. In mainstream anthropology, there is a clear divide between the self and other, with the balance of power tipped in favor of the ethnographic self. In halfie anthropology things are more complicated. When halfies do research within their own community, the self and other are synonymous. But as in the case of feminist anthropology, a different kind of other, negative in connotation, always lurks in the shadows: mainstream, dominant society. In this context, the self and other are not only separate, but antagonistically opposed. One consequence is that halfie anthropology is pulled between two audiences: the halfie community, which demands to be celebrated, and the wider anthropological profession, which takes off from a different position regarding the relationship between self and other.[2]

Given the dynamics of globalization, it is reasonable to suggest that the number of people who fall into the halfie category will increase over the next decades. Not only, therefore, will ethnographies on halfies become even more relevant, but also the theoretical articulation of the halfie perspective. It may be useful to create a more general category which subsumes halfie, native, indigenous and feminist anthropology. Let us call it Oriental anthropology. What I have in mind is something similar to but not identical with Said's reverse *Orientalism* (1979), in which aspects of culture previously undermined are valorized. Oriental anthropology will promote the indigenous worldview rather than the one imposed on it by the West. But it will profile not only what is admirable and pleasant, but also what is mean and miserable. Following Said, Oriental anthropology will not be confined to a specific geographic location; instead it will express the perspective of people who do not fit into the mainstream.

Similar to what was said earlier about feminist anthropology, in order for Oriental anthropology to take off it may be necessary for its message to trickle down into the textbook. Once again, a text that draws primarily from non-Western sources will not be any more one-sided than our conventional texts. An anthropology for which the distinction between the Occident and the Orient is meaningless is the long-range goal. Oriental anthropology, promoting the perspective of the historically dominated, may be one step towards obtaining it.[3]

8. Analysis of Qualitative Data

An enormous, and still expanding, literature on qualitative methodology exists. Advice abounds about entry into the field, impression management, participant observation and other techniques; light has been shone on the epistemology of ethnography, the literary devices employed by fieldworkers, and on a range of pertinent issues such as stress and ethics. Yet there remains a missing link: the analysis of qualitative data. This is what I call the last frontier, the part of ethnographic inquiry still cloaked in mystery, an example of what was earlier labelled "unfinished business."

It is not difficult to understand why progress in the analysis of qualitative data has not remotely matched that of quantitative analysis, with its codes, scales, and statistical measurements. In quantitative work, a questionnaire may be precoded, but to a very great degree data collection and data analysis constitute separate stages, with the latter constituting the larger, more time-consuming chore. In qualitative work, the collection and analysis of data are inseparable. Ethnographers on a daily basis juggle concepts, search for themes, and attempt to interpret what is going on in front of their eyes, as well as what they are hearing. Above all else, ethnographic research revolves around writing—documenting, describing, interpreting and explaining. The analytic procedure, in other words, simply refuses to wait until the investigator leaves the field. The implication is that fieldwork is more than a test of rapport, charm, and endurance; it is a complex theoretical exercise in its own right.

The challenge of showing how to analyze qualitative data has been rendered more complex by recent theoretical directions in the discipline. What will our orientations look like in the next generation? Will post-positivism wither away, or will a synthesis of positivism and post-positivism eventually emerge? Should we attempt to erect separate procedures of qualitative data analysis for the positivistic and post-positivistic traditions? Regardless of the answers to these questions, a place to begin is to divide analysis into two parts. One involves the organization of data into categories, and another the search for significant themes. Most recommendations in textbooks about how to proceed analytically with qualitative data focus on these steps (e.g. Agar 1980), and in my judgment computer programs, such as NUDIST, for the analysis of qualitative data lack the capacity to do any more.

The other part of analysis involves the interpretation of data. As I have suggested elsewhere (1996), interpretation consists of three operations. One is building models from one's data. Such models relate the parts of one's project to the whole; they provide a coherent overview of the research scene, and thus fit well with positivism. A second operation is the burst of insight. My argument is that a most significant aspect of qualitative research is the quick and penetrating understanding of social action. The burst of insight depends on one's perceptiveness. This subjective dimension of fieldwork resonates with assumptions intrinsic to postmodernism and feminist methodology. A third operation concerns the sheer act of writing. To repeat what was stated earlier, when one writes one does not just record or report. Writing always involves interpretation. Writing and analysis are synonymous. For example, as I write these words I am attempting to analyze the analysis of qualitative research. For obvious reasons, the emphasis placed on writing is compatible with the postmodernist program.

Finally, about one thing there can be little doubt: the scholar who is able to demystify the analysis of qualitative data will find a warm welcome in the anthropology hall of fame.

9. Gap between Theory and Method

One way to examine the history of anthropology is to divide it into three phases: building the scientific foundation of the discipline (roughly from the days of Boas until the 1950s), patching the cracks that had emerged (roughly the 1960s), and demolition and reconstruction (the decades since then). During the first phase, British structural functionalism represented a strong version of science, American historical particularism a weaker version, but the goal of science itself was shared equally in both the theory literature and the methods literature on both sides of the Atlantic. During the second phase it was American cultural ecology that attained the strong version of science. The main models that emerged in British social anthropology, transactional analysis and conflict theory, introduced a degree of complexity that made nomothetic inquiry more difficult to realize. While the goal of science remained alive, and was certainly reflected in the upsurge of methods texts, in Britain a gap had begun to emerge between the methods literature and the theoretical literature. During the third phase it no longer made sense to think in terms of strong and weak versions of science in the discipline, at least in relation to theoretical orientations. The postmodernists pronounced science dead, and the feminists, at least the feminist methodologists, dismissed science as a male story that propped up patriarchy, eschewed grand theory and generalization, and advocated a politically astute anthropology woven around fragmentary data and subjectivity. While all this was going on, the methods literature remained, if anything, even more committed to nomothetic inquiry. The upshot has been a huge gap between our literature on theory and our literature on methods, with the former aligned with the humanities and the latter with the sciences.

Obviously, this is an unhealthy state for the discipline, and it cries out for resolution. This is one writing project, however, that may be rendered purposeless before anyone can manage to pull it off. The forces gathering against post-positivism may by themselves reduce the gap between theories and methods, in the process undermining some of the most attractive features of the post-positivist program.

10. No-Name Anthropology

In a recent study (Barrett 1996:178-179), I coined the term no-name anthropology, a sort of underground version that continued in the 1980s and 1990s to follow the conventional assumptions and models that were prominent before the era of post-positivism. My impression was that while most anthropologists were at least paying lip service to the new approaches, especially postmodernism, many of them in their fieldwork activities were simply ignoring the current theoretical literature, and the literature on methods as well. It was as though they could not stomach the radical message of the postmodernists and feminists or the scientism of the methods texts, and were unpersuaded by the novel conceptual alternatives to the natural science model advocated by Lévi-Strauss and Geertz. Instead they continued to undertake research which respected empirical data, relied on long-term participant observation, and sought out generalizations, correlations and causes.

What may be admirable about no-name anthropology is that it kept the fieldwork tradition alive in an era dominated by meta-theory and library studies. No-name anthropology may even possess a broader significance. In a sense, it did not just begin as a reaction to the recent literature on theory and method. There has always been some expression of no-name anthropology. Many ethnographers draw a sharp line between the library and the fieldwork setting. The literature on theory and method may be interesting for its own sake, but fieldwork has its own (common sense) rules. Often anthropologists are skeptical about the value of theory, especially grand theory, and unwilling to allow it to shape their research. They may not even be fully conscious of the theoretical underpinnings of their research. To the extent that they do think about the broader theoretical picture, they tend to be unapologetically eclectic.

It would seem, then, that a book that addresses the actual manner in which much of ethnography is produced is long overdue. From my point of view, there is little to be gained by obfuscating the ethnographic tradition in order to promote a misleading, albeit elegant, portrait of the discipline.

Conclusion

If I am right about the significance of globalization for the discipline, there probably will be a spate of books addressed to the new problematic. Some academics will prove once again that scholars are experts in legitimation, providing apologies for the global economy. Others, exhibiting a critical stance, will focus on social problems emanating from globalization, and may even question what constitutes the good society, although that runs counter to the relativistic standpoint. It would be marvelous if someone would produce the grand synthesis, pulling all our models and approaches under a master plan. I doubt, however, if this will ever be achieved, even if another genius appears on the scene. The contributions of Lévi-Strauss and Geertz were stunning, but they were also one-sided and incomplete.

If there is to be a successful grand synthesis, I only hope that I live long enough to see it. No doubt some of the key theoretical works for the future will never get written, or will appear too late to play a critical role. That is the way it always has been. Then, too, there will be books that will alter the course of the discipline that I have not anticipated, both because of the limits of my imagination and because of changes in society that simply cannot be foreseen. What is predictable, however, is the eventual emergence of new models of society. It is not, let me make clear, a question of whether we will want to build new models. In this we have no choice. Society will not stay still.

Notes

1. Located somewhere in between the original theoretical work and the textbook is the reflective commentary or thought piece. Examples are Murphy's *The Dialectics of Social Life* (1971) and Sahlins's *Culture and Practical Reason* (1976).

2. Abu-Lughod points out that "wholies," essentially the dominant Western male, also occupy a position from which they write.

3. Incidentally, as in the case of feminist anthropology, there is no reason why Western anthropologists from the dominant group cannot contribute to Oriental anthropology, as long as they are willing to express its perspective.

References

Abu-Lughod, Lila
    1991   "Writing Against Culture." In Richard G. Fox, ed., *Recapturing Anthropology*. Santa Fe, NM: School of American Research Press.
Agar, Michael H.
    1980   *The Professional Stranger*. Orlando, FL: Academic Press.
Appadurai, Arjun
    1991   "Global Ethnoscapes: Notes and Queries for a Transactional Anthropology." In Richard G. Fox, ed., *Recapturing Anthropology*. Santa Fe, NM: School of American Research Press.
Bachrach, P. and M. S. Baratz
    1962   "Two Faces of Power." *American Political Science Review* 56:947-952.

1963   "Decisions and Non-Decisions: An Analytic Framework."
        American Political Science Review 57:632-642.
Bailey, F. G.
    1969   *Stratagems and Spoils*. Oxford: Blackwell.
    1980   "The Exercise of Power in Complex Organizations." Un-
            published paper for Burg Wartenstein Symposium No. 84.
Baldus, B.
    1975   "The Study of Power: Suggestions for an Alternative."
            Canadian Journal of Sociology 1:179-201.
Barrett, Stanley R.
    1984   *The Rebirth of Anthropological Theory*. Toronto: Universi-
            ty of Toronto Press.
    1994   *Paradise: Class, Commuters, and Ethnicity in Rural
            Ontario*. Toronto: University of Toronto Press.
    1996   *Anthropology: A Student's Guide to Theory and Method*.
            Toronto: University of Toronto Press.
Bourdieu, Pierre
    1984   *Distinction: A Social Critique of the Judgement of Taste*, R.
            Nice, trans. Cambridge, MA: Harvard University Press.
Clifford, James, and George E. Marcus, eds.
    1986   *Writing Culture*. Berkeley: University of California Press.
Cox, Oliver
    1948   *Caste, Class and Race*. Garden City, NY: Doubleday.
Dahl, R. A.
    1961   *Who Governs?* New Haven, CT: Yale University Press.
Dahrendorf, Ralf
    1959   *Class and Class Conflict in Industrial Society*. Stanford,
            CA: Stanford University Press.
Dunk, Thomas W.
    1991   *It's a Working Man's Town: Male Working-Class Culture*.
            Montreal and Kingston: McGill-Queens University Press.
Eichler, Margrit
    1986   "The Relationship Between Sexist, Nonsexist, Women-
            Centred, and Feminist Research." *Studies in Communication*
            3:37-74.
Festinger, Leon
    1957   *A Theory of Cognitive Dissonance*. Evanston, IL: Row,
            Peterson.
Frank, A. G.
    1975   "Anthropology = Ideology; Applied Anthropology =
            Politics." *Race and Class* 17:57-68.

Friedrichs, R.
    1972a "Dialectical Sociology: Towards a Resolution of the Current
           Crisis in Western Sociology." *British Journal of Sociology*
           13:263-274.
    1972b "Dialectical Sociology: An Exemplar for the 1970s." *Social
           Forces* 50:447-455.
Gacs, Ute et al.
    1988 *Women Anthropologists: A Bibliographical Dictionary.*
          Westport, CT: Greenwood Press.
Geertz, Clifford
    1973 *The Interpretation of Cultures*. New York: Basic Books.
Giddens, A.
    1979 *Central Problems in Social Theory*. London: Macmillan.
Golde, Peggy, ed.
    1970 *Women in the Field*. Chicago, IL: Aldine.
Harding, Sandra
    1992 "Subjectivity, Experience and Knowledge." *Development
          and Change* 23:175-193.
Harris, Marvin
    1968 *The Rise of Anthropological Theory*. New York: Crowell.
Hunter, Floyd
    1953 *Community Power Structure: A Study of Decision Makers.*
          Chapel Hill: University of North Carolina Press.
Kardiner, A., and E. Preble
    1961 *They Studied Man*. New York: Mentor.
Kroeber, A. L., and C. Kluckhohn
    1952 *Culture: A Critical Review of Concepts and Definitions.*
          Cambridge, MA: Harvard University Papers of the Peabody
          Museum of American Archaeology and Ethnology (Vol.
          47).
Kuhn, T. S.
    1970 *The Structure of Scientific Revolutions*. 2nd edition. Chi-
          cago, IL: University of Chicago Press.
Leach, E. R.
    1954 *Political Systems of Highland Burma*. Boston, MA: Beacon
          Press.
Lévi-Strauss, Claude
    1978 *Myth and Meaning*. Toronto: University of Toronto Press.
Lukes, S.
    1974 *Power: A Radical View*. London: Macmillan.

McDonald, Lynn
  1993   *The Early Origins of the Social Sciences.* Montreal and
          Kingston: McGill-Queens University Press.
  1994   *The Women Founders of the Social Sciences.* Ottawa: Car-
          leton University Press.
Merrington, J.
  1968   "Theory and Practice in Gramsci's Marxism." *Socialist
          Register* 5:145-176.
Messerschmidt, Donald A., ed.
  1981   *Anthropology at Home in North America: Methods and
          Issues in the Study of One's Own Society.* Cambridge:
          Cambridge University Press.
Murphy, Robert
  1971   *The Dialectics of Social Life.* New York: Basic Books.
Nader, Laura
  1972   "Up the Anthropologist. Perspectives Gained from Studying
          Up." In Dell Hymes, ed., *Reinventing Anthropology.* New
          York: Pantheon Books.
Ortner, Sherry B.
  1991   "Reading America: Preliminary Notes on Class and Cul-
          ture." In Richard G. Fox, ed., *Recapturing Anthropology.*
          Santa Fe, NM: School of American Research Press.
Rabinow, Paul
  1986   "Representations Are Social Facts: Modernity and Post-
          Modernity in Anthropology." In James Clifford and George
          E. Marcus, eds., *Writing Culture.* Berkeley: University of
          California Press.
Rex, John
  1970   *Race Relations in Sociological Theory.* New York: Schock-
          en Books.
Sahlins, M.
  1976   *Culture and Practical Reason.* Chicago, IL: University of
          Chicago Press.
Said, Edward W.
  1979   *Orientalism.* New York: Vintage Books.
Strathern, Marilyn
  1987   "An Awkward Relationship: The Case of Feminism and An-
          thropology." *Signs* 12:276-292.
Tyler, Stephen A.
  1969   *Cognitive Anthropology.* New York: Holt, Rinehart, and
          Winston.

van den Berghe, Pierre
    1967   "Dialectic and Functionalism: Toward a Synthesis." In N.
               J. Demerath and R. A. Peterson, eds., *System, Change and
               Conflict*. New York: Free Press.

Warner, W.
    1949   *Social Class in America: A Manual of Procedure for the
               Measurement of Social Status*. Chicago, IL: Science Re-
               search Associates.

Warren, Carol A. B.
    1988   *Gender Issues in Field Research*. Newbury Park, CA:
               SAGE Publications.

White, Leslie
    1949   *The Science of Culture*. New York: Grove Press.

Whittaker, Elvi
    1994   "Decolonizing Knowledge: Towards a Feminist Ethic and
               Methodology." In J. S. Grewal and Hugh Johnston, eds.,
               The India-Canada Relationship. New Delhi: SAGE Pub-
               lications.

INDEX

Aborigines, 27-29

Abu-Lughod, Lila, 91, 214-215, 261, 266, 272, 277

Adaptive, 4, 7, 58-59, 62-63, 65, 69, 71, 204, 206-207

Affirmative theory, 180-182, 188, 190-191

Africa, 23, 36, 46, 67, 79-82, 213, 219, 230, 256

Africanists, 79

Agricultural, 26, 93, 197, 202, 207-208

Alienation, 62, 85, 99-100, 106

Alterity 213, 217-218, 231

American culture, 28-29

American Indian, 197

Anatolia, 67

Ancestor, 13, 19-20, 22, 24-30, 94

Anglo-Saxon anthropology, 9

Animistic beliefs, 198

Anthropology Newsletter, 14

Anthropology-of-science, 13

Anthropomorphic, 36, 39

Anti-Darwinian, 40, 43

Anti-Hegelian, 96

Antipositivist, 145

Anti-science, 80, 261

Anti-Vietnam War movement, 81

Arab, 217, 227, 240-241

Archaeology, 4

Art, 71, 86, 187, 236

Asia, 1, 46, 179, 240

Asian historians, 40

Australian, 27-29

Aztec, 64, 67

Bacon, Francis, 247

Bajuni, 217, 221

Balinese, 61

Baseball, 98

Bateson, Gregory, 151, 175, 177, 182-187, 190

Bedouin, 248

Behaviorism, 87, 150, 154

Benedict, Ruth, 55-56, 86, 202

Bias, 20, 36, 42, 45-47, 61,

78, 96, 108, 160, 190, 265
Big-game hunter, 60
Bilateral inheritance, 24, 29
Bimin-Kuskusmin, 66
Biocultural, 202-203
Biodiversity, 180
Bioenergy, 185
Biological anthropology, 46
Biosemiotics, 187, 190
Biosphere, 177-178, 183, 188, 190
Boas, Franz, 2, 6, 55, 86, 125, 183, 203, 255, 268-269, 274
Boasian, 3, 6-8, 11, 13, 110
Bohra 217
Bourdieu, Pierre, 91, 109, 117-118, 122, 267
Brazil, 81-82
British social anthropology, 101

Canada, 215-216
Canadian, 12-13, 46, 268
Capitalism, 216-217, 225, 230, 242-243, 258-259, 266, 270
Causation, 13, 106-107, 118, 130, 134, 145, 157
Chaco Canyon, 67
Chaos theory, 185-186
Charismatic, 239
Cheyenne Indians, 65
China, 67, 216
Chinese, 25-26, 29, 215-216
Chinese-Canadian, 215
Christian, 219, 221, 226, 229
Clans, 25, 28
Class, 10, 24, 60, 64, 79, 85, 125-126, 238, 241-243, 258, 267-268, 270

Climate, 177, 238
Clinical psychology, 183
Cognition 89, 111-112, 159, 161, 204
Cognitivist, 153
Cold War, 56
Collectivist, 182
Collectivity, 149, 152, 156, 205
Colonialism, 6-7, 26, 61, 68, 81, 99, 258-259
Colonization, 213
Colostrum, 64-65
Community, 5, 21, 24-26, 28, 34, 41, 46, 60-61, 85-86, 94, 181, 197, 206-208, 213, 216-217, 227, 245, 272
Comparativism, 6, 12
Conceptual constructs, 236
Condorcet, Marie Jean de, 83
Conflict theory, 260, 275
Conformity, 206, 245
Consciousness, 115, 261
Consensus, 101, 110, 144, 157, 163, 260
Conservatism, 207, 242
Constitutive culture, 89
Constructionism, 88
Constructivism, 144, 151
Contestable, 96
Counter-hegemonic, 9
Crete, 67
Critical anthropology, 80-82
Critical issues, 6, 12-13
Cross-cultural, 5-7, 271
Cultural adaptation, 60, 71
Cultural anthropology, 2, 6-8, 10-12
Cultural ecology, 176
Culturalist, 92, 99
Cultural materialism, 4

Cultural practices, 7
Cultural relativism, 2-3, 6-7
Cultural studies, 8-9
Cultural-system focus, 148
Culture-bound, 40
Culture contact, 60
Culture of poverty, 85
Culturology, 105
Cybernetic, 175-178, 183, 191, 202

D'Andrade, Roy, 12, 14, 77-78, 81, 85, 111, 147, 158
Darwin, Charles, 186
Darwinism, 159, 175, 186
Descartes, René, 149
Descent, 24-29, 248
Deterritorialization, 266, 271
Dialectic 163, 192, 200, 205, 238, 259-260, 262, 265, 277
Diasporic, 215
Discursive, 98, 214, 218, 220
Diversity, 2, 5, 39, 60, 158-162, 164
Double bind, 184
Dreaming being, 28
Dualism, 4, 107, 124, 149, 184-185, 190, 216
Dumont, Louis, 108-110
Durkheim, Émile, 110, 113, 160-161, 163, 235, 259, 265, 270
Dutch, 33, 67-68

Earth Summit, 189
East Africa, 213
Eco-feminists, 187, 192
Ecological anthropology, 40

Ecology 40, 59, 129, 175-176, 178-180, 182-185, 187-189, 260, 275
Ecosystem, 122, 175-177, 179, 189, 191, 198-199, 202, 206
Education, 47, 228, 251, 272
Egypt, 67
Elite, 26, 181, 239, 241, 243-245, 247-248, 251
Emergent, 110, 119
Emic, 115, 259
Emotion, 89-92, 241
Empiricism, 111, 145, 199-201, 261
Enactment, 95, 222, 230
Enlightenment, 82-83, 258-259
Environmental ethics, 197, 199, 201, 207
Environmentalism, 176, 189, 191
Epistemology 13, 35, 42, 113-114, 175-176, 178, 183, 186, 188-189, 214-215, 273
Essentialism, 5, 159
Estonia, 267
Ethics, 189, 197, 199, 201-202, 204, 206-209, 247, 273
Ethiopia, 59
Ethnic, 10, 34, 42, 45-46, 60, 215-216, 270, 272
Ethnic anthropologies, 34, 42, 46
Ethnic identity, 216
Ethnicity, 64, 79, 216, 268
Ethnocentrism, 55, 270
Ethnographers, 43, 44, 256, 267, 268, 271, 272, 273, 276
Ethnographic present, 29

Ethnographic writing, 4, 8
Ethnography 7-9, 14, 20, 39, 56, 59, 62-63, 78, 116, 132, 213, 257, 262, 267, 269, 272-273, 276
Ethnolinguistic studies, 198
Ethos, 208
Etic, 259
Eurocentric, 215
Europe, 1, 61, 67, 93, 180
European, 26, 33-34, 36-37, 39, 43-44, 46-47, 61, 198, 219, 228, 244, 270-271
Evans-Pritchard, E. E., 23-24
Eventamental, 133
Event-laws, 107, 130-131
Evolutionary biologist, 58-59
Evolutionism, 260, 262
Exemplar, 36, 45, 99, 255, 257
Experiential realism, 144

Faction, 241
False consciousness, 115
Fauna, 198-199
Feedback, 129, 176, 184-185, 202, 244
Feminist anthropology, 260, 261-262, 268, 272-273, 277
Feudalism, 258
Feuding 62, 68
Fieldwork, 4, 8, 20, 23, 29, 116, 153, 255-257, 271-276
Flora, 198, 199
Folk societies, 56, 60-62, 65
Folk taxonomies, 89
Folkways, 9
Force-field, 143-144, 162-163
Formalist, 200
Foucault, Michel, 82, 97-100,

117-118, 122
Fox culture, 114
Fractal geometry, 186
Frankfurt School, 96
Frazer, James, 23, 29, 152
Freudians, 235
Functionalism, 3, 5, 7, 11
Fur trade, 198

Gaia hypothesis, 177-178, 183, 187, 189
Galton's problem, 263
Geertz, Clifford, 4, 8, 57, 87-89, 98-101, 112, 154-156, 202, 239, 255-256, 261-262, 264, 271, 276
Gellner, Ernest, 92-93, 115-116
Gender, 64, 79, 214, 218, 262-263, 268-269
Gendered, 213-215, 217, 221, 227
Genes, 64, 117, 146
Genetics, 190
Ghost in the machine, 151
Globalization, 258-259, 266-267, 270, 271-272, 276
Goldschmidt, Walter, 63
Gramsci, Antonio, 9, 243, 269
Greece, 67

Halfies, 272
Harris, Marvin, 4, 12, 20, 58-59, 77, 79, 107-108, 113, 115-117, 123-124, 129-130, 132-133, 153, 203, 235-237, 242, 255-256, 266
Health, 64, 69, 71
Hegelian, 96, 163

Hegemonic, 218, 220
Hegemony, 2, 164, 213, 262
Heredity-environment, 147-149
Herodotus, 55
Herskovits, Melville, 55, 56
Hierarchy, 124, 153, 156-157, 163, 186, 205, 218, 238, 244, 266
Historical particularism, 255, 260, 275
Historicism, 3
Hohokam, 67
Holism, 106, 108-110, 118-119, 175-179, 183-184, 186-187, 189-190, 202-203
Holists, 112, 118
Homo sapiens, 258, 265, 270
Hopi, 19, 57
Humanism, 106, 131-132, 235, 246, 250, 255, 258
Human materialism, 235-236, 239-241, 244, 246-248, 251
Human rights, 180-182, 189
Hume, David, 55, 121
Hungry ghosts, 25-26, 29-30
Huxley Memorial Award, 47
Huxley Memorial Lecture, 9
Hybridity, 215-216
Hydramont, 217
Hyperreality, 182
Hyphenated identities, 215-216
Hypoplasia, 64

Idealism, 62, 96, 98, 199-200
Identification, 81
Identity 2, 9-10, 125, 163, 201, 214-216, 218, 272
Ideology 26, 93, 108, 130, 178, 199, 204, 207, 239, 242-245, 248-249, 250-251, 266
Ilahita Arapesh, 66
Imanishi, Kinji, 40, 43, 47
Immanent holism, 175, 177-178, 184-188, 190
Immune system, 64
Immunoglobins, 64
Imperialism, 258
Incest, 241, 250
Incommensurable, 8
Indigenous anthropology, 42-43
Indigenous groups, 198
Individualism, 11, 262
Indonesia, 179, 189, 191
Industrializing, 179, 191
Industrial Revolution, 258
Indus Valley, 67
Informant, 4, 220-221
Infrastructural, 237, 240-241, 243-244, 246, 249-250
Insider anthropology, 272
Instrumental, 186
Interdisciplinary, 4
Interface, 217, 237, 243, 246
Interpretive anthropology, 260-261
Interpretive approach, 8
Involution, 4, 202
Ireland, 81
Irian Jaya, 63, 68
Irrationality, 200
Ishida, Eiichiro, 36-37, 47
Islamic, 217, 225, 251
Isms, 199
Isomorphism, 216
Ituri Forest, 249
Japan, 33-34, 36, 41, 43, 46-48, 177, 179
Japanese, 12, 33, 48, 85, 157, 160, 215-216

Japanologists, 41
Journal, 36-39, 41, 43, 44, 46-
47

Kant, Immanuel, 149
Kenya, 213, 217, 219-220, 222
Kinship, 13, 22-25, 27-30,
157, 160, 240-241, 251,
256, 267-268
Kluckhohn, Clyde, 55-56, 86-
87, 266
Konso, 59
Koryak, 250-251
Kroeber, Alfred, 56, 86, 147-
149, 152, 156-157, 202,
266
Kuhn, 20-21, 24, 207, 236,
257, 263-264
!Kung San, 65
Kuper, Adam, 24, 101
Kuru, 128
Kuwayama, Takami, 34-36,
38, 40-41, 43-47
Kwashiorkor, 249-250
Kyoto, 41, 47-48, 177-179

Lakoff, George, 108, 114-115,
144-146, 163
Lamu, 213, 217-220, 223, 225-
230
Land wisdom, 197, 199
Latin America, 240
Laws, 61-62, 106-107, 110,
118, 121-124, 126, 130,
134, 187, 201
Leach, Edmund, 4, 256, 269
Lebenswelt, 146
Life expectancy, 64
Literary criticism, 19

London School of Economics,
23
Lyotard, Jean François, 189

Macro, 11, 13, 113, 119, 187,
190, 263
Mae Enga, 65
Maize, 67-68
Maladaptation, 55, 60, 63-65,
71
Malinowski, Bronislaw, 3, 20,
23-24, 29, 111, 113, 183,
203, 255, 268
Malnutrition, 64, 81
Marginalization, 35-37, 43-44,
46
Marind-Anim, 69
Maring ritual, 129
Market economy, 218, 224-
225, 229-230
Marx, Karl, 10, 92, 96, 129,
235, 268-270
Marxists, 175-176, 235, 240-
242, 270
Masses, 99, 242-245, 248, 251
Mass media, 191
Materialist, 4-5, 10-11, 23, 96,
153, 185, 202, 236-238,
249-251
Mayan civilization, 67
Mead, George Herbert, 198-
199
Mead, Margaret, 8, 22, 55
Mercantilism, 258
Mesopotamia, 67
Meta-theory, 257, 276
Methodology 4-5, 11, 36, 42,
145, 230, 261, 273-274
Methods, 3, 6, 10-11, 63, 77,
119, 151, 186, 248, 251,

262, 266, 268, 274-276
Micro, 11, 13, 113, 119, 121,
    187, 224-225, 263
Middle-class, 262
Middle East, 219, 240
Mind/body, 149
Mississippi Valley, 67
Modernity, 143-144, 189, 213,
    215, 217-219
Modernization, 219, 262
Modern/postmodern, 143, 162
Mombasa, 218, 224, 228-229
Montezuma, 67
Moral-ethical, 77, 79-80
Moralism, 6, 199, 200-201
Moral-subjective, 78
Mores, 55
Morgan, Lewis Henry, 20, 24,
    203
Mozambique, 79
Multicultural discourse, 216
Multiple realities, 152
Murdock, Peter, 9, 56, 110,
    117, 121

Nairobi, 218, 222
Nakane, Chie, 7, 42
Narrative, 217, 219, 222, 226,
    229
Native anthropology, 272
Native North Americans, 197
Natural sciences, 246
Natural selection, 239
Nature's Veto, 179
Ndembu, 248
Neo-Darwinism, 186
Neo-evolutionism, 260
Neolocal residence, 24-26, 29-
    30
Neo-positivist, 80

Nietzsche, Friedrich, 99-100
Nihilism, 1-2, 4, 6, 8, 10-11,
    82, 100
Nihonjinron, 42, 48
Nineteenth century, 2
Nomothetic, 130, 250, 275
No-name anthropology, 5, 275-
    276
Non-linear, 185-186
Non-native, 41, 43, 48
Non-Western, 7, 42, 56, 58,
    61, 215, 217, 273
Nordic Institute of Anthropol-
    ogy, 43
Normative, 87, 156-157, 180,
    186, 200-201, 206-207
North America, 1-2, 4, 12, 14,
    44, 67
Nurture, 81

Objectivism, 81, 114, 146, 162
Observer, 77-78, 116, 130,
    155
Occident, 273
Occult, 154
Omani, 217
Ontological, 112, 115-117,
    146-147, 152, 215
Open system, 246
Organic solidarity, 160, 163
Organism, 147-149, 151-152,
    156-157, 160, 184-185,
    187-190
Orient, 94, 214, 273
Oriental anthropology, 272-
    273, 277
Orma, 217, 221, 226
Ortner, Sherry B., 3, 10, 109-
    110, 112, 117, 267
Othering, 214

Paleolithic, 60
Pan-Hegelian, 175
Papua New Guinea, 59, 65-66
Paradigm 2-3, 5-8, 11, 19-22, 24, 26-27, 38, 40, 42-43, 69, 80, 87, 114, 125, 177, 191, 214, 235-237, 247, 249-251, 258, 263, 268
Parsons, Talcott, 89, 147-149, 152, 156-157, 161
Participant observation, 4, 33
Pathogenic, 63
People of color, 5, 270-271
Peripheral countries, 34
Personality, 78, 147-149, 152-153, 156-157, 239
Peru, 67
Phenomenalism, 133
Phenomenology, 80
Philosophical idealism, 96
Philosophic realism, 144
Philosophy, 25, 132, 144-145, 149-150, 178, 186
Physicalism, 133
Platonic, 159
Pleuropneumonia, 67
Political economy, 176
Portugal, 79
Positivism, 82, 144-145, 154, 189, 260-261, 274
Positivist, 81, 133, 144-145, 155, 263
Post-Gramscian, 9
Postmodern, 1-2, 4-11, 14, 20, 77, 143, 147, 162, 164, 176, 180-182, 189
Postmodernism, 4-5, 9, 13
Postmodernist, 8, 78, 82, 271, 274
Postmodernity, 143-144
Post-positivism, 260-263, 274-275
Practice theory, 11
Praxis, 10, 190
Primate behavior, 35-38, 47
Primatologists, 36-40, 43-44, 48
Primatology, 12, 33, 35-41, 43-46
Primitive, 7, 56-57, 59-60, 62, 70, 258
Prophecy, 67-68
Prophets, 67, 235
Protest, 62, 65, 108
Protestant ethic, 262
Pseudo-behavior, 131
Psyche, 89-90, 92, 101-102, 129
Psychiatrists, 61
Psychic unity, 6
Psychobiology, 91-92, 101
Psychological anthropologists, 100
Psychology, 9-10, 36, 47, 59, 87, 101, 110, 128-129, 145, 161, 183, 239
Puberty, 79
Pygmies, 249

Qualitative, 256, 262, 273-274
Quantum Theory, 123-124, 126
Quasi-organism, 112
Quetzalcoatl, 67

Race, 45, 64, 79, 125, 266, 270
Racism, 60, 81, 99, 181, 263, 269, 270-271
Radcliffe-Brown, A. R., 23
Rape, 62

Rappaport, Roy, 10, 129-130, 157, 175-176, 191, 203, 248
Rationalism, 199-201
Rationality, 4, 8, 70, 109, 200, 204, 206, 208, 258
Realism, 13, 70, 143-147, 149-153, 155, 157, 159, 162-164
Reciprocity, 208
Recursion, 185-186
Recursiveness, 13
Reductionism, 110, 112-113, 150, 203
Reflective, 277
Reification, 215
Relationships, 25, 27, 28
Relativism, 2-3, 6-8, 12, 55-58, 60, 71, 82, 151, 180, 190
Religion, 24, 92, 94, 249, 251, 263
Representation, 4
Reviews, 21, 38, 41
Rhetoric, 110, 175, 199, 205
Rome, 64, 67
Rosaldo, Renato, 57, 109, 158
Rousseau, Jean-Jacques, 55, 83
Russian, 93

Sahlins, Marshall, 109, 113, 129, 240, 256, 277
Salvage theory, 262-263
Samoa, 22
Sapir-Whorf hypothesis, 57
Sarhili, 67-68
Saudi Arabia, 224-225
Scandinavian, 43
Scapegoating, 270
Schneider, David, 57, 87-88, 98-99, 113, 154-157, 160, 200
Scientism, 10, 275
Script, 217-218, 220-222, 226-231
Scriptural, 221, 225, 227-228
Sebei, 63
Semiology, 105
Semiosphere, 188, 190
Semiotics, 190
Slavery, 56
Snow Mountains, 63
Social anthropologist, 35-36, 44, 79
Socialization, 22, 266
Social sciences 10, 260
Social system, 92-93, 98, 101-102, 147-148, 151-152, 156, 158
Sociocultural anthropology, 2, 4
Sociologist, 55, 61, 155
Sociology, 35, 59, 105, 111, 113, 125, 161, 246, 258, 262, 267-268
Somali, 217, 221
Sophists 55
South, the, 180-182, 188-189, 191
South Africa, 79, 81-82, 256
Southeast Asia, 179
Soviet Union, 92-93, 243
Spaniards, 67
Spencer, Herbert, 202-203, 264
Spirits, 25
Spiritual, 245, 247
Steward, Julian, 175-176, 203, 256, 259
Storytellers, 230
Stratigraphic, 156-157

Structural-functionalism, 79
Structuralism, 251, 257, 260-261
Subjective, 77-78, 123, 150, 269, 274
Subsistence, 4, 20, 69, 157, 182
Substantivist, 200
Suicide, 62, 65-66, 124, 265
Sumner, William Graham, 55
Supernaturalism, 131
Superorganic, 105-109, 112, 119, 121, 131-132, 202, 264
Superstructural, 237-238, 240, 249-250
Supra-physical, 106-108, 110, 112, 118, 120, 122, 125, 130-131, 133
Surplus value, 265
Swahili, 217, 220, 224
Sweden, 47
Symbol, 88, 113
Symbolic interactionists, 199
Symbolism, 111, 245, 251, 266
Synthesis, 162, 202, 274, 276

Tambaran initiation ritual, 66
Tanzania, 213
Tauade, 59
Teach-In, 81
Technology, 20, 56, 70-71, 178, 207-208, 238, 241, 251
Teleology, 246-247, 249-250
Teotihuacan, 64
Text, 4-5, 7-8, 12-14, 112, 126-129, 132, 162, 181-182, 190, 222, 262, 268-269, 273, 275

Textbook, 4, 58, 159, 190, 256, 263, 269, 273-274, 277
Thatcher, Margaret, 261
Therapists 183-184
Thick description, 154-155
Third World, 45, 230, 259, 271-272
Tiv, 23
Token internationals, 39, 44, 47
Totalities, 189
Traditional societies, 64, 66, 71
Transactional analysis, 275
Transactionalism, 176
Transcendentalism, 131, 133
Translation, 36, 40, 48
Transnational, 45
Trobriand, 24
Turkey, 251
Turks, 241
Twentieth century, 61
Twenty-first century, 180
Tylor, Edward Burnett, 8, 20, 27, 58-59, 81, 86, 105, 202-203

Uganda, 63, 213, 219
Under-development, 262
Uniformism, 160
United States, 2, 22, 34, 43, 180, 271
Urban, 61, 63-64, 217
U.S. Forest Service, 198, 205
Utilitarian conservation, 197, 199, 201

Value-free, 263

Vernacular, 96
Voice of America, 1
Voodoo, 248

Wardaman, 27-28
Warfare, 59, 65, 70
Weber, Max, 87, 235, 239,
    268-270
West, 33-34, 37-39, 93-94, 99,
    180-181, 189, 213-215,
    267, 273
Wholies, 277
Wife battering, 62

Witchcraft, 62, 67-68, 248
Womanhood, 227
Women's groups, 222
World system, 33-34, 44, 246
World War II, 56, 81, 183
World Wildlife Fund, 179
Writers, 214, 230, 268

Xhosa, 67-68

Yankee City, 267
Yanomamo, 22, 30, 65

CONTRIBUTORS

Pamela J. Asquith
Department of Anthropology
University of Alberta
Edmonton
Alberta T6G 2H4, Canada

Stanley R. Barrett
Department of Sociology and
Anthropology
University of Guelph
Guelph
Ontario N1G 2W1, Canada

Paul Bohannan
Department of Anthropology
University of
Southern California
Los Angeles
CA 90089

Daniel M. Cartledge
Department of Humanities
Ferris State University
Big Rapids
MI 49307

E. L. Cerroni-Long
Anthropology
S.A.C. Department
Eastern Michigan University
Ypsilanti, MI 48197

Roy D'Andrade
Department of Anthropology
University of California
at San Diego
La Jolla
CA 92093

Parin A. Dossa
Department of Sociology and
Anthropology
Simon Fraser University
Burnaby, British Columbia
V5A 1S6, Canada

Robert B. Edgerton
Department of Psychiatry and
Bio-Behavioral Sciences
UCLA, N.P.I. Box 62
Los Angeles, CA 90024

Peter Harries-Jones
Department of Anthropology
York University
North York
Ontario M3J 1P3, Canada

Marvin Harris
Department of Anthropology
University of Florida
Gainesville
FL 32611

Paul J. Magnarella
Department of Anthropology
University of Florida
Gainesville, FL 32611

Joseph A. Maxwell
Graduate School of Education
George Mason University
Fairfax
VA 22030

Tim O'Meara
Obermann Center
for Advanced Studies
University of Iowa
Iowa City, IA 52242

Karen Saenz
Department of Anthropology
UCLA
Los Angeles, CA 90024

Mari Womack
Mandala Communications
4034 South Pacific Avenue
Suite 32
San Pedro, CA 90731

ISBN 0-89789-684-X

90000>

EAN

9 780897 896849

HARDCOVER BAR CODE